POP
in Latin America

MW01052361

POPULISM
in Latin America

Second Edition

Edited by

Michael L. Conniff

Preface by

Kenneth Roberts

THE UNIVERSITY OF ALABAMA PRESS

Tuscaloosa

Copyright © 2012
The University of Alabama Press
Tuscaloosa, Alabama 35487-0380
All rights reserved
Manufactured in the United States of America

First edition published 1999. Second edition 2012.

Typeface: Garamond, Copperplate & Corbel
Cover photo and design: Rebecca Todd Minder

∞

The paper on which this book is printed meets the minimum requirements
of American National Standard for Information Sciences—Permanence of
Paper for Printed Library Materials, ANSI Z39.48-1984.

Library of Congress Cataloging-in-Publication Data

Populism in Latin America / edited by Michael L. Conniff ; preface by
Kenneth Roberts. — 2nd ed.
p. cm.
Summary: "This updated edition of Populism in Latin America discusses
new developments in populism as a political phenomenon and the
emergence of new populist political figures in Mexico, Argentina, and
Venezuela in particular"— Provided by publisher.
Includes bibliographical references and index.
ISBN 978-0-8173-5709-2 (pbk. : alk. paper) — ISBN 978-0-8173-8613-9
(ebook)
1. Populism—Latin America. 2. Latin America—Politics and government. I.
Conniff, Michael L.
JL966.P66 2012
320.56′62098—dc23
2012021211

Contents

vi / Contents

List of Illustrations

Preface

Kenneth Roberts

Few political phenomena are as adaptable and resilient as populism in Latin America. Political opponents and detractors routinely proclaim populism's demise, if not its extinction, reflecting a belief, perhaps, that populism is rooted in historical political and economic conditions that are no longer present in the region. "Modern" Latin America, it is often thought, holds no place for such relics from bygone historical eras. Yet time and time again, populism has not only returned to the political center stage, but also adapted its form and content to the realities of a new political era. From Víctor Raúl Haya de la Torre, Lázaro Cárdenas, and Juan Perón to Alberto Fujimori and Hugo Chávez, populism has spawned many of Latin America's most colorful, powerful, and polarizing political figures. These leaders not only transformed their own countries—for better or worse—but also left indelible marks on the politics of the region.

Historically, populism was associated with the onset of mass politics during the early stages of industrialization in twentieth-century Latin America. The first generation of populist leaders played a critical role in the political incorporation of urban working and middle class groups as oligarchic rule gradually—and often fitfully—yielded to mass democratic participation. These classical expressions of populism were later undermined by military repression, the debt crisis, and the collapse of state-led development in the 1980s. Nevertheless, populism made a surprising comeback in the 1990s by providing political cover for free-market reformers and neoliberal technocrats who set out to dismantle forms of state intervention that had been erected by the earlier generation of populist figures. Then, since the late 1990s, a more radical brand of populist leadership has emerged as part of a broader leftward shift in Latin American politics. With Chávez at the forefront, this new generation of populist leaders and movements has challenged neoliberal orthodoxy, revived nationalist and redistributive policy goals, and given new voice to popular discontent with traditional parties and political elites. Once again, the prospects for democracy and development in much of Latin American rest in the hands of populist leaders. This revised and updated book places these new populist figures in a larger historical and comparative perspective, making it clear that populism did not belong exclusively to a specific historical stage of political and economic development in Latin America. Neither is it wedded to any particular set of economic policies, a fixed group of social constituencies, or a singular guiding ideology (whether of the left or the right). The essays in this volume cut through different meanings and expressions of populism to identify the common core of both classical and contemporary populist movements—a charismatic bond between political leaders and mass followers. By analyzing this common core in different national and historical settings, the essays shed new light on the ways in which charismatic bonds adapt to the shifting contours of Latin America's social, economic, and political landscapes.

Readers of this volume will learn that populist leaders have emerged in highly varied national contexts and appealed to strikingly diverse social and political constituencies, including organized labor, the urban and rural poor, and diverse middle classes. They have adapted their political discourse and ideology to the challenges of their time, and they have pursued a broad range of public policies. Some populist leaders, for example, have opened markets, whereas others have closed them, and many have redistributed property or income. Populists have increased democratic participation and expanded the range of democratic alternatives, while often limiting the rights of opponents or undermining democratic checks and balances. But whatever they do in public office, populist leaders always claim to represent the common people—*el pueblo*—in a redemptive struggle against established elites (whether these are domestic or foreign, political, or economic). It is this common thread that links together the movements and leaders who are analyzed, in vivid detail, in the portraits of this volume.

Introduction

Michael L. Conniff

Looking back upon Latin American politics in the last century, we can see certain patterns in leadership styles. In some countries, military dictators predominated. In others, old-fashioned parliamentarians rose to commanding positions. Occasionally a reformer or socialist gained dominance in the political arena. In all, Latin America displayed a wide variety of leaders of all stripes.

In the long view, populists were the most characteristic leaders of the twentieth century. From the earliest years in the La Plata region until the end of the 1990s, populists proved amazingly successful at gaining high office, holding onto power, maintaining their followings, and renewing their careers. Their imprint will continue for decades to come.

In this book you will find lively introductions to some of Latin America's outstanding leaders—the populists. These men, and sometimes women, stood out from the ranks of the ordinary politicians.[1] They displayed flair, daring, broad appeal, and uncanny timing. They campaigned for public office early, often, and almost always successfully. They constitute one of the most important groups of leaders in twentieth-century Latin America. Their impact on politics has been profound yet not fully recognized.

By "outstanding," we do not necessarily mean moral, wise, constructive, or representative leaders. Some corrupted their countries, others manipulated their followers, and still others disgraced themselves. Still, they were extraordinarily effective in reaching masses of voters, whom they convinced to cast ballots for them. And some left positive legacies for generations to come. Later in the text we offer a working definition of just who these people were.

We designed and wrote this book with the general reader in mind, especially college students and the intellectually curious. We set aside many social scientific debates in the field in order to keep our focus on the leaders and their followers. In particular, we have steered clear of the argument that populists were simply irresponsible big spenders who used public moneys to win mass support.[2] Rather, we see populism basically as a political phenomenon: a question of who gains public office and how they govern. That is subject enough for one book.[3]

Since our purpose is to introduce the subject to readers, we have limited our notes in number and length, providing references only to the most important sources. We give preference to those in English and Spanish that are likely to be available in university libraries.

The authors of these chapters have devoted decades to studying the populists and the countries they governed. Here, they survey the populist experiences in those nations most profoundly influenced by this distinctively Latin American way of conducting the people's business. Their intent is to provide authoritative accounts of the whole sweep of the twentieth and the early twenty-first centuries. They do so in ways that invite generalization and comparison, which we attempt to do in this introduction.

In chapter 1, Joel Horowitz examines Argentina's strong legacy of populism, beginning with the remarkable Hipólito Yrigoyen, moving through the archetypal Juan and Evita Perón, and ending with President Cristina Fernández de Kirchner. He finds that these leaders built upon others' careers, using and improving methods of mass politics. They were particularly adept at creating images, myths, and rituals that furthered their own careers. Horowitz's treatment of Evita Perón, in particular, brings to life Latin America's best-known woman. His main finding is that populists divided society and antagonized those who dissented, creating strong feelings of anger. He concludes that the era of populism continues in Argentina.[4]

The chapter on Brazil by Michael Conniff picks up the story in the late 1920s, when metropolitan Rio de Janeiro surpassed a million inhabitants. That country's first populist, who served as mayor of Rio in the mid-1930s, showed that leaders could win elections by convincing the common people that he cared about their interests and well-being. He abandoned the old-style boss politics and created a mass following that might have led to the presidency itself had he not run afoul of the military. Others followed suit, in particular Adhemar de Barros in São Paulo and Getúlio Vargas, when he campaigned for president in 1950.[5] During the next fifteen years, which historians call the Populist Republic, this style dominated state and national politics. Even when the military took power in 1964 and attempted to eradicate populism, they were unsuccessful, because the political culture had embraced the ballot box and account-ability of leaders. In the 1980s and 1990s, the populist tradition was revived in the person of President Fernando Collor, whose brief and disastrous term fore-shadowed the end of an era. Despite a lull in populism, the style underwent a revival under President Luiz Inácio "Lula" da Silva.[6]

Paul Drake examines several key episodes in Chile's modern history, finding elements of populism that nevertheless did not develop into a strong tradition. The first presidency of Arturo Alessandri, the socialist interlude of Marmaduke Grove, and the front government of Pedro Aguirre Cerda might have evolved into a dominant style of electioneering and governance.[7] However, Drake finds that Chile's strong party system prevented such a development. Moreover, ideo-logical platforms ranging from conservative to Marxist grabbed voters' atten-tions and loyalties, leaving little room for populist appeals. Thus Chile was ex-ceptional among the larger countries of the region in not sustaining populism.

In Mexico, according to Jorge Basurto, the formative experience of populism was the extremely powerful administration of Lázaro Cárdenas in the 1930s. While drawing on revolutionary goals and rhetoric, Cárdenas forged a populist coalition that allowed him to sideline the military and dedicate his resources to helping the masses.[8] That legacy was revisited by President Luis Echeverría in the 1970s, yet the latter could not prevail over the conservative forces that had emerged in the 1950s. Instead, populism failed, and until 2000 Mexico's poli-tics were controlled by antidemocratic leaders in the Revolutionary Party (PRI). Basurto sees populism as a redemptive force in the 1990s, led by Cárdenas's son, Cuauhtémoc, who lost two presidential bids but later governed the metropolis of Mexico City. The surprise victory of conservative candidate Vicente Fox com-pletely disrupted national politics in 2000. In 2006 the next mayor of Mexico City, Andrés Manuel López Obrador mounted a populist campaign that nearly gave the reformers control of the presidency.

Steve Stein's chapter on Peru finds a long, often rocky history of populism in that country, beginning with the rise of the American Popular Revolutionary Alliance (APRA) party in the 1920s and the clash of young titans in the 1930 presidential election. APRA's longtime populist leader, Haya de la Torre, epito-mized the drive, style, appeal, and staying power of populism, yet he never won the presidency due to military opposition.[9] Another Peruvian, Fernando Be-laúnde Terry, chose the mantle of populism when campaigning in 1960 and 1961 and for a time enjoyed some success, with U.S. support. Amazingly, how-ever, a military government adopted many of the techniques and appeals of populism after taking power in 1968. Without a charismatic leader, or even a strong vocation for leadership, this unique experiment in "military populism" failed. Haya de la Torre's protégé, Alan García, led APRA into the presidential palace only after Haya died, yet he made a mockery of administration. The most extraordinary twist to the story is the triumph of Alberto Fujimori, a Peruvian of Japanese descent, when he was elected president in the 1990s. Stein finds that Fujimori is a textbook case of the neopopulists of the 1990s.

Venezuelan populism began with Rómulo Betancourt, who led his party to power in 1945, according to Steve Ellner. A forceful, charismatic figure, Betancourt almost single-handedly forged alliances and fostered democratic procedures that would orient Venezuelan politics for another generation.[10]

Ximena Sosa provides a fascinating view of populism in Ecuador, a country often overlooked by students of modern politics. Two leaders, José María Velasco Ibarra and Abdalá Bucaram, deeply influenced national affairs from the 1930s to the 1990s. Others arose to challenge them. Besides engaging portraits of these leaders, Sosa supplies background and analysis for understanding politics in her country.

Panama's sole experience with populism came during the career of Arnulfo Arias, three-time president, according to William Francis Robinson in chapter 8. Active from the 1930s to the 1980s, Arnulfo continues to influence Panama through his widow and the heir to his Arnulfista Party, Mireya Moscoso.

Kurt Weyland challenges the notion that neoliberal, or monetarist, economic policies are incompatible with populism. Instead, as he argues in chapter 9, several figures in recent history have adroitly used neoliberal economics to strengthen their appeal, thereby becoming neopopulists. He examines Carlos Menem in Argentina, Fernando Collor in Brazil, and Alberto Fujimori in Peru as prototypes of this new leadership.

A General Definition

Populism was an expansive style of election campaigning by colorful and engaging politicians who could draw masses of new voters into their movements and hold their loyalty indefinitely, even after their deaths. They inspired a sense of nationalism and cultural pride in their followers, and they promised to give them a better life as well. Populists campaigned mostly in the big cities, where tens of millions of people gained the franchise and exercised it at the ballot box. The vast majority of these new voters belonged to the working classes, which gave some of the populists a decidedly pro-labor image. Yet populists also attracted middle-class voters, who applauded the social and economic programs these leaders championed and who also obtained jobs and benefits from them. Even some wealthy and powerful citizens joined with the populists, believing that their programs and leadership would be good for their interests and the national destiny. Put simply, the populists raised more campaign money, got more voters to the polls, and held followers' allegiances far better than traditional politicians.

The populists exhibited charisma—that is, special personal qualities and talents that, in the eyes of their followers, empowered them to defend the interests of the masses and uphold national dignity. The masses no longer trusted oligarchical families, political parties, the church, established newspapers, or business elites. Previously, these privileged sectors selected presidents and legislators by giving them their blessing. When the privileged classes could no longer confer legitimacy, however, charismatic figures could claim the right to exercise power on behalf of the people.

The special attributes that made the populists charismatic varied widely: they exhibited such diverse traits as great intellect, empathy for the downtrodden, charity, clairvoyance, strength of character, moral rectitude, stamina and combativeness, the capacity to build, or saintliness. They also possessed power and did not hesitate to use it for their own purposes and for the benefit of their followers. Qualities such as these set the populists apart from and above the ranks of common politicians.

As the populists' successes and fame grew, their followers became even more devoted, convinced that their leaders could bring salvation in troubled times. Faith in their leaders' special attributes helped followers imagine that personal bonds joined them, transcending the limits of space and time. It is no exaggeration to say that at times a mass hypnotic state united leader and followers.[11] Upon the populist's death, his or her charisma often metamorphosed into myth, becoming a legend that lived on for decades. Charisma, though hard to define, was a crucial element in populism.

The populists promised to reform their societies and to improve the lives of the masses. They stood for change and betterment, both material and spiritual. The slogan for Juan Perón's Justicialismo was simply, "economic growth and social justice." Psychic rewards were important, especially during adverse times, when sacrifice was required. Populists could not be easily categorized as to ideology, however, because their programs rarely fit existing doctrinal schemes (for example, conservatism, liberalism, socialism). In fact, the most common label for their programs derived from simply adding *ismo* to their names: Peronismo, Getulismo, Adhemarismo, Velasquismo, Gaitanismo, etc.

The populists drew from existing sociopolitical models, like socialism, communism, democratic capitalism, fascism, and corporatism, for example. No single doctrine prevailed among them, however, and many recombined ideas inconsistently. Not a few changed their approaches sharply over time. Populists' ideas, then, were eclectic and flexible, designed to appeal to the largest number of voters at a given time.

National pride also infused populist rhetoric. Panama's three-time president Arnulfo Arias even called his credo "Panameñismo," the ultimate patriotic appeal (see chapter 8). The populists preached that the state should be strengthened in order to fulfill a great national destiny. The individual could take pride in being a citizen of this nation. By the same token, populists held themselves up as defenders of the popular sovereignty against foreign pressures and exploitation. Major international companies, in particular, came under attack by the populists, who claimed they squeezed the workers and bled the country of resources, with little commitment to economic development. National pride could turn xenophobic in times of general hardship, because foreign enemies were easier to blame than domestic ones.

The populists promised, and sometimes delivered, a better life for the masses. To do so, they used a variety of mechanisms to distribute favors (called patronage) and raise the general standard of living (which they termed economic development). They created government jobs, financed neighborhood improvements, authorized easy loans, subsidized food staples, set low fares for public transportation, decreed new and higher employment benefits, spent lavishly on charity, supported free education, and stoked economic growth with deficit spending. When they achieved positive results, the populists were revered by the masses for redistributing income in favor of the working class. Cárdenas, Perón, and Vargas did so during parts of their administrations and were credited with economic miracles.

Expansive economic policies often led to inflation, indebtedness, and charges of malfeasance, however, and the populists as a group have been blamed for irresponsible borrowing and spending. In fact, among some economists the term *populist* has come to mean opportunism and fiscal mismanagement exclusively.[12] It is certainly true that many populists took unorthodox directions and committed economic errors. They were not alone, however, because many traditional politicians also embraced innovative theories and actions and likewise failed at times. In fact, throughout much of the industrializing world, new economic concepts took hold in the 1940s, 1950s, and 1960s. Known generally as structuralism, these ideas led to government intervention, increased spending, public ownership, property reforms, and price regulation. By these means, government leaders sought to catch up with the economic powerhouses of North America and Europe.

The seeming triumph of more orthodox economics in the 1990s, variously known as neoliberalism, monetarism, or business capitalism, should not lead us to accuse populists alone for taking unorthodox paths a generation ago. Nor should we assume that they always did so for corrupt or irresponsible motives. Highly respected economists in the Keynesian tradition—for example, Galbraith, Hirschman, Prebisch, Sunkel, and Furtado—gave respectability to structuralism. The important point to remember is that expansive economic policies, legitimized by structuralist theories, served populist leaders especially well by offering both an expanding GDP pie—more for everybody—and more equitable distribution. It was a win-win economics that, unfortunately, did not succeed in the long run.

Not only were populists in step with the new political economy of the mid-century, they were also moderate in their application of it. When it came to redistributing wealth, power, and prestige to achieve the maximum benefits for all, populists did not go overboard. None advocated genuine revolution or the violent overthrow of the existing government followed by radical restructuring of society. Instead, they insisted on coming to power through elections and on changing society by the rule of law, according to the will of the people. Popular sovereignty, in fact, became something of an incantation for the populists.

Latin American populists promoted democracy even though they did not always behave in democratic ways. The very definition of the populists as representatives of the people required election and public approval of the leader. Still, many exhibited autocratic traits and abused their powers. While lawfully elected, some did not abide fully by the laws. In their quest for high office, they sometimes infringed others' rights of political expression and office. This seemingly paradoxical relationship between the leader as people's choice and as locus of authority is explored later in our discussion of elections.

The populists appealed to the common men and women, to the poor and working classes, and to the humble and downtrodden not only for votes but for legitimacy. To gain acceptance, they appropriated elements of folklore to show their nearness to the masses, and they were in turn embraced by popular culture. Haya de la Torre and Arnulfo Arias expressed pride in Indian heritage; Perón and Vargas evoked the ethos of the gaucho; Adhemar de Barros posed as a *caipira,* or country bumpkin; and Jorge Gaitán and Leonel Brizola always stressed their own poverty as youths to explain their identification with the poor. The most vivid examples of the folk acceptance of populists were their celebration in popular verses and songs throughout the region—sambas, cordeles, tangos, corridos, and other forms. This cultural approval of the leader, while impossible to quantify, was crucial for the lasting success of the populists.

The closest we will come to a synthetic description of Latin American populism may be expressed thus: Latin American populists were leaders who had charismatic relationships with mass followings and who won elections regularly. Reducing it to a formula, it might look thus:

populism = leader ↔ charismatic bond + elections ↔ followers

The Setting

Populism arose in Latin America during the early twentieth century in response to deep-going socioeconomic changes. In most countries, the huge expansion of exports to European markets of that era provided capital for urban reforms and growth, infrastructure development, and industrial expansion. Capitals and port cities, in particular, underwent major improvements complemented with massive redevelopment programs. Rio, Buenos Aires, Lima, Caracas, Santiago, Mexico City, and Bogotá all became major metropolises in the early years of this century, and dozens of other cities grew rapidly as well. Manufacturing and population growth went hand in hand, concentrating people and resources in big cities.

Migrants and immigrants crowded into these cities—as workers and employees or simply a new generation of young people—and they became available to activists of all sorts. Labor organizers, evangelists, military enlisters, retail hawkers, politicians, and myriad others recruited these newcomers for their movements and products. For those recently arrived, urban life was liberating and invigorating yet also dangerous and sometimes oppressive. Slums burgeoned with urban poor, riots erupted, services broke down, workers struck, and people began to feel out of touch with their families and regional origins. A generalized sense of rootlessness and malaise, which sociologists call *anomie,* afflicted many city dwellers.

The generalized sense of alienation in big cities affected virtually all groups. Workers toiled in sweatshops for meager wages, with little hope of sharing the fruits of the booming economies. Children of immigrants felt ostracized because of their foreign surnames and family traditions. Youths growing up in the cities could not expect to live as well as their parents. People of color—mestizos, Indians, and Afro-Latinos—experienced discrimination in schools, workplaces, government offices, and even commercial establishments. Women suffered multiple disadvantages, except for those who belonged to upper-class families. Migrants from rural areas found limited chances to advance in the cities. These sectors shared nothing but their common lack of opportunities, and they often fought among themselves for minor benefits. In short, although it offered advantages over rural and small-town existence, life in early-twentieth-century cities was harsh.

About the time large numbers of poor people began to experience anomie, political elites increased their control over the lives of middle- and working-class people. They rigged elections to stay in power and then used the police to regulate day-to-day life in the cities. They developed corrupt organizations to gather votes on election day and to preserve their power. A veritable rogues' gallery of election riggers ran early-twentieth-century Latin American politics. Rarely was the popular will expressed through honest elections.

Meanwhile, new methods of surveillance made it easier to police the masses. Automobiles, telephones, telegraph, recording devices, photography, radios, automatic weapons, and espionage allowed police departments to monitor and control the citizenry as never before. Police watched for and suppressed any activities that threatened the monopoly of power wielded by the elites. The agents of law and order paid little attention to individual rights, because their actions were sanctioned by higher authority. Police targeted organizations as well as individuals, especially labor unions, student groups, radical parties, and leaders of minority groups in general. Persons suspected of disrupting the peace were routinely harassed and jailed, and foreigners were often deported.

After the turn of the twentieth century, then, most urban Latin Americans lived under what today would be regarded as very undemocratic conditions. In earlier times, things had not been any more democratic, to be sure, but landowners were likely to be the agents of control and repression, not governments. Moreover, Latin America lagged behind Europe and North America in the gradual expansion of individual rights and self-governance.

Conditions were ripe in Latin America for leaders who could give the masses a sense of belonging, provide a semblance of representative government, and undertake changes that would improve daily life. These leaders did emerge and took the initiative in urban politics. Their style of campaigning and administration was later dubbed populism, after its earlier counterparts in Russia and the United States.

Urbanization and industrialization are often cited as causes of populism in Latin America, because they amassed millions in the cities and made them available to politicians who could appeal to them. We cannot, however, point to any direct causality, because urban and industrial growth did not always lead to populism and because populism sometimes arose in their absence. More accurately, we can state that these factors created sociopolitical conditions highly favorable to the rise of populist leadership.

The Impact of New Technologies

The general expansion of Latin American economies in the early twentieth century aided the rise of populist politics. It made possible new systems of transportation and communication, thereby allowing candidates to reach large audiences of potential voters more easily. The advent of streetcars, ferries, commuter trains, and buses made urban campaigning much more effective. Telephone and telegraph services helped party managers to schedule candidate appearances and bargain with local representatives. Gradually whole cities became single-voter precincts available to ambitious and adroit politicians. Skillful use of these new media was an important attribute of the populists.

In the 1920s and 1930s radio made its debut in politics. Radio not only reached tens of thousands but also broadcasted candidates' words and promises in appealing ways, with sound effects, music, background audience, and clarity unattainable otherwise. Candidates who mastered the radio seemed modern, competent, and appealing. Latin American cities became laboratories of campaign innovation using radio waves.

By the 1950s television began to appear in a few large markets, and populist leaders immediately embraced it. TV made the candidates' faces familiar, their gestures and expressions recognizable, and their slogans and symbols more immediate. Indeed, the advent of television brought on the marketing of candidates using the most modern techniques available.[13]

In addition, long-distance transportation service and communications media brought politicians into contact with voters throughout their national territories. The airplane began to revolutionize campaigning after World War I. Populists barnstormed in small planes, and in many towns and villages it was the first time people had ever seen or heard a national politician, much less an airplane. Air travel also became a metaphor for modernization that enhanced candidates' images.

By the 1950s radio broadcasters developed national chains, and a decade later their television counterparts did the same. Truly national campaigns, while costly, could present candidates in appealing ways to audiences all over the country. Cadres of professional media experts came to manage elections. The populists were more talented in media communication than their competitors and hence were able to forge national followings drawn from the big cities as well as the towns of the interior.

Phases of Populism

The sweep of over a century of populist politics in the region may be conveniently broken down into periods. The first two decades of the century saw the advent of early populism by precursors like José Batlle y Ordóñez (1903–7, 1911–15) in Uruguay and Guillermo Billinghurst (1912–14) in Peru. In addition, Hipólito Yrigoyen in his 1916–22 administration pioneered the style later dubbed populist.

During the 1920s and 1930s populism became more widespread as the conditions for it matured and newly available media made it feasible to amass large electoral followings. Yrigoyen's politics in and out of power confirmed his place as a leading populist. Arturo Alessandri's election and first administration (1920–25) revealed populist elements. Air force colonel Marmaduke Grove, briefly leader of a Socialist government in Chile during 1932, aspired to a populist leadership. Víctor Raúl Haya de la Torre launched his career in Peru during these years, although he did not win any elections. The mayor of Rio de Janeiro from 1931–36, Pedro Ernesto Baptista introduced populism into Brazil, and later it was adopted by Adhemar de Barros during his first term as governor of São Paulo (1938–41).

Lázaro Cárdenas, the president of Mexico from 1934 to 1940, was a populist. Cárdenas campaigned vigorously for his election, going beyond the official backing provided by the incumbent party. He carried out vast programs to achieve goals written into the Constitution of 1917. He remodeled and strengthened the multiclass party his predecessor had founded. He eased the powerful Mexican army out of its preeminent role in politics. His outstanding qualities were deep concern for the peasants and workers, plus steady pursuit of constructive reforms. Recognition of his charisma spread mostly by word of mouth. The only modern technologies he used extensively were the radio, airplane, and telephone. Like several other populists, he was not a bombastic, crowd-pleasing orator. His influence grew quietly through thousands of face-to-face meetings. No Mexican leader since has been able to forge the kind of charisma Cárdenas achieved in the 1930s.

The second period, the heyday of Latin American populism, began in the 1940s and ended in the 1960s. This era saw populism emerge as the main form of politics in many countries; in others, it challenged traditional leaders to become more representative.

In 1944, a number of Latin American leaders began to advocate free elections and widening the franchise, a classic populist appeal. Democratization was triggered by the accumulating victories of the Allied forces in World War II. Whirlwind campaigning ensued in many countries, and populism reached its apogee in the 1950s. In most countries, women gained the vote following the war and became a potent force for change.[14]

In Brazil, Getúlio Vargas adopted the approaches pioneered by Pedro Ernesto and Adhemar and eventually conducted that country's first modern election in 1950. He was soon challenged not only by Adhemar but by other populists, such as Jânio Quadros, Juscelino Kubitschek, and Carlos Lacerda. By the late 1950s they were joined by others, such as Miguel Arraes, Leonel Brizola, and João Goulart. Little wonder that Brazilian historians refer to the 1945–64 era as the Populist Republic.

In Argentina, the foremost populist leaders of the region, Juan Perón and his wife, Evita, began their political campaigns in 1944 and captured power in

1946 with a stunning election victory. Perón would only be removed by a military coup in 1955.

In 1940, Panama's president Arnulfo Arias launched what would become a long and tumultuous career in populist politics. In 1944 the former president of Ecuador, José María Velasco Ibarra, returned to office, this time as a populist without equal in his country. The energetic leader of Venezuela's Acción Democrática, Rómulo Betancourt, led a coup in 1945 and established a regime considered populist by most analysts. The front-runner in Colombia's 1950 election, Jorge Gaitán, was gunned down before the election, ending the first populist campaign in that country's history.

A young populist in Cuba, Eddie Chibás, considered a strong contender for the presidency, instead took his own life in 1951 out of frustration with electoral corruption. During the 1950s Gen. Carlos Ibáñez of Chile resurrected his career with a distinctly populist administration as president (1952–58). Populists dominated Brazilian national politics until the military took over in 1964. Arnulfo Arias returned to power (1949–51), as did Velasco Ibarra (1952–56, 1960–62). Víctor Paz Estenssoro's revolutionary government in Bolivia took on frankly populist overtones in the mid-1950s. Only dictatorial regimes or firmly rooted democracies were immune to the expansive politics of the era.

By the early 1960s, however, populism seemed to falter as a major form of politics. For one thing, the triumph of Fidel Castro's revolution in Cuba polarized the hemisphere and reduced the room in which mainstream politicians could maneuver for votes. Increasingly, military groups removed presidents whom they accused of stirring up the masses and encouraging leftists. The coups against Arturo Frondizi in 1962 and Goulart in 1964 were of this nature. In addition, most people had become registered voters in preceding years, so that populists could not find as many new recruits as before. In short, the conditions that had favored the rise of populism in the 1920s, 1930s, and 1940s had eroded.

From the mid-1960s on, a wave of military governments took power, the onset of a period of authoritarian regimes. These governments were diametrically opposed to populism and justified their existence on the grounds that the populists had encouraged strikes, communism, inflation, and corruption. Military leaders promised to restore order and good administration and to carry out socioeconomic reforms from above. This was an era of antipopulist government.[15]

A few populist leaders and movements persisted but did not prosper. Juan Perón returned to the presidency in 1973 but promptly died, leaving his inexperienced widow, María Estela Perón (1974–76), to cope with deteriorating conditions in Argentina. The daughter of Colombian dictator Gustavo Rojas

Pinilla, María Eugenia Rojas, revived her father's National Popular Alliance or ANAPO party in the 1960s and ran credible populist campaigns. Several governors and congressmen in Brazil managed to defy the military and resurrect populism. Michael Manley's term as prime minister of Jamaica in the 1970s was decidedly populist, yet he was unable to convert early support into effective administration. In Ecuador, Jaime Roldós and Assad Bucaram took their populistic Concentration of Popular Forces (CFP) organization into the presidency in the late 1970s, but within two years both died. Mexican president Luis Echeverría (1970–76) consciously tried to recreate the politics that Cárdenas had employed so successfully, but he failed utterly. Populism seemed to be dying out.

In the last period, following *apertura* (redemocratization) in the late 1970s, populism experienced a revival in some countries. Most notably, when the military stepped down in Peru, APRA's candidate, Alan García, won the presidential election with a frankly populist campaign. His term (1985–90) proved disastrous, however, due to poor leadership and rough relations with other APRA leaders. The subsequent government of Alberto Fujimori, while neoliberal in its economics, took a frankly populist approach that was at first both successful and viable.

When the Brazilian military decreed amnesty for exiles in 1979, several former populists staged successful comebacks, mostly at the state level. By the mid-1980s, Leonel Brizola, Jânio Quadros, and Miguel Arraes had won governorships or mayoral races in the states of Rio de Janeiro, São Paulo, and Pernambuco, respectively. None was able to advance to the presidency, however, or build a national constituency.[16]

Carlos Menem, president of Argentina from 1989–95 and reelected for a second term, became a neopopulist. Although he campaigned on the traditional pro-labor, economic interventionist platform of his Peronist party, once in office he enacted very different policies, consonant with the neoliberal ideas current in the world. Despite this flip-flop, Menem became for a time Argentina's most successful leader in several generations.

Brazil's Fernando Collor de Melo (1990–92) also employed a populist style during his campaign and first year in office. Youthful, handsome, athletic, and well spoken, Collor ran virtually without a party, on a platform stressing honesty, renewal, and neoliberal economics. This image, conveyed effectively to the masses through overweening media, proved captivating, and he won a close runoff against the Workers' Party candidate, Luiz Inácio "Lula" da Silva. Collor's pose as an outsider ready to overhaul the corrupt system of previous generations transformed into an inchoate charisma early in his administration. During his second year in office, however, Collor was implicated in a major fraud scheme involving kickbacks on government contracts. In 1992 he was impeached and resigned from office, a failed populist at best. His 1994 acquittal of corruption charges did not lead to his rehabilitation.

Some writers have debated whether or not populism will die out in this new century. Those predicting its demise argue that electoral expansion has ended, since most people now have the vote. The dominance of electronic media and techniques of political marketing have rendered nearly all candidates charismatic and "sellable," given enough money. Personal attributes and quasi-mystical connections with the masses no longer seem relevant to urbanized masses. And perhaps most important, the globalization of new economic, social, and environmental policies have rendered the old populist measures obsolete. These analysts argue that populism is finished in Latin America.

Other observers point to the continued attraction of old-timers like Leonel Brizola and Miguel Arraes, and the evocative power of names like Perón, Batlle, Bucaram, and Cárdenas, as proof of the renewed viability of populism. They note the cult worship, even among young people, of figures like Evita, Lázaro Cárdenas, and João Goulart and the popularity of leaders who can manipulate the old symbols of cultural nationalism. Perhaps Menem and Fujimori have shown how to adapt populism to the changing times. After all, populists were always adept at bridging the gap between traditional and progressive measures. These analysts believe that conditions may soon be ripe for a major resurgence of populism, citing the emergence of Hugo Chávez, Rafael Correa, and Evo Morales in recent years.

Therefore, it may be premature to declare that populism is either moribund or on the rebound.

Structural Characteristics

Organizational aspects of populist movements, in addition to leadership and means of reaching the masses, have struck observers as very important in distinguishing them from other forms of political mobilization. The multiclass makeup of populism stood in contrast to most other parties in the region, which drew from restricted social strata, for example, the workers, middle sectors, or rural landowners. Populists' broad appeals gave their parties heterogeneous followings that were unwieldy yet also very effective in reaching newly enfranchised voters, a something-for-everyone approach. Only very clever leaders could manage this without tripping over discrepant planks in their platforms.

In his classic article on populist coalitions, Torcuato Di Tella diagrammed various possibilities, reproduced in figure 1. The Peronist alliance, he believed, was the closest to pure populism. Many other observers have taken these sug-

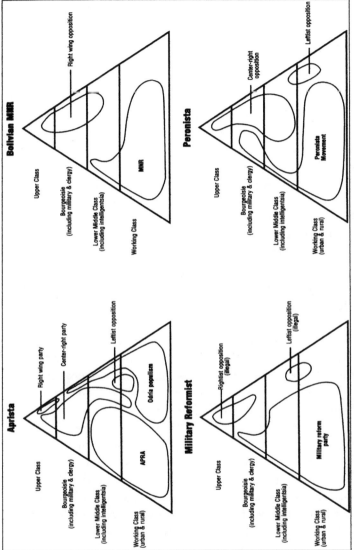

Figure I.1. Torcuato Di Tella's Four Models of Populist Parties. (From Torcuato S. Di Tella, "Populismo y reforma en America Latina," *Desarrollo economic* 4, no. 16 [1965]: 391–425.)

gestions and applied them in other settings. His most powerful finding was that all the variations drew on at least two classes and often from three. Since 1964 most theoretical writing has emphasized this feature.

Others have noted that the populist parties of Latin America did not meet criteria by which parties in the United States and Western Europe are judged, especially regarding aggregation of interests and adjudication of conflicts. Rather, personalismo and centralization, lasting features of Latin American leadership, infused populist movements as well. All decisions, appointments, and initiatives required action by the leader. This tendency undermined the effectiveness of populist leaders once in office, because no mechanisms had been created for shared decision making and delegation of power. Moreover, personalismo condemned these movements to instability when the leader died or was removed from the scene, as happened frequently.

Despite their reluctance to bureaucratize their parties, populists were astute coalition builders. They formed alliances between existing interest groups and newly enfranchised sectors. The growing cities contained diverse groups recently active in politics—such as factory workers, white-collar employees, tradesmen, and the self-employed—as well as politicized sectors of professionals and public servants. The populists imaginatively constructed broad, heterogeneous followings by appealing to diverse groups in different ways. They also formulated vague programs and doctrines with which many sectors and classes could identify—Perón's Justicialismo and Vargas's Trabalhismo are good examples.

Populists also pioneered new enlistment methods that displaced traditional clientelism. The clientelist party relied on individuals' self-interests, offering a little something for everyone. Each person in a complex network of relationships claimed a degree of autonomy vis-à-vis others in the system. Clientelist recruitment, then, incorporated voters more slowly and broke down when presented with major policy demands. Clientelism had the further disadvantages of being expensive to sustain and unreliable in times of crisis.

In the populist mode, initiative and responsibility gravitated to the leader, whose charisma bridged the space occupied by clientelist intermediaries. The leader delegated the usual work of politics to aides: speech writing, managing the media, rallies, and fundraising. These anonymous staffers could not rival the leader; their only hope for advancement was to enhance the leader's popularity and win elections. In this manner, well-directed campaigns reached out and won over new voters rapidly.

Populists' campaign organizations did not have to dispense as much patronage as their clientelist rivals because the psychic rewards and security provided by the leader largely replaced tangible payoffs. The populists could also respond more quickly to changes and opportunities than traditional leaders, since they did not have to consult elaborate councils and committees. Finally, populists actually flourished in times of crisis, because their charisma reassured and calmed their followers.

Election Results

Populists, like most politicians in the Western world, measured their initial successes in terms of votes won. Elections were central to populism in Latin America, simultaneously as cause, means, and result. Populists first had to fight for fair elections to be held. Then they developed innovative ways to reach and win over ever-growing numbers of voters. Finally, in order to win subsequent election campaigns, they pressed to broaden further the franchise and assure impartial procedures.

In the early days populists like Batlle, Yrigoyen, and Alessandri had to struggle to affirm the sovereignty of the popular will, because free elections had never been held before. The early campaign slogans conveyed the urgency of their demands: Yrigoyen's "Intransigencia" until clean elections were held, Francisco Madero's "Effective Suffrage and No Reelection," and Batlle's "No More Deals." Without honest elections, these and many other candidates had no hope of gaining office.

Once clean elections were assured, later populists pushed to expand the suffrage and improve the administration of elections. Gradually they extended the vote to younger and unpropertied persons and to women. Their campaigns prospered because many of the newly enfranchised were loyal to the leaders who gave them the vote. By the 1950s and 1960s, populists urged better methods of polling voters, using simple, secret, uniform ballots. These reforms were often accompanied by the creation of independent judicial boards to supervise elections and certify their results. Even after the authoritarian turn of government in the 1960s, these procedures remained in effect, thanks largely to their institutionalization.

Finally, by the 1970s and 1980s the trend toward even greater inclusion in the electoral process had produced near-universal suffrage. In most countries, eighteen-year-olds vote. Brazil even lowered the voting age to sixteen and enfranchised illiterates. Peru and Chile did so as well. Moreover, most countries now require that voters exercise that right or face fines and bureaucratic hassles. The obligatory vote undoubtedly causes larger turnouts.

These election improvements had a number of outcomes. Most notably, they increased the volume of voting many times over. Elections went from virtually nonexistent to mass participation in the course of the last century. Table I.1 demonstrates the dramatic increase experienced in most countries. Surpris-

Table I.1. Voter Turnout in Latin America, 1900–2010
(year, turnout in millions—rounded to nearest 100,000)

Decade	Argentina	Bolivia	Brazil	Chile	Colombia	Ecuador	Mexico	Peru	Uruguay	Venezuela
1900			'02, .6 '06, .3			'01, .1 '05, .1			'07, .5*	
1910	'16, .7		'10, .6 '14, .6 '18, .4	'15, .1		'11, .1 '12, .1 '16, .1	'10, >.1 '11, >.1 '17, .8		'14, .1*	
1920	'22, .9 '28, 1.5		'22, .8 '26, .7	'20, .2 '25, .3 '27, .2		'20, .1 '24, .2	'20, 1.2 '24, 1.6 '29, 2.1		'26, .3	
1930	'31, 1.6 '37, 2.0		'30, 1.9	'31, 1.3 '32, .3 '38, .4	'30, .8 '34, .9 '38, .5	'32, .2 '34, .2	'34, 2.3	'31, .3 '36, .2 '39, .3	'30, .3	
1940	'46, 2.9		'45, 6.2	'42, .5 '46, .5	'42, 1.1 '46, 1.4 '49, 1.1	'40, .1 '48, .3	'40, 2.3	'45, .5		'46, 1.4 '47, 1.2
1950	'51, 7.6 '58, 9.1	'51, .1 '56, 1.0	'50, 8.3 '55, 9.1	'52, 1.0 '58, 1.3	'57, 4.4 '58, 3.1	'52, .4 '56, .6	'52, 3.7 '58, 7.5	'56, 1.3	'50, .9 '54, .9 '58, 1.0	'58, 2.7

1960	'63, 9.3	'60, 1.0; '64, 1.3	'60, 12.6; '66, 17.0*	'62, 2.6; '66, 2.5	'64, 2.5	'60, .8; '68, .9	'64, 9.4	'63, 2.0	'62, 1.2
1970	'73, 12.1		'70, 22.0*; '74, 29.0*; '78, 38.0*	'70, 4.0; '74, 4.8; '78, 4.9	'70, 3.0	'79, 1.7	'70, 14.1; '76, 16.7		'71, 1.7
1980	'83, 15.4; '89, 17.0	'80, 1.5; '85, 1.7; '87, 1.3*; '89, 1.6	'82, 48.0*; '84, 55.0*; '86, 69.0*; '89, 70.0	'82, 6.8; '86, 7.1	'89, 7.2	'84, 3.0; '88, 3.6	'82, 22.5	'80, 4.0; '85, 7.6	'84, 1.8; '89, 2.3
1990	'94, 15.4*; '95, 17.9; '99, 19.0	'93, 1.7; '97, 2.3	'94, 94.0	'90, 6.4; '94, 7.7	'93, 7.3	'92, 4.2; '96, 4.8; '98, 5.0	'94, 35.5	'90, 7.2; '95, 9.1	'94, 1.9; '99, 2.2
2000	'03, 19.6; '07, 19.4	'02, 3.0; '05, 3.1; '09, 4.9	'02, 91.7; '06, 95.8	'02, 11.2; '06, 12.1	'00, 7.3; '06, 7.1	'02, 5.1; '06, 7.0; '09, 7.9	'00, 37.6; '06, 41.8	'01, 12.1; '06, 14.5	'04, 2.2; '09, 2.3
2010			'10, 111.0	'10, 13.3	'10, 7.2				

(Final column — '63 series)

1960	'63, 3.1; '68, 3.7
1970	'73, 4.4; '78, 5.3
1980	'83, 6.8; '88, 7.5
1990	'93, 5.8; '98, 7.0
2000	'00, 6.6; '06, 11.8
2010	

*Congressional only

Note: actual votes cast, including blank and null ballots

Sources: 1900–1999, Michael L. Conniff, ed., *Latin American Populism in Comparative Perspective* (Albuquerque: University of New Mexico Press, 1982), 18–19; James W. Wilkie, ed., *Statistical Abstract of Latin America* (Los Angeles: UCLA Latin American Center, annual), vols. 24–30; *Keesing's Record of World Events*, annual, 1985–95.

2000–2010: http://www.idea.int/vt/; *Keesing's Record of World Events*, annual, 2000–2011.

ingly, elections even affected military governments indirectly in the 1970s and 1980s. Contests for state and local offices became informal plebiscites on government performance. In many places, large numbers of blank and invalid ballots served as indictments of the governments' conduct. In Argentina, Brazil, Peru, and Chile, declining fortunes at the polls helped convince military rulers to remove themselves from power.

Populists did not dominate, much less win, every election in Latin America, of course, but it seems fair to attribute much of the growing importance of the ballot box and improved procedures to populist campaigns earlier in the century.

The populists' contribution to establishing fair, broad elections does not mean that they were necessarily democratic themselves or that they would forgo victories to protect popular sovereignty. Many populists had earlier careers as traditional, even oligarchical, leaders. Several imposed dictatorships—Vargas from 1937 to 1945 and Perón (from behind the scenes) from 1943 to 1945, for example. A number conspired against duly constituted governments from exile. And in office, a number of the populists regularly violated the laws under which they were elected.

To some extent, the populists' devotion to electoral means of winning office ran against the grain of their personalities. Virtually all were driven, ambitious, even obsessed with gaining power. They sacrificed their families and health in order to campaign for office. Such win-at-all-cost motivation led them to unethical and undemocratic behavior. Many ran their parties as little more than personal fan clubs and campaign organizations. Paradoxically, though, they felt obliged to win popular approval through elections and thus contributed to the consolidation of democratic procedures.

Populism in the Twenty-First Century

Given the perspective of more than a hundred years of populist experience, historians and political scientists continue to search for its core essence, especially today in a Latin America more democratic and developed than ever before. Paul Drake's text, *Between Tyranny and Anarchy*, argues that the neopopulist label does not help delineate a coherent group of leaders following policies from the classic era—rather, they act as opportunists who follow the global policies of the day. Even the leftists Hugo Chávez and Evo Morales fail to achieve the solid coalitions of their predecessors. Mitchell Seligson, on the other hand, analyzed recent opinion surveys from around the region to chart ideological drift and openness to populist measures. With regard to the latter, he found that younger, poorer, and less educated citizens were more tolerant of populism than others. He did not find a necessary connection between the rise of left-wing leaders and populism.[17]

Yet another take on the issue comes from the edited book, *Leftovers*, by Jorge Castañeda and Marco Morales. Their introduction focuses on the surge of leftist leaders in the region since 2000 and attempts to both understand and explain this phenomenon. While cognizant of populist behavior among some of these leaders, Castañeda and Morales emphasize their ideological leanings and treat populism as something of a stylistic overlay. They show that elections have given a decided preference for leaders on the left, yet trend toward the more moderate ones fairly consistently over radical ones. They believe that a moderate/radical dichotomy is observable and important, because the politics they reflect are far too complex for the single category "leftist."[18]

Given these considerations, we may conclude that populism may not disappear in the twenty-first century as much as fade away, to be replaced by other leadership behaviors. Thus Hugo Chávez may be compared to the neopopulists of the 1990s, yet the most salient features of his regime may be his radicalism and confrontational style.

In the 1982 predecessor volume to this book, John Wirth began his preface with the incantation, "Populism is dead . . . Long live populism." Since then we have learned to be careful in pronouncing populism's death, and indeed we chronicled the rise of neopopulism in our 1999 volume. So caution leads us to the conclusion that populism may once again arise, probably in new guises.

This introduction has offered a broad overview of the populist experience in Latin America. It conveys a sense of the writing about leading populists, their campaigns, and the eras in which they flourished. The nine original essays that follow comprise the core of this book. They give more detailed studies of individual countries and leaders, taking into account their political cultures and chronologies. The campaigns, the excitement, the disappointment, and the individuals come alive in these chapters.

Notes

1. On women in populist politics, see Karen Kampwirth, ed., *Gender and Populism in Latin America: Passionate Politics* (University Park: Pennsylvania State University Press, 2010).

2. In this vein, see Rudiger Dornbusch and Sebastian Edwards, eds., *The Macroeconomics of Populism in Latin America* (Chicago: University of Chicago Press, 1991).

3. Our earlier volume, Michael L. Conniff, ed., *Latin American Populism in Comparative Perspective* (Albuquerque: University of New Mexico Press, 1982), helped elucidate the field in the 1980s. Alan Knight's article, "Populism and Neopopulism

in Latin America, Especially Mexico," *Journal of Latin American Studies* 30 (1998): 225–48, provides a valuable survey emphasizing Mexico.

4. See his *Argentine Unions, the State, and the Rise of Perón, 1930–1945* (Berkeley, CA: Institute for International Studies, 1990) for further background.

5. Michael L. Conniff, *Urban Politics in Brazil: The Rise of Populism, 1925–1945* (Pittsburgh: University of Pittsburgh Press, 1981).

6. Kurt Weyland, *Democracy without Equity: Failures of Reform in Brazil* (Pittsburgh: University of Pittsburgh Press, 1996).

7. Paul W. Drake, *Socialism and Populism in Chile, 1932–52* (Urbana: University of Illinois Press, 1978).

8. Jorge Basurto, "Populismo y movilización de masas en México durante el régimen Cardenista," *Revista mexicana de sociología* 31, no. 4 (1969): 853–92; Marjorie Becker, *Setting the Virgin on Fire* (Berkeley and Los Angeles: University of California Press, 1995).

9. Steve Stein, *Populism in Peru: The Emergence of the Masses and the Politics of Social Control* (Madison: University of Wisconsin Press, 1980).

10. Steve Ellner, *Los partidos políticos y su disputa por el control del movimiento sindical en Venezuela, 1936–1948* (Caracas: Universidad Católica Andrés Bello, 1980).

11. Francisco Weffort makes this point in *O populismo na política brasileira* (Rio: Paz e Terra, 1978).

12. See Dornbusch and Edwards, *Macroeconomics.*

13. Thomas E. Skidmore, ed., *Television, Politics, and the Transition to Democracy in Latin America* (Washington, D.C.: Woodrow Wilson Center, and Baltimore: Johns Hopkins University Press, 1993) explores the impact of this medium in recent decades.

14. Leslie Bethell and Ian Roxborough, eds., *Latin America between the Second World War and the Cold War, 1944–1948* (New York: Cambridge University Press, 1992).

15. Brian Loveman and Thomas M. Davies Jr., eds., *The Politics of Antipolitics: The Military in Latin America* (Wilmington: Scholarly Resources, 1997).

16. On the transition in Brazil, see Thomas E. Skidmore, *The Politics of Military Rule in Brazil, 1964–1985* (New York: Oxford University Press, 1988).

17. Paul Drake, *Between Tyranny and Anarchy* (Stanford: Stanford University Press, 2009), 204–5; Mitchell A. Seligson, "The Rise of Populism and the Left in Latin America," *The Journal of Democracy*, 18, no. 3 (July 2007): 81–95.

18. Jorge G. Castañeda and Marco A. Morales, eds., *Leftovers: Tales of the Latin American Left* (New York: Routledge, 2008), 3–18.

1

Populism and Its Legacies in Argentina

Joel Horowitz

Populism and its aftermath have dominated the political history of modern Argentina. Much of the style and rhetoric of politics derives from populism. More important, some seemingly unbridgeable schisms in today's society can be traced directly to populism. While populist movements attracted the support of masses of people, they simultaneously repelled major sectors of society. Populists defined themselves as the saviors of the nation and their opponents as enemies of the people. Thus politics revolved around movements that won strong allegiances but excluded their enemies. This contributed to a cycle of military takeovers that ultimately produced massive violence, involving both the military and civilians. Populism addressed certain problems, but it also produced new ones. The answers that it provided, or perhaps the style of the answers, deeply divided Argentina.

A key populist legacy is leadership style. The leader, whether in power or exile, dominates his party for long stretches. The party might undergo internal struggles, but once the leader has settled them, his rule is almost unchallengeable. Within the Peronist Party, this role of caudillo was borne by three men; the baton of Juan Perón was eventually picked up by Carlos Menem and then by Néstor Kirchner. This pattern of leadership is more noticeable within the Radical Party, which even after ceasing to be populist retains its style. Hipólito Yrigoyen was followed by Marcelo T. de Alvear, Ricardo Balbín, and Raúl Alfonsín. They continued to dominate their party after their popularity had faded with the public at large. Even when the parties adopted attributes of "modern" politics, such as conventions, they continued to be dominated by strong-willed leaders.

At the outset, a working list of populist characteristics in Argentina will be helpful. Populist movements claimed not to be class based. Ideologically they were incoherent but they tried to be inclusive. Their leaders were overwhelmingly personalistic and also charismatic. Their style was nationalistic, so they drew on native traditions or at least pseudo-traditions of the country. They evinced a deep concern for reform, social justice, betterment of the working class, and integration of the poor into society. They portrayed class conflict as alien. The core populist message promised change without altering the fundamental nature of society. Populist parties also claimed to have the answers to the problems of the nation and argued that those who opposed them were unpatriotic. They tended to ally with unions and to build a strong centralized state with power focused on the president.

What is crucial is that the populists threatened the elites' control over their world more than their economic interests.[1] It is the populists' style, their confrontation of the elite, and their rejection of the elite manner of behavior that sets them apart from other movements.

Early Argentine Populism

At the end of the nineteenth century Argentina underwent a prodigious economic change that transformed it from a relatively poor country to the richest in Latin America, and a wealthy nation by any standard. It became rich enough to attract large-scale immigration from southern and eastern Europe.

Argentina's economic miracle was made possible by the sudden opportunity to use the fertile lands of the Pampas, some of the best in the world. Rising world demand, the ability to attract hundreds of thousands of immigrants, and the building of railroads and other types of infrastructure permitted Argentina to become a major exporter of meat and grain. While this rapid economic transition went on, politics remained largely unchanged. Elite elements governed behind a facade of democracy, but fraud reigned in the voting process. This continued despite rapid urbanization, population growth, and the emergence of a middle class.

The modern political system began in the wake of a failed attempt to overthrow the government in 1890. The country's first modern political party, the Radical Party (Unión Cívica Radical, also called the Radicals or the UCR) emerged out of the coup. The Radical Party opposed the political system by refusing to participate in it and by calling for fair elections. Behind its push for fair elections lay the threat of revolution, which it attempted several times. The party's primary base of support was in the middle sectors of society. Much of the leadership, however, came from the elite, but appeals were directed toward the working class.[2] The man who came to dominate the party was Hipólito Yrigoyen (1852–1933), a strange leader for a modern party. He was the illegitimate son of a Basque blacksmith and of a woman from the elite. He never married but had at least six children with different women. He used the title "doctor" without having earned it. He infrequently appeared, and even more rarely spoke, in public. He wrote little for popular consumption, and what he wrote was difficult to understand.[3] There was little consistent political philosophy behind his utterances. When he reached the presidency in 1916, he seemed much more interested in power and expanding it than in any program.

Yrigoyen, however, was a master politician. He created the machinery of a modern political party and outmaneuvered all his rivals. Despite his quirky nature and his secretive behavior, he made himself into a symbol of the Radical Party. He represented the hopes of the party faithful. Crowds detached the horses from his carriage at his inauguration in 1916 and pulled it through the streets. A cult of personality developed around him.

The Radical Party apparatus generated adoring works. For example in 1929 the Radical Party daily, *La Epoca,* carried the following poem, entitled "To the Great Argentine President Dr. Hipólito Yrigoyen":

The Country adorns itself with your name triumphant,
And the Fatherland praises you deservedly and with love,
Because always, your slogan was forward!
And your creed nobility, ideal and ardor.

I that knew to mock the people a moment,
Learned from your lips the best word,
The word that says: a brilliant Fatherland
I will leave as the inheritance of my effort and honor.

The workers of all the Argentine region
Today bless your name and the battle that culminates
In the supreme progress of this immense Nation.

The Nation that tomorrow will judge your memory
As the limpid page of your clear story
Of one who was an apostle and an eminent man.[4]

This poem was not unusual. Radical Party publications were filled with doggerel and statements that sung Yrigoyen's praises.

It is difficult to fully comprehend what evoked such popular support for Yrigoyen and whether his conduct can be called populist or simply popular.

He did not campaign with the flamboyant gestures or oratory of most populists. In many ways he simply built a traditional political machine by dispensing patronage and creating jobs. The bureaucracy and the scope of government
expanded quickly. His opponents considered this one of his chief defects. He
used older political techniques and was not especially innovative, but he pushed
those methods to their limit.

Police chiefs had always played central political roles in Argentina, and Yrigoyen strengthened the tradition. His chiefs of police of Buenos Aires, for example, functioned as key operatives, even settling labor conflicts. Their importance was shown by the career path of Elpidio González, a key Yrigoyen ally. He
went from minister of war, to candidate for governor of the important province
of Córdoba, to police chief of Buenos Aires, to vice president, and to minister
of interior. A good police chief was a man for all seasons.

Yrigoyen did appeal to new groups and spoke about altering society without
changing its underlying nature. His rhetoric stressed change. While scorning the
idea of class conflict, he continually attacked the oligarchy, the ill-defined rural-
based elite of which he was a marginal member. One way he attracted support
was by treating the middle and working classes like true members of society.
(This approach was later used by Juan Perón in the 1940s.) Under Yrigoyen,
middle-class politicians held considerable power for the first time.

Sometimes Yrigoyen's gestures were obvious. During a 1917 strike at a meatpacking plant, he turned down an interview with the leaders of the Sociedad
Rural, the cattlemen's association, the most important economic and social group
in the country. One of the nation's leading newspapers lamented that these men
were not received with the same attention as strikers.[5] These types of gestures
along with the opening of the political system created a special relationship with
a large segment of the population.

Yrigoyen reached the presidency because the governing segment of the conservative elite feared a Radical Party revolt and the constant labor agitation
and believed that they could win a fair election. In 1912 they passed the Sáenz
Peña law, which made voting obligatory for all male citizens and made voter
fraud more difficult. Despite the conservatives' hopes, Yrigoyen won the first
fair presidential election in 1916. His margin in the electoral college, however,
was extremely narrow, and therefore, he needed to widen his base of support.
Yrigoyen turned to the rapidly growing native-born working class as a potential source of voters. This was possible because Syndicalism had become an influential ideology among Argentina's vigorous labor movement in the years after
1910. The Syndicalists proclaimed their disdain for bourgeois politics and stated
that the revolution would come through a general strike. They displayed a willingness, however, to deal with political authorities in an ad hoc fashion. This

was perfect for Yrigoyen and the Radicals, since Syndicalists had no political ties and their growth would block the expansion of the Socialist Party, which had become a serious rival in the city of Buenos Aires.

Yrigoyen used a two-pronged approach with the Syndicalists. The initial thrust was to tolerate strikes led by Syndicalists and to be sure they were rewarded by favorable agreements. The most dramatic strikes occurred on the railroads and in the port of Buenos Aires in the first years of Yrigoyen's term. Government intervention considerably improved conditions and forced employers on the waterfront to accept the union's role in hiring workers for ships. As late as the 1927–28 presidential campaign, Yrigoyen's publicity stressed his role in settling these early strikes.[6]

Yrigoyen would not, however, pursue these labor tactics beyond a certain point. He did not support strikes from ideological conviction but rather from a desire for votes. When upheavals threatened to alienate key sectors of public opinion, he shifted directions. In January 1919 a strike in a Buenos Aires steel plant erupted into violence between strikers and police, which led to a general strike. Betraying labor, the administration tolerated and perhaps encouraged middle- and upper-class attacks on working-class neighborhoods, attacks that resembled pogroms against Jews and Catalans. The death toll rose to several hundred. This was the so-called Tragic Week. Threatened with losing middle- and upper-class support, Yrigoyen used force against the strikers.[7]

Despite the real danger to his regime's stability, however, Yrigoyen continued to back some labor groups, and unrest rolled across Argentina even after the Tragic Week. His tolerance ended, though, when strikes threatened to reduce export earnings and to undermine his coalition. With presidential elections coming up, in mid-1921 Yrigoyen shifted tactics. He abandoned the port workers and broke a general strike started in their support. Extreme violence was also used against workers in Patagonia.[8]

Yrigoyen's attempts to woo the urban working class went beyond supporting certain strikes. He pressed Congress to pass labor laws, especially in 1921 and 1922. This, coupled with the fact that he was more accessible to members of the working class than his predecessors, helped earn him continued popularity with the average Argentine.

The constitution did not permit direct reelection to the presidency, so Yrigoyen had to step aside in 1922. He chose Marcelo T. de Alvear to be his party's nominee, and Alvear won easily. An aristocrat, Alvear was far from being a populist. While desirous of obtaining working-class support, he preferred moving through bureaucratic channels instead of along the personalistic and populist trails that Yrigoyen trod. Soon a rift developed between Yrigoyen and Alvear, and the Radical Party split.

In 1928 Yrigoyen won reelection and attempted to restore the policies he had followed earlier, backing certain types of labor and expanding the state—for example, trying to make the national oil company a monopoly. He accomplished little, however. Aged and lacking in energy by then, he even appeared senile to some observers.[9] The depression soon made any new initiatives unlikely, and problems mounted. Opposition to Yrigoyen surged, as many sectors felt threatened by the professional politicians who surrounded him and by the Radicals' use of the power of the state to increase their hold on the government. The anti-Yrigoyen political class felt threatened by the Radical expansion of power. With considerable civilian encouragement, the military overthrew Yrigoyen in September 1930.[10]

In many ways Yrigoyen set the pattern for future regimes, populist and nonpopulist alike. Perón was going to further expand the connection with labor. While populist regimes expanded bureaucracies and the scope of the state faster than other types of governments, all, until the 1990s, essentially accepted this populist legacy.

The Interregnum

The regime that emerged from the 1930 military coup helped create conditions that, a decade later, produced the most celebrated wave of populism in Argentina. The neoconservative governments that ruled from 1932 to 1943 kept up a pretense of democracy but depended on voter fraud to remain in power. Members of the traditional landed elite ruled directly.

Paradoxically, the exigencies brought on by the Great Depression forced this ruling landed elite to favor a policy of import substitution industrialization (ISI) that not only undermined their own power but also produced rapid expansion of the urban working class. The number of blue-collar workers employed in manufacturing nearly doubled between 1935 and 1943, from 418,000 to 756,000.[11] This surge in urban employment was made possible by massive flows of migrants from the interior to the bigger cities, especially Buenos Aires. Despite myths to the contrary, recent research has not uncovered any marked difference in political behavior between the migrants and longtime urban residents.[12] The rapidly growing urban working class remained largely invisible to the political elite, shielded from public view by voter fraud and their own prejudices. Even leftist parties such as the Socialists and the Communists failed to recognize the changes that had occurred.

Organized labor, moreover, could not capitalize fully on the economic transformation under way. Many employers refused to negotiate with unions, and the government, although at times willing to mediate labor disputes, was inconsistent. Unions needed to use strikes or political mobilization to attract government attention, but they never could be sure of whether such actions would bring repression or help. By 1943 many labor leaders had become deeply frustrated with the lack of aid from left-wing parties. Many began to search for alternative sources of support.

The unions' political potential had grown significantly. Between 1936 and 1941 union membership had risen by nearly a fifth, to more than 440,000 members. While this represented only 12 percent of the economically active urban population, unions had spread from their original redoubts in transportation firms to manufacturing and services.[13] This increase occurred despite great difficulties for unions. Frequently, nonideological workers preferred not to join unions, since belonging could mean dismissal and blacklisting. In addition, given meager salaries, dues represented a significant burden, especially because little immediate benefit could be seen. Still, by 1943, many workers had been exposed to what unions could do and were willing to join under the right circumstances. By the same token, many more were willing to go on strike when the situation demanded, even though they were not union members.

A sense of alienation gripped much of the urban working class, and the general population partly shared this sentiment. Scandals occurred in all major political parties. Disillusionment with democracy set in—this was shared by much of the Western world during the 1930s—but was also due to the nature of Argentina's political system. Some years later writers referred to the 1930s as the "infamous decade." The general mood can be summed up by some lines of a tango, the popular urban music of the era:

Today it makes no difference
Whether you are honest or a traitor
Ignorant, wise or a thief,
Generous or crooked;
All's the same, nothing is better.[14]

The working class felt even a deeper sense of alienation. In Buenos Aires the expected norms of behavior were extremely middle class. As early as the turn of the century, a Spanish visitor noted the lack of workers' distinctive dress, such as was seen in the streets of Paris or Barcelona. Men not wearing jackets were not permitted on the sidewalks of the fashionable shopping street, Calle Florida, until the Peronist era. Workers carried their work clothes rather than wearing them on the streetcars.[15] Male workers venturing into downtown Buenos Aires dressed like the middle class, in a tie and jacket.

Perón's Rise to Power

In June 1943, dramatic political changes were introduced by a group of army officers who seized power. Initially, the military cracked down on unions. While focusing on Communists, they also targeted other tendencies. One of the two major labor confederations was closed. The government took over the two railroad unions, the strongest organizations in the country, and appointed a military officer to run them. It became almost impossible to call strikes.

A countervailing force emerged from within the military, however, one anxious to deal creatively with labor issues. Almost from the beginning of military rule, a group of army officers began summoning union leaders to find out what workers wanted. They spoke with leaders of all ideological hues, even Communists. Their true motivation remains unclear, but they did want to block the spread of communism and solve problems causing social unrest before they became more serious. Argentina's next major populist leader, Col. Juan Domingo Perón (1891–1974), emerged from this group.

Perón, a tall, commanding figure and a powerful speaker, had the ability to charm people and win them to his side. He was one of those rare politicians imbued with genuine charisma. Perón's motivations in helping the working class were complex, since ideologically he was eclectic. He had been influenced by right-wing European ideologies and by a desire for order, but he also wanted power for himself.[16] He excelled at the bureaucratic maneuvering by which one rose through the ranks in the army. Nevertheless, he always wanted to obtain power through popular support and legitimate means. While mostly unsuccessful, he did make major efforts to attract support from the largely middle-class Radical Party and from the business community. His real success came in recruiting support from unions and the urban working class.

With his bureaucratic astuteness, Perón became a major force in the army by late 1943. He soon became vice president and minister of war—a predictable trajectory for an ambitious, skillful, and lucky officer. He also concentrated his efforts in a surprising arena. In October 1943 he took over as head of the National Department of Labor, a post hitherto of little importance, since its powers were limited and it only had authority in the capital and in the more backward, underpopulated regions. Perón used the department of labor, however, as a platform from which to win over the hearts and minds of much of the working class. The position allowed him to legitimize his approaches to labor, and it provided him with a staff that had well-established contacts with unions and unsurpassed knowledge of their needs and desires. By the end of November 1943, Perón had transformed the agency into the Secretariat of Labor and Social Security, with expanded powers and national jurisdiction.

Prospects for the labor movement improved only slowly, however. Perón did place his close friend Col. Domingo Mercante in charge of the two rail unions. Mercante was in some sense a railroader: his father had been an engineer and a cousin belonged to one of the unions. He called internal union elections. The government created a hospital for railroaders and addressed several long-standing grievances. Still, the aid to the rail unions remained an exception and most unions received little or nothing.

Repression by government agents gradually became more selective, but it was only after May 1944 that Perón began seriously to favor unions. Labor leaders had been playing a difficult game. They opposed the regime while constantly seeking help from the secretariat. With unprecedented unity, almost the entire labor movement planned a May Day 1944 protest against administration policies. Not surprisingly the regime banned the rally. At this point Perón, stung by his inability to court the Radical Party and his seeming failure with labor, began a major effort to woo unions.[17] He was remarkably successful.

Perón's policies always had two edges: assistance that permitted many unions to achieve long-sought goals, and repression against uncooperative organizations. On the pro-labor side, the government began enforcing labor laws for the first time. With state backing, the number of contracts between labor and management soared. In the last six months of 1944, 228 contracts were signed in the city of Buenos Aires alone. Many secretariat-mediated contracts merely set wages, but others addressed crucial issues. Contracts often stipulated seemingly minor changes in work rules but afforded workers more dignity, such as separate changing rooms for male and female employees. For the first time, workers had a say in setting shop-floor rules. In addition, contracts frequently contained clauses committing the secretariat to enforce them, and Perón saw that it did so.[18] Labor contracts finally had meaning, and the balance of power between capital and labor began to shift. Real wages for the unskilled rose 17 percent between 1943 and 1945, while those for skilled workers rose 10 percent.[19]

Before 1944 it had been extremely difficult to organize and sustain unions outside the city of Buenos Aires. This changed when the secretariat began actively to favor their establishment. For example, the telephone workers in Buenos Aires had long sought to help organize their counterparts in other regions, but with little success. In 1944 and 1945, however, thirteen phone-worker unions across the country were organized, some with direct help from the government.[20]

The other side of Perón's labor strategy was repression. All organizations close to the Communist Party had to go underground to survive. The government supported rival anti-Communist unions. This destroyed several important unions, including those in textiles, meatpacking, and the metal trades. Repression was used against any union that refused to cooperate. The Socialist-controlled municipal workers union was taken over and run by a government agent. Individual leaders always faced the threat of arrest or harassment.

Perón's ties to unions provided him with entrée to the working class and with a legitimacy he could not have obtained otherwise. This was especially important, because traditionally workers harbored a deep suspicion of the military. Also, as we will see, unions could provide crucial assistance with mobilization.

Unions and their members did not blindly support Perón; in many cases they did so reluctantly. For decades they had struggled to secure a place in society and for material gains but had usually failed. They saw this moment as a chance to achieve their long-standing dreams, because Perón needed the union leaders as much as they needed him.

Just as important as concrete rewards was the sense workers had that they now formed a legitimate part of the larger society. For the first time, union leaders were assigned to important posts, both political and bureaucratic. A former secretary general of the largest labor confederation, Luis Cerutti, held a conspicuous job in the secretariat. A Socialist and longtime lawyer for the largest railroad union, Juan Bramuglia, received an appointment as acting governor of the Province of Buenos Aires.

Perón made intense personal appeals to unions. His charisma gave his actions a decided impact. In speaking to unions, he stressed their importance to him. "I come to the house of the railroaders as if it were my own. I profess a profound gratitude to them, because I am convinced that many of the successes of the Secretariat . . . are due precisely to the railroad workers." He also suggested that he was almost one of them, since he was an honorary president of the largest rail union. Perón attempted to show that he cared about the workers.[21] This appeal was especially effective because workers had been socially and politically isolated prior to 1943. At some point in 1945 psychological links were forged between Perón and many workers that proved powerful and long lasting.

The relationship between many workers and Perón was sealed by the dramatic events of October 1945, which became a founding myth of Peronism. While Perón had built a following within the working class, he had become extremely unpopular with some sectors of the society. In the minds of many, the military regime was identified with Fascist Italy or Nazi Germany. (The regime contained many who sympathized with the Axis.) The opposition saw themselves as resembling the citizens of occupied France. The end of World War II made the situation of the regime difficult and obliged military leaders to reduce censorship and repression. Students and the middle class responded with frequent antiregime demonstrations. Many military officers disliked Perón's policies and removed him from all of his positions on October 9.

Perón's dismissal created a vacuum. His enemies hesitated, unsure of what to do next. Workers and their union leaders, however, responded rapidly, afraid that they would lose the gains of the previous two years. Employers canceled recently won concessions, and the newly created Columbus Day holiday was ignored. Some union leaders went to the government seeking reassurances, which they received. Others met secretly outside of Buenos Aires to plan a general strike.[22] On October 16, the National Labor Confederation (CGT) voted to hold a general strike in two days.

On October 17, a hot spring morning, thousands of workers surged into downtown Buenos Aires, especially from working-class suburbs to the south. Later, when the bridge across the Riachuelo River was raised, they crossed on improvised rafts. The crowd congregated in the plaza in front of the presidential palace and called for Perón's return. The crowd was remarkably well behaved and (legend notwithstanding) well dressed: photographs show most men in ties and jackets despite the heat. Some did take off their jackets and shirts, and a few waded in the fountains. This led to the scornful use of the term *descamisados* (shirtless ones) for Perón's supporters. Soon it became a proud symbol of Peronism, and rallies often saw the doffing of jackets as a sign of solidarity and pride in being working class (though many were not). The elite and middle class became uneasy, not so much because of the actual behavior of the crowd, but because the city was no longer totally theirs. Only in a society so middle class in mores could this symbolic rejection of bourgeois values appear threatening. This kind of social tension is extremely important in understanding both the attraction and the repulsion that was felt for populist measures.

Faced with the prospect of having to clear a plaza filled with perhaps a quarter of a million Perón supporters, the military relented and released Perón. This opened the way for his participation in presidential elections.[23]

What had happened? Legend has it that Perón's friend and soon-to-be wife, Eva Duarte (better known as Evita), rallied the workers on his behalf. Marysa Navarro has demonstrated that Evita lacked the contacts and the public persona to do so.[24] The demonstration was planned, because simultaneous protests occurred in working-class suburbs and in various places around the country. It could not have been the direct result of the CGT's strike call, which was issued too late and for the following day.

The fact is that some union leaders had been pushing for a strike since October 9 and the workers were primed for action. During the 1930s the union movement had developed legitimacy and connections that stretched across all the worker barrios of greater Buenos Aires. Workers did not need much encouragement and poured out into the streets. Although the participants and many others were extremely proud, some felt distress and even distaste for the events of the day. For the first time the working class had reshaped the history of Argentina. The October 17 experience created a bond between workers and Perón that still exists. By returning Perón to power, workers had changed the course of politics and given themselves a greater sense of pride, a realization of their power, and a new identification as Peronists.

Presidential elections were called for February 1946, and although Perón was a candidate, he was not expected to win. Virtually all the traditional parties supported the candidate of the Radical Party, José Tamborini. The United States openly opposed Perón. People thought that workers would follow the wishes of the parties that had traditionally claimed their support, the Socialists and the Communists. Perón's principal backing came from the Partido Laborista, founded in the wake of the October 17 demonstrations. Modeled on the British Labour Party and based on some labor leaders' dreams of an independent organization that could push for social reform, the party relied on unions.[25] Perón also received support from dissident Radicals, some conservatives, and the Catholic Church.

With the Partido Laborista doing much of the organizational legwork in urban areas and with heavy union support, Perón won a solid 52.4 percent of the vote. Moreover, candidates allied with him swept into both houses of Congress in overwhelming numbers. Even in provinces in which modern working classes had not yet developed, Perón won handily.[26] There, dissident politicians, with material help from the state, had used traditional methods to obtain votes. As in many populist regimes, traditional politics combined with new forms of mobilization.

Perón in Power

Perón had the option of ruling democratically. His majority in Congress allowed him to do almost anything he desired. In the fashion of Argentine populists, Perón pulled power to himself and refused to share it, even in symbolic terms, with those who did not support him. The regime gradually became more authoritarian, especially after 1950, when the economy began to deteriorate. The process began very early. In May 1946, under considerable pressure from Perón, the Partido Laborista was dissolved. The CGT was soon obligated to shed its independent secretary general, Luis Gay, and submit to a Perón appointee.[27] Perón never had room for people who were not totally devoted to him. With the 1951 seizure of *La Prensa,* a serious and traditional newspaper that catered to the elite, only one important daily, *La Nación,* remained independent of the government. Opposition to the regime became increasingly dangerous. Jailings and generalized repression became extensive.

Still, Perón was never content to be a dictator. He was a populist and as such always anxious to expand his bases of support, and he was highly successful. An important reason for Perón's growing popularity was the rapid economic growth that occurred during the first years of his presidency. Real hourly wages went up 25 percent in 1947 and increased almost as much the following year. The percentage of national income going to workers increased 25 percent between 1946 and 1950. While not all sectors benefited—agriculture was being squeezed for the advantage of the urban sectors—the economy grew at high rates in both 1946 and 1947 and only slowed down somewhat the following year.[28]

Prosperity allowed Perón to expand his political base. Many businessmen began to support him, partly because he was in power but also due to the new opportunities he offered. Perón also moved to consolidate his support with workers through enactment of better pension plans, health care, and vacation resorts. These were provided through the unions.

Symbolic gains were often as important as material ones. During the 1930s resentment had spread against foreign ownership of key public utilities. (In addition to having nationalist sentiments, many believed that the state could provide better and more efficient service.) With the money Argentina had earned during World War II, Perón set about buying many of them, including the telephone and railroad companies. This was extraordinarily popular with wide sectors of the population.

Eva Duarte de Perón (Evita) played a crucial role in the development of the symbolic side of Peronism. An actress when she met Perón in 1944, she rapidly developed an interest in politics. Her influence on Perón and their open relationship was so unconventional that it helped spur the military coup against Perón in October 1945. In a society where women did not have the vote and where their public role remained traditional, Perón and Evita stood out as people willing to defy social norms. She not only displayed an interest in politics and played an active part, but Perón accepted and perhaps encouraged it. Moreover, he defied convention by marrying a woman with "a past," shortly after October 17, 1945.[29]

Once Perón became president, Evita rapidly emerged as a political force. While she never held an official post within the newly created Ministry of Labor, she became the power broker. She played much the same role as Juan had during the period when he built support in 1944 and 1945. It was Evita who obtained for a union whatever improvement it sought. She was increasingly loved by large sectors of the poorer classes. Evita could not be perceived as a threat by Perón, however, as she could not be separated from him. This she expressed in her autobiography: "In different ways we both wanted to do the same thing: he with intelligence; I with the heart; he, prepared for the fray; I, ready for everything without knowing anything; he cultured and I simple; he great and I small; he master and I pupil. He the figure and I the shadow. He sure of himself, and I sure only of him!"[30]

Although not a particularly good actress, Evita, like Ronald Reagan, found her perfect role in the public arena. Her speeches were very effective, touching the hearts of many (and raising the ire of others). While Perón gradually became more presidential and less strident, Evita, on the other hand, was frequently vituperative. Her denunciations of the oligarchy seemed heartfelt. She too had charisma, and Marysa Navarro has argued that the special interaction between the Peróns prevented his charisma from being routinized by the exercise of power.[31]

In 1947 Evita opened the Eva Perón Foundation (it was formally established the following year). The foundation was supported mostly by tax revenues, but it also received donations, some given freely and some not so freely. The foundation took over social welfare institutions from an already discredited organization that had been poorly run by women from the elite.

Evita's foundation did everything from managing orphanages and building hospitals to organizing boys' soccer tournaments. It became a bridge between the people and Evita. She became the personal intercessor to whom one went when in need. She would regularly hold court and give petitioners what they wanted. Access to her was relatively simple. She was pictured as quasi-saintly in this largely Catholic nation. She was described as kissing on the mouth, for example, a woman with syphilis or leprosy and not worrying about catching it. She became the subject of widespread propaganda and popular beliefs.[32] The foundation was unique, since it combined the resources of a large state institution with the personal leadership of Evita. The sewing machine given to a needy woman came not from the institution but from Evita herself.

Argentine women received the vote for the first time in 1947. Evita was very influential in the last stages of the campaign for women's suffrage. She was given more credit than she deserved by both supporters and enemies. After the vote was obtained, Evita insisted on creating and leading a separate Peronist woman's party. Women's branches soon stretched across the country. When Perón ran for reelection in 1951, he received a much higher percentage of votes from women than from men.[33] Evita's role in this feat was enormous.

Perón also attempted to establish a cultural hegemony to revise Argentina's vision of itself. This was particularly difficult since Peronism, like other populist movements, had no consistent ideology. The movement did, however, spawn a subculture that thrived long afterward. Rituals such as the celebration of May Day were reformed and "Peronized" to stress the benefits that workers had received and the harmony that existed under Perón. School curricula stressed Catholic values and glorified the Peróns.[34] Cities and even provinces were named after the Peróns. Monuments were erected.

The Peronists' efforts to redefine the culture produced tremendous tensions in the society. The Catholic Church, an early ally, felt that the Peronist culture impinged on its arena and began to distance itself from the regime. The opposition of much of the middle and upper classes also intensified as they saw their vision of the country challenged. This lay atop the repression, the symbolic and real challenge to upper- and middle-class dominance of Argentine society, and the resentment at the enlarged role of the working class.

After 1948 the economy began to deteriorate, in part due to shifts in Argentina's international terms of trade. Many economic gains were reversed. Those earlier drawn to the regime by prosperity withdrew their support. After Evita's death in 1952, there remained no one close to Perón strong enough to give sound advice, and he seemed intoxicated by power. Repression intensified. By 1954–55 tensions in the society were extremely high. There were no neutrals. Military officers with considerable civilian assistance overthrew Perón in September 1955.

Like the Radicals before them, the Peronists saw themselves as the only viable option for the nation. This exclusivity and lack of tolerance intensified resistance by excluded sectors, helping to cause the regime's downfall.

After the Fall

The lines etched into society by Perón's populist regime were not erased by the leader's fall from power. Society became even more divided between those who believed that Peronism needed to be expunged from Argentina and those who supported it. Other legacies of Peronism were numerous. The unions had emerged as crucial political actors; regimes defied them at their own risk. The state's role in the economy had become extremely large with many sectors dominated by government corporations. The bureaucracy had grown even more bloated and inefficient.

After a brief interlude in which the military attempted a policy of "neither victors nor vanquished," harsh repression began against those who sided with Perón. The mere public mention of his name was forbidden. Symbols and images of Peronism were banned. The government aided efforts to take unions away from the Peronists and barred old leaders from office.[35]

The results were not at all what those in power hoped, as commitment to Peronism increased. A resistance movement emerged, which for a number of years organized sabotage and terrorist activities. New militant leaders fiercely loyal to Perón took power in the unions. Later, restrictions were eased but Argentina remained divided. Approximately one-third of the population—mostly working class and poor—remained deeply Peronist and were loyal to a culture very different from that of the majority. Meanwhile, middle-class supporters of Peronism had largely fallen away. A large portion of the citizenry viewed Peronism as anathema.

The military did not wish to continue to rule and advocated a return to democracy. Yet democracy became, in Guillermo O'Donnell's words, "an impossible game."[36] The military, backed by a considerable segment of the civilian population, refused to permit the Peronists to take part in elections or, when they did, to hold office. Since the Peronists were the largest party in the country, their exclusion rendered electoral politics a sham. From 1958 to 1966 the ground trembled under the feet of the elected governments, with the military constantly intervening to block the Peronists. Periodic waves of labor unrest and a disappointing economic performance added to the uncertainties and prevented the formation of wider coalitions. No political force was capable of challenging the legacies of populism and winning. In addition, Fidel Castro's Cuban Revolution spurred the growth of the left, which produced tremendous anxiety among the elites.

From exile Perón continued to wield his influence, first backing one faction within his movement and then another, but not allowing any person to garner enough prestige to supplant him as leader. He blocked the emergence of a Peronism without Perón. In the same fashion, he maneuvered to regain power while simultaneously trying to prevent other forces from achieving stability and legitimacy.

When the military seized power in 1966, it attempted to clean out what it saw as a putrid economic and political system. It began to restructure and "rationalize" the economy. The regime also banned politics and tried to curb union power. A combination of economic and political frustrations and the worldwide rebelliousness of the late 1960s led to a series of violent urban riots. The most famous, the Cordobazo of 1969, lasted two days, left as many as sixty dead, and seriously undermined the regime.[37]

Several guerrilla groups also challenged the military. Guerrillas avowed loyalty to various left-wing ideologies as well as to a curious fusion of left-wing ideology and Peronism. Perón gave the latter guerrillas his blessing. Revolution became chic. Mannequins in boutiques were dressed as revolutionaries. Primarily based in the universities, a leftist-leaning Peronist youth movement sprouted overnight. Again, Perón became the man of the hour. Those hoping for a Socialist and Peronist Argentina supported him, as did those who yearned for stability, including many of his traditional enemies. His traditional supporters, especially the unions—his principal allies since 1955—still eagerly backed him despite increasingly bloody clashes with the Peronist left.

In hope of stanching the violence, the military turned to elections. Ultimately, Perón was reelected to the presidency in 1973, and he offered many of the same solutions as before. He was stymied, however, by the swirling conflicts of ideology. His movement's right and left wings could not possibly be reconciled, and he repudiated his left wing. Then, after little more than eight months in office, he died.[38] He was succeeded by his third wife and vice president, María Estela, nicknamed Isabelita, who lacked his prestige and savvy. Her time in office was marked by runaway inflation, as well as violence by the right, the left, and the security forces.

In March 1976 the military took over and inaugurated a period of terror unmatched in the country's history. The military made the word *disappear* into a transitive verb, and documented evidence exists of almost ten thousand disappeared people. The real death toll was much higher, probably in the neighborhood of thirty thousand.[39]

Democracy returned in 1983, brought on by the military's total loss of legitimacy. The ruling junta had decided to invade the Malvinas Islands (The Falklands), in a desperate attempt to salvage a rapidly deteriorating economic situation and its loss of authority. The islands had been a British colony since the early nineteenth century, but Argentina had always claimed them. A British counterattack retook the islands, and military prestige disintegrated.

The Radical Party government of Raúl Alfonsín, which won the presidential elections of 1983, cannot be called populist. It did, however, retain elements of populist appeal. All parties used folkloric motifs, such as large drums, in their demonstrations. In addition, the Radicals had the hegemonic vision of populism: during the heady moments of their greatest popularity they talked of the third historic movement (the first two were those of Yrigoyen and Perón). Power was increasingly concentrated in the hands of Alfonsín, and the Radicals spoke of changing the constitution so he could be reelected.

These dreams faded quickly. Alfonsín had come to office promising to open the political system and make it conform to the rules of law. To a surprising extent, he succeeded. The key military commanders of the preceding dictatorship were tried and convicted. A series of military revolts, however, sharply limited the government's power in this area. Still, it was the poor performance of the economy that destroyed Alfonsín's popularity. During the first exciting months of the return to democracy, the staggering economic problems created by an unpayable foreign debt, high inflation, and the expectation of further high inflation were largely ignored. Argentina was going to grow its way out. By the

Figure 1.1. This poster, commemorating the thirtieth anniversary of the general strike that freed Perón to run for president, evokes the image of Evita and Juan to enhance the popularity of Isabelita Perón. (Courtesy of Carol Hirschfeld Horowtiz.)

time the danger of the situation was realized, much political capital had been expended, and the government lacked the popularity to overcome vested interests and an increasingly hostile labor movement. Despite valiant efforts, it failed to overcome either inflation or the debt.

Peronist Carlos Menem won the 1989 presidential election with a populist campaign that garnered him slightly under half the votes. A provincial governor with a colorful lifestyle, he promised the redistributive policies that characterized populism, especially Peronism. Once in office, Menem reversed direction and instituted policies firmly rooted in neoliberalism. His models were Margaret Thatcher and Ronald Reagan, who believed that government involvement in the economy should be sharply limited.

Populism had left a legacy of a large state role in the economy and a bloated bureaucracy. Even repressive military regimes failed in attempts to change this situation. What permitted the reversal of this tradition was an outbreak of hyperinflation (during 1989 the cost of living rose some 5,000 percent) while Alfonsín was a lame duck. Food riots and waves of fear swept over urban areas, and Alfonsín felt obliged to turn over power to Menem before the end of his term. (Nonetheless, it still marked the first time since the 1920s that a democratically elected president turned over the sash of office to his legitimately elected successor.) Still, the country was gripped by fear, and this permitted or perhaps pushed Menem to change course.[40] People wanted to believe that that type of inflation could not happen again.

Menem drastically opened up the economy to global competition and sold off most of the numerous state enterprises. Inflation was tamed through the introduction in 1991 of the convertibility plan, in which the peso was tied to the value of the dollar, and pesos could be issued only when they had backing. The changes in economic policy necessitated a major shift in governing style. The old populist measures were no longer possible. The sale of state companies and the shrinkage of the bureaucracy made government employment much less important, and the general shortage of government funds meant that wages in the public sphere were much lower than in the private sector. Other ways of helping the poor also were limited severely by fiscal constraints. The continual expansion of the state sector of the economy that began under Yrigoyen and under Perón had been reversed. Clearly, traditional populism ceases to be possible under this type of economy.[41]

Other vestiges of populism in Argentina were deeply altered. The union movement was weakened greatly because it could not effectively resist compression of real wages and higher unemployment. In part this was due to a shrinking industrial base and the challenges produced by an economy opened to world competition, but it was also due to Menem's ability to divide and conquer a movement that was paralyzed by its own blind loyalty to Peronism. It did not know how to oppose a Peronist leader who continued to enjoy considerable support from the rank and file.

Still, legacies of populism remained. Like Yrigoyen and Perón before him, in what can be called populist style, Menem amassed power, stretching the constitution. He frequently bypassed Congress and issued decrees, issuing more of the latter than all his predecessors combined. Also, Menem packed the Supreme Court and limited the autonomy of the court system. Again like his populist forebears, he made himself the center of all attention, appearing frequently on television. He cavorted with sports teams and with super models. While he used less rhetoric about hegemony over other political sectors than Alfonsín did, the hegemonic overtones to the regime were stronger. Menem had the constitution rewritten so that he could win reelection to a second term, which he did with slightly less than half the votes cast. Despite Menem's dismal showing in later polls, some Peronists called for a further amendment to the constitution so that Menem could run for a third term. Ultimately, Menem had to reject these attempts. The policies of Menem are clearly not traditionally populist, but the political style has left its mark.

The lack of flexibility produced by the convertibility plan and economic crisis in other developing countries helped produce a recession, and in 1999 Fernando de la Rúa led a center-left coalition to victory over the Peronists. Populism seemed dead, but infighting in the governing coalition and more importantly the belief that the peso needed to remain tied to the dollar led to economic, social, and political collapse. Due to an ever deepening depression, de la Rúa was forced to resign amid mounting violence in December 2001. This led to breaking the tie to the dollar and a quick devaluation of Argentine currency. After a brief period of chaos, Eduardo Duhalde, the leading Peronist in the crucial province of Buenos Aires, emerged as the interim president.[42] Previously he had governed the Province of Buenos Aires with populist gestures such as trying, without a great deal of success, to turn his wife, Hilda, into an Evita-like figure. He governed the country in a more sober fashion, and with the help of his economic minister, Roberto Lavagna, stabilized an economy that had gone through its worst collapse ever. Numbers cannot do justice to the misery and loss of hope that occurred, but the poverty rate stood at 50 percent and unemployment at 20 percent in 2002.[43]

In order to block the reelection of Menem to the presidency, Duhalde backed a relatively obscure Peronist governor from the Patagonian province of Santa Cruz, Néstor Kirchner, who won the election largely because of the president's backing. Kirchner unexpectedly became the dominant figure in the Peronist party, and he was undoubtedly a populist. Although some commentators have labeled Kirchner a left-wing populist, to this author he was a traditional Peronist populist. He concentrated power in the executive branch. He used nationalism. He ignored and criticized international organizations such as the International Monetary Fund; this criticism was immensely popular because of the role the IMF had played in encouraging the economic policies in the era before the collapse. Similarly he attacked U.S. policies, especially those of George W. Bush, who was extraordinarily unpopular. Kirchner also encouraged the prosecution of military leaders for crimes committed during the most recent dictatorship.

Kirchner benefited as well from a rapidly expanding economy helped along by heterodox policies and high prices for agricultural exports. The economy grew 9 percent per year between 2003 and 2007, while real wages rose and unemployment dropped sharply. He used clientelism, especially in the latter years of his term, to expand his base of support and provide employment. In 2007, the presidential election year, government expenditures rose 30 percent.[44] He also pressured foreign corporations to sell out to local entrepreneurs with good political connections, and the scope of the government began to increase again. An alliance with unions was less important than in previous populist periods, but it was replaced by alliances with certain groups of *piqueteros*, groups of the unemployed who banded together to protest by blocking traffic and similar tactics. The Kirchner government was mostly tolerant of these disruptions and allied itself firmly with certain groups through giving jobs, housing, and the like. These groups became militant Kirchneristas.[45]

The constitution now allowed for two consecutive terms, but Kirchner, perhaps afraid that during a second term his lame duck status would hurt him, supported the presidential candidacy of his wife, Cristina Fernández de Kirchner, a politician in her own right, who won easily in 2007. Although frequently compared to Evita, during the campaign she compared herself to Hilary Clinton. Her presidency has been made more difficult by the worldwide recession, drought, and inflation that began under her husband. The attempts to keep food prices low in order to appeal to the working class base and high taxes on agricultural exports have led to heated and continuous conflicts with the agrarian sector, the motor of the economy. Attempts to further centralize power in the presidency and the feeling that Néstor Kirchner, not his wife, was running the country helped splinter the Peronist Party. The administration has become extremely confrontational with those that it perceives as its enemies. Still, Christina Kirchner remains extremely popular with many traditional Peronist constituencies.

Populism has returned to Argentina, though at times what is a populist trait and what is a national political tradition are difficult to differentiate. A tradition of the strong party leader—which may be a populist trait—lingers. There is a reluctance to accept other parties as legitimate political contenders. The populist faith that only their movement knows the truth remains. In addition, many sectors of society remain highly suspicious of Peronism in part because of lack of faith in its commitment to democratic beliefs and in part because of its class and cultural basis. There is also a fear that no other party will be allowed to govern. While much has changed in Argentine society in recent years, the divisions left by populism remain. Populism helped create a society where the opposition was viewed as lacking essential virtues. It helped create a large state and bureaucracy. Populism may have brought new groups into the society, but it also divided the nation and made it more unstable.

Notes

1. See Joel Horowitz, "Industrialists and the Rise of Perón, 1943–1946: Some Implications for the Conceptualization of Populism," *The Americas* 47, no. 2 (October 1990): 199–217, especially 216.

2. For the Radical Party, see Joel Horowitz, *Argentina's Radical Party and the Mobilization of Popular Support, 1916–1930* (University Park: Penn State University Press, 2008).

3. Félix Luna, ed., *Los radicales* (Buenos Aires: Todo es Historia, 1976).

4. The poem by Emilio Uttinger appeared in *La Epoca,* March 14, 1929.

5. Ricardo Sidcaro, *La política mirada desde arriba: Las ideas del diario La Nación, 1909–1989* (Buenos Aires: Editorial Sudamericana, 1993), 59.

6. David Rock, *Politics in Argentina 1890–1930* (London: Cambridge University Press, 1975), 143–52; Paul Goodwin, *Los ferrocarriles británicos y la UCR* (Buenos Aires: Ediciones La Bastilla, 1974), 69–148; Jeremy Adelman, "State and Labour in Argentina: The Portworkers of Buenos Aires, 1910–1921," *Journal of Latin American Studies* 25, no. 1 (February 1993): 84–93; *La Epoca,* August 28, 1927, March 22, 1928.

7. Edgardo Bilsky, *La semana trágica* (Buenos Aires: Centro Editor de América Latina, 1984).

8. See Joel Horowitz, "Argentina's Failed General Strike of 1921: A Critical Moment in the Radicals' Relations with the Unions," *HAHR* 75, no. 1 (February 1995): 57–79.

9. Roberto P. Korzeniewicz, "Labor Politics of Radicalism: The Santa Fe Crisis of 1928," *HAHR* 73, no. 1 (February 1993): 1–32. For a claim of senility, see for example, Ysabel F. Rennie, *The Argentine Republic* (New York: Macmillan, 1945), 221–22.

10. The best analysis of the regime's breakdown is Peter H. Smith, "The Breakdown of Democracy in Argentina, 1916–1930," in *The Breakdown of Democratic*

Regimes: Latin America, ed. by Juan J. Linz and Alfred Stepan (Baltimore: Johns Hopkins University Press, 1978), 3–27.

11. Dirección Nacional de Estadística y Censos, *Cuarto censo general de la Nación,* III (Buenos Aires: n.p., 1949), 26.

12. Joel Horowitz, *Argentine Unions and the Rise of Perón, 1930–1945* (Berkeley: Institute of International Studies, University of California, 1990), 3–4, 221. See also for an overview of the entire period between 1930 and 1943.

13. Departamento Nacional del Trabajo, División de Estadística, *Organización sindical: Asociaciones obreras y patronales* (Buenos Aires: n.p., 1941), 27; Carlos F. Díaz Alejandro, *Essays on the Economic History of Argentina* (New Haven: Yale University Press, 1970), 428.

14. Enrique Santos Discépolo, "Cambalache" (1934) as translated by Nicolas Fraser and Marysa Navarro in *Eva Perón* (New York: W. W. Norton & Co., 1980), 19.

15. Federico Rahola, *Sangre nueva: Impresiones de un viaje a la América del Sud* (Barcelona: La Académica, 1905), 83; Christopher Towne Leland, *The Last Happy Men: The Generation of 1922, Fiction and the Argentine Reality* (Syracuse, NY: Syracuse University Press, 1986), 30; James R. Scobie, *Buenos Aires: Plaza to Suburb* (New York: Oxford University Press, 1974), 220.

16. The two best biographies of Perón are Joseph Page, *Perón* (New York: Random House, 1983), and Robert Crassweller, *Perón and the Enigmas of Argentina* (New York: W. W. Norton & Co., 1987).

17. This analysis is based on Horowitz, *Argentine Unions.*

18. *Revista de Trabajo y Previsión* (July–September 1944): 1016–67; (October–December 1944): 1546–660. For the importance of this, see Horowitz, "Industrialists and the Rise of Perón."

19. Miguel Murmis and Juan Carlos Portantiero, *Estudios sobre los orígenes del peronismo* (Buenos Aires: Siglo Veintiuno Argentina, 1971), 106.

20. *Federación,* May 11, July 14, September 30, 1945.

21. Juan Perón, *El pueblo ya sabe de qué se trata* (no publication information), 46, 60.

22. Author's interview with Luis Gay, Buenos Aires, June 29, 1984.

23. See Juan Carlos Torre, ed., *El 17 de Octubre de 1945* (Buenos Aires: Ariel, 1995).

24. Marysa Navarro, "Evita and the Crisis of 17 October 1945," *Journal of Latin American Studies* 12, no. 1 (May 1980): 127–38.

25. See Horowitz, *Argentine Unions,* 190–91; Juan Carlos Torre, *La vieja guardia sindical y Perón: Sobre los orígenes del peronismo* (Buenos Aires: Editorial Sudamericana/ Instituto Torcuato Di Tella, 1990), 148–86; Elena Susana Pont, *Partido Laborista: Estado y sindicatos* (Buenos Aires: Centro Editor de América Latina, 1984).

26. See the essays in Manuel Mora y Araujo and Ignacio Llorente, eds., *El voto peronista* (Buenos Aires: Editorial Sudamericana, 1980).

27. Juan Carlos Torre, *La vieja guardia sindical,* 205–50.

28. Thomas E. Skidmore and Peter H. Smith, *Modern Latin America,* 3d ed. (New York: Oxford University Press, 1992), 88.

29. The best biography in English is Fraser and Navarro, *Eva Perón.* See also Marysa Navarro, *Evita* (Buenos Aires: Corregidor, 1981).

30. Eva Duarte de Perón, *Evita by Evita* (New York: Proteus, 1980), 41. She did not actually write this work, and it is impossible, as it is with any married couple, to know the internal power dynamics of the relationship. She clearly was much more powerful than she portrays herself here.

31. Marysa Navarro, "Evita's Charismatic Leadership" in *Latin American Populism in Comparative Perspective,* ed. Michael L. Conniff (Albuquerque: University of New Mexico Press, 1982), 47–66.

32. Mariano Plotkin has hypothesized that the foundation was created in part to fill a gap created by a failure to establish an all-encompassing social welfare system. The best discussion of the foundation is Plotkin, *Mañana es San Perón* (Buenos Aires: Ariel, 1994), 215–55. For the need to separate beliefs from propaganda, see J. M. Taylor, *Eva Perón: The Myths of a Woman* (Chicago: University of Chicago Press, 1979).

33. Navarro, *Evita,* 169–84, 207–24. The constitution had been rewritten so Perón could be reelected.

34. Plotkin, *Mañana es San Perón.*

35. See Daniel James, *Resistance and Integration: Peronism and the Argentine Working Class, 1946–1976* (Cambridge: Cambridge University Press, 1988); Oscar R. Anzorena, ed., *JP: Historia de la Juventud Peronista (1955–1988)* (Buenos Aires: Ediciones del Cordón, 1989); Juan Carlos Torre and Liana de Riz, "Argentina since 1946," in *The Cambridge History of Latin America,* vol. 8, ed. Leslie Bethell (Cambridge: Cambridge University Press, 1991), 93–101.

36. Guillermo O'Donnell, *Modernization and Bureaucratic-Authoritarianism: Studies in South American Politics* (Berkeley: Institute of International Studies, University of California, 1979), 167–201.

37. James Brennan, *The Labor Wars in Córdoba, 1955–1976* (Cambridge: Harvard University Press, 1994), 136–69.

38. Perhaps the best picture of this period is given by a work of fiction, Tomás Eloy Martínez, *The Perón Novel,* trans. Asa Zatz (New York: Pantheon, 1988). See also Torre and de Riz, "Argentina since 1946," 129–57.

39. Comisión Nacional sobre la Desaparición de Personas, *Nunca más* (Buenos Aires: EUDEBA, 1984). For the haunted nature of the period, see Andrew Graham-Yooll, *A State of Fear: Memories of Argentina's Nightmare* (London: Eland, 1986).

40. For a discussion of the riots, see Sergio Serulnikov, "When Looting Becomes a Right: Urban Poverty and Food Riots in Argentina," *Latin American Perspectives* 21, no. 3 (Summer 1994): 69–89. For 1989 as a major break with the past, see Tulio Halperín Donghi, *La larga agonía de la Argentina peronista* (Buenos Aires: Ariel, 1994).

41. For differing but interesting visions of this period, see Jeremy Adelman, "Post-Populist Argentina," *New Left Review* 203 (1994): 65–91; José, Nun, "Populismo, representación, y menemismo," *Sociedad* 5 (October 1994): 93–121.

42. All the changes followed the form of the constitution, and the army stayed in the barracks.

43. Steven Levitsky and María Victoria Murillo, "Argentina: From Kirchner to Kirchner," *Journal of Democracy* 19, no. 2 (April 2008), 16–30.

44. Ibid.

45. Carlos Escudé, "Piqueteros al gobierno: Un experimento populista argentino, 2003–2007," *Estudios Interdisciplinarios de América Latina y el Caribe* 20, no. 1 (January–June 2009).

2

Brazil's Populist Republic and Beyond

Michael L. Conniff

Populism began late in Brazil because entrenched antidemocratic political leaders resisted opening up the system to broader participation. But by midcentury populism reached a fever pitch. During the 1950s nearly a dozen figures fought for national office in populist fashion, and they left a major imprint on the political culture. The military takeover of 1964 brought the demise of the so-called Populist Republic, the most intense political arena in the Americas at the time.

After a decade of repressive government, the military began to allow more open participation again, and a few of the old-timers returned and managed to win state-level offices. None of the elder populists could get a clear shot at the presidency, however, and the promising career of newcomer Fernando Collor de Melo crashed two years into his term as president. By the mid-1990s the populist style in politics seemed destined to fade from the scene, replaced by more moderate approaches. To be sure, the very successful presidency of Luis Inácio "Lula" da Silva from 2003 to 2011 had many characteristics of the populists, although analysts disagree.[1]

Proto-Populists

During the 1920s several elected officials in Rio de Janeiro began to conduct what would later be called populist politics. Maurício Lacerda, Adolfo Bergamini, and João de Azevedo Lima broke with the usual neighborhood clientelism and appealed to larger constituencies in the city. They promised to reform government and to fight for the greater good of society as a whole. Just as important, they began to find independent voters and organizations that would support their elections. They pioneered a style of leadership that would flourish during the populist heyday of the 1950s.[2]

Rio's proto-populists of the 1920s represented working- and lower-middle class precincts, where public services lagged behind more affluent districts. They spoke often and loudly to citizens throughout the city, drawing crowds with their flamboyant manners. They were nonconformists, fed up with doing things the way they had always been done. They championed the underdog and attacked the powerful. In the city council and federal congress they made headlines by denouncing the cozy deals and minor corruptions that kept the wheels of government greased. They always had a social measure to push or some miscarriage of justice to decry.

These reform-minded, outspoken leaders in Rio made an important innovation by recruiting groups as well as individuals. They represented labor unions, employee associations, retired persons, and neighborhoods, thereby expanding their electoral followings. Their constituents were often less well-to-do than those of traditional politicians, but they were more numerous, which counted most on election day. To critics, this broad-based representation was demagoguery, because it "converted individual corruption into that of groups, classes, and special interests." This simple but powerful breakthrough would make possible the great populist movements of the 1940s and 1950s. The reformers opened the doors to politics for the masses.

The 1930 presidential election, which pitted Getúlio Vargas against official candidate Júlio Prestes, witnessed a major increase in voter recruitment. Vargas ran on a reform platform that had great appeal in the cities and among middle-class voters. Rio's reformers, in particular, campaigned heavily for Vargas, as did opposition leaders in other cities. As a result, the turnout was much higher than it had ever been. Still, Vargas lost, because most politicians did not go along with him and kept their voters in the loyalist camp. The country did not, however, return to politics as usual.[3]

When Vargas and his supporters carried out a revolution in late 1930, many of the reform-minded politicians supported him and ended up in his new government. Bergamini became mayor of Rio, and Lacerda was appointed city attorney, for example. The disarray of the new government, however, and the financial exigencies caused by the New York stock market crash of 1929 prevented Vargas from accomplishing anything serious in his early months. He had too few jobs and too little patronage to spread around.

Soon, a revolution within the revolution occurred. Tough-minded men who had risked their lives fighting to install Vargas now formed a pressure group, the Club 3 de Outubro (named for the date the revolution began). They were called the *tenentes,* since many were former lieutenants who had been cashiered in the 1920s for their revolutionary activities. They supported Vargas in hopes of restoring their commissions and promoting the nationalistic reforms they had championed earlier. The pressure they exerted put Vargas in a bind, forcing him to choose between them and the civilian reformers. In order to survive, Vargas chose the tenentes, in what amounted to a coup. One of the tenente leaders, Pedro Ernesto Baptista, became mayor of Rio de Janeiro in mid-1931.[4]

The First Populist

Pedro Ernesto, as he would be known later, became Brazil's first genuine populist. His background would hardly have suggested such a career. A Pernambucan youth who had migrated to Rio to study medicine, Pedro Ernesto stayed and developed into a gifted surgeon. With the backing of some Portuguese investors, he built the largest and best-equipped surgical clinic in South America. For personal reasons, he became embroiled in the struggles of the tenentes during the 1920s and with them joined Vargas's revolution in 1930. Because of his aid to them over the years, the tenentes chose Pedro Ernesto as president of the Club 3 de Outubro in 1931.

Vargas, who united with the tenentes temporarily during 1931 and 1932 in order to retain power, soon distanced himself from their brash and unpopular actions and encouraged allies to do the same. Pedro Ernesto accepted Vargas's advice to form a party and run for mayor of Rio. The platform of his new group, called the Autonomist Party of the Federal District, stressed local self-rule for Rio de Janeiro. Pedro Ernesto, meanwhile, underwent a major transformation in the eyes of the public, from revolutionary to social democrat.

Inspired by the experiments of the 1920s reformers, Pedro Ernesto began inviting organizations into his party. The easiest to recruit were federal and municipal employees, whose associations received benefits in exchange for their votes. Next he turned to unions and workers in major utilities companies. In each case, a delegate of the group was taken into the party hierarchy. Soon the core of the movement was firmly secured by employee and workers organizations representing tens of thousands of voters. Not coincidentally, the new federal election law authorized unions and employers to register their members and present them en masse to election officials. In a matter of months, Pedro Ernesto's party easily dominated local elections.[5]

While party lieutenants were lining up organizations to vote for Pedro Ernesto, his associates helped him create a new public persona. He returned to his civilian clothing and was addressed as *doutor,* in deference to his medical career. His clinic treated hundreds of people free each week, so that he became known for his compassion and charity. He began to speak on a radio station owned by the city. His party even founded a newspaper to publicize its program and candidates. In fact, the Autonomist Party was the first to operate a modern campaign in Brazil, albeit on a municipal level.

Early in his administration, Pedro Ernesto appointed a brilliant educational reformer, Anísio Teixeira, to be director of schools in Rio. With enthusiasm and zeal, Teixeira set out to provide a place for every child in the city. He built twenty-eight new schools and put the entire system on two shifts a day, so that all children could be accommodated. The city even built a school in a shantytown, the infamous favela of Mangueira. Teixeira introduced a new philosophy, called the New School, which placed the child at the center of the learning process. In all, Teixeira inspired devotion and respect from teachers and school officials.

Pedro Ernesto, meanwhile, expanded the city's health service by constructing six new hospitals in poor and outlying districts. He appointed hundreds of new physicians and nurses. This was a natural initiative for a doctor-politician to pursue, and it made him very popular. He became known throughout the city as the builder of schools and hospitals. His image became that of a benevolent doctor. His administration had a center-left appeal, as did many other regimes formed during the 1930s.

In order to penetrate lower-class precincts and register voters, the Autonomist Party divided the city into zones and designated chiefs to find new recruits in each area. Here patronage came into play, as local constituents signed up in exchange for favors of the most varied sorts. Party agents promised jobs, medical treatment, pensions, street paving, water and sewer lines, electric service, schools, and police protection. Pedro Ernesto, as head of the party, reaped the popularity while his chiefs and lieutenants concentrated on adding new voters to the rolls.

The results were spectacular. In 1930, during the most intense election ever held in Brazil, 64,000 people voted in Rio de Janeiro. Four years later, after new voter lists had been developed, nearly twice as many, 110,000 people, voted. Pedro Ernesto, the reformist mayor who built schools and hospitals, became enormously popular. His appeal reached from the favelas to government offices and from lower-middle class neighborhoods to the highest chambers of business and finance. In the 1934 election, his party took eight out of ten council seats and then chose him for the 1934–38 mayoral term.

By 1935 Pedro Ernesto became a national figure courted by politicians from other states. His very success, however, made him a target for both friends and enemies: leftists tried to take advantage of his popularity, and rightists attacked him as a dangerous radical. The Communists who plotted the November revolt of that year, for example, tried hard to recruit him to their cause. By the same token, right-wing groups targeted him because of his friendship with leftists and his tolerance of their causes.

When the 1935 communist revolt broke out, police and military investigators attempted to link Pedro Ernesto with the conspirators. They rounded up intellectuals and writers and succeeded in shutting down the Federal District University that Anísio Teixeira had founded. But the mayor had actually forewarned President Vargas and so he remained in the clear.

In early 1936 Pedro Ernesto seemed destined for higher office, and his name circulated as a possible 1938 successor to Vargas, who was ineligible for reelection. But the capture of communist leader Luís Carlos Prestes in March 1936 and the discovery of letters (unanswered) to the mayor led to the latter's arrest on charges of conspiracy. He had clearly become too popular and ambitious to be allowed to govern Brazil's capital city any longer. Vargas allowed the police to arrest him.

Pedro Ernesto spent several years defending himself against charges of treason, and he was eventually absolved. By that time, however, Vargas had already launched his New State (1937–45), an autocratic regime that erased most vestiges of democracy. When Pedro Ernesto succumbed to cancer in 1942, he received the largest funeral in the history of Rio de Janeiro.

The Rise of Populism

One of Vargas's appointees in 1938 was another physician, Adhemar de Barros, scion of a wealthy coffee family in São Paulo and dabbler in politics during the 1930s. Brilliant, outgoing, and ambitious, Adhemar used his appointment to launch himself into a career in politics. He immediately began building hospitals, schools, and highways to impress his constituents. He published glossy magazines touting his projects and sent his wife out to visit charity organizations. Imitating Franklin Roosevelt, he even broadcast fireside chats over the radio. This was the beginning of one of Brazil's most extraordinary populist careers.[6]

Adhemar de Barros was neither liked nor trusted by the traditional political leaders of his state, who hated Vargas for defeating them in a brief civil war in 1932, and in 1941 they succeeded in having him removed from office. That did not deter Adhemar for long, however. With his family money and connections, plus faithful aides from his three-year stint as governor, he would begin politicking again in the newly democratic environment of postwar Brazil.

Vargas himself began a career makeover in 1943 and 1944, anticipating a transition to democracy after the war. He addressed his speeches increasingly to the workers, and he rhetorically allied himself with their interests. His labor ministers remained in the background, allowing Vargas to get the credit for new social and labor programs. The 1943 Consolidation of Labor Laws (CLT), in particular, established Vargas as a friend of the Brazilian worker. By 1944 a veritable media blitz vaunted the benefits Vargas had bestowed on the masses. The culmination was his order in early 1945 that the labor minister create a party to capitalize on this popularity. Thus was born the Brazilian Labor Party (PTB). Even though he did not embrace the populist style wholly, Vargas began to experiment with it. Perhaps he secretly admired the approaches that Pedro Ernesto and Adhemar had pioneered. From all indications, Vargas succeeded in winning the lasting support of Brazil's workers and poor.[7]

Before he could put his new party to the test in elections, Vargas was overthrown by the army in late 1945. He took refuge on the family ranch in Rio Grande do Sul, in a self-imposed exile. Vargas did win a senate seat the following year, however, and he kept up a modest presence in Rio de Janeiro. He nursed his pride and pondered his chances of returning to power someday to vindicate his record as president.

The Heyday of Populism

In the meantime, Adhemar formed the populist-style Social Progressive Party in São Paulo and ran for governor in 1947. Finding his upper-class background a hindrance, he adopted the image of a rough-and-tumble provincial (*caipira*). Spending his own money as well as others', he expanded his following by hiring publicity experts, commissioning polls, purchasing radio stations and newspapers, and flying his own airplane to far-flung towns. In office he stressed more building programs—schools, hospitals, highways, and dams—that glorified his image as "the Manager." Tempted by the presidency in 1950, he nonetheless withdrew in favor of Vargas, on the understanding that the latter would support him in 1955.[8]

Vargas came out of his quasi-retirement to run for president in 1950 in what became the first truly modern election in the country. It also established his credentials as a full-fledged populist. He chose to be a reluctant candidate who could only be coaxed into the arena again by the will of the people. He remained at his ranch until just months before the election, aloof from the usual byplay of campaigning. Instead, he held quiet consultations with visitors, making deals and waiting for the right moment to go public with his candidacy. Meanwhile, he kept up an intense correspondence with his daughter Alzira, who lived in Rio and acted as his campaign manager and strategist. Alzira Vargas do Amaral Peixoto (married to an important figure in the government party, the conservative Social Democratic Party—PSD) conducted Vargas's campaign from her apartment in Rio, staying in close touch with her father by courier mail. She assembled a campaign team to coordinate with other candidacies, raise funds, prepare speeches, organize trips, issue press releases, and prepare ballots (a responsibility of candidates before official ballots were adopted). Her apartment became the unofficial headquarters for Vargas's election.[9]

Perhaps the most important role Alzira played was helping her father create just the right image for the masses in 1950. Vargas would be a solitary figure, maligned by ungrateful politicians and parties, who nonetheless held a covenant with the common people. He had brought about economic development and industrialization, and more importantly, he had protected the interests of the workers in that process. Under his leadership, Brazil had played an important part in world affairs, respected and courted by the great powers. Especially important was his sponsorship of a wide array of rights and social programs for the working class.

Now in his late sixties, Vargas considered returning to office to finish the job by protecting the country's new wealth from rapacious elites and greedy foreigners. The nationalism of his stance complemented his earlier stress on economic development and labor. Yet he would only run for office if the people demanded this ultimate sacrifice from their beloved leader.

The candidate's visual images proved very appealing. Photographs and caricatures showed Vargas on his ranch, wearing cowboy garb and drinking the traditional yerba mate tea of the region. He often posed while he smoked cigars. He always smiled and exuded an air of confidence, thoughtfulness, and pleasure at being around friends. The people needed him, not vice versa. The campaign staff distributed tens of thousands of publicity sheets depicting Vargas in this way.

Simultaneously his daughter Alzira directed the activities of the feminine branch of the PTB. Vargas had given women the vote in 1932, making Brazil the third country in the hemisphere to recognize women's suffrage. By the late 1940s women worked in myriad jobs throughout the economy, from industry and finance to teaching and health services. Those in manufacturing were becoming quite active in labor disputes. Although the PTB women's branch was staffed largely by well-to-do activists, its appeal penetrated deep into the social pyramid. Working women were especially appreciative of the protections provided for them under the CLT of 1943. Polls showed that Vargas enjoyed a substantial lead in preferences among women.

Once Vargas decided to announce himself a candidate, he moved quickly to consolidate his popularity. Meanwhile the organization Alzira had assembled translated the people's preferences into votes on election day. The centerpiece

Figure 2.1. Getúlio Vargas campaigns in 1950, with his wife, Darcy, and daughter Alzira at his side. (Courtesy of Arquivo Adhemar de Barros, São Paulo)

of the campaign was a bruising two-month tour of eighty-four cities in a rented DC-3. At each stop, Vargas had a tailor-made speech drafted by staff and vetted by himself. Seen everywhere as a smiling, warm, grandfatherly figure, Vargas became the best-known and most-liked person in the country. When the votes were finally counted, Vargas had won 48 percent in a contested three-way race, the highest plurality ever received in Brazil.

Vargas tried hard to carry out his promises to the masses, especially regarding protection of natural resources, economic planning, and a fair distribution of wealth. He created a national development bank tasked with channeling public loans to basic and critical industries. He proposed nationalizing all petroleum development and refining, a sector notorious for high profits and excessive remittances abroad. This passed in 1953 and gave rise to Petrobras, today one of the world's largest government-owned companies. Vargas also submitted to Congress a bill that would have nationalized electric power utilities so they could push service into poor and rural areas. This effort failed due to heavy lobbying from the industry. Finally, Vargas continued to give special attention to labor laws, social security, unemployment, and welfare services.[10]

In all, Vargas's second administration produced some major social progress, yet it did so in a climate of heightened political and economic conflict. Vargas's PTB-PSD coalition in Congress began to unravel. The military became restive over advances made by labor unions. The economy plunged into a recession in 1952, and Vargas, sixty-nine years old, had lost some of the deft touch he had shown earlier. His administration began to founder in early 1954.

No one rocked Vargas's boat more than a young and brilliant newspaper writer named Carlos Lacerda. The only populist born in a major city (Rio), Lacerda was the son of Rio's 1920s reformer, Maurício Lacerda. Writing at first for the sensational press and later in his own paper, *Tribuna da Imprensa,* Lacerda became an indefatigable crusader who despised politics as usual. A man of deep and conflicted emotions, Lacerda plunged into every controversy as if Brazil's destiny depended upon him. Graced with a high and versatile intellect, plus exquisite speaking abilities, Lacerda became the enfant terrible of 1950s Brazilian politics. President Vargas was on the receiving end of most of Lacerda's attacks.[11]

Lacerda entered politics in the 1930s as an ally of Luís Carlos Prestes but was forced to bow out after the 1935 revolt failed. In the 1940s he began a long migration toward the right of the ideological spectrum, by repudiating his father, renouncing communism, converting to Catholicism, and devoting himself to protecting the public trust. In 1947 he won election to Rio's city council, where he perfected his skills as an orator and crusader. He eventually found a home, not very comfortable, in the opposition National Democratic Union (UDN) party.

Lacerda campaigned for any cause, large or small, on the grounds that the public must be served by honest men. Uncompromising, flamboyant, outspoken, and outrageous at times, Lacerda became famous for his attacks on the establishment. After 1950 Vargas symbolized the establishment, and hence he was the target of Lacerda's most concentrated criticism.

In mid-1954 Vargas's bodyguard, probably acting alone, hired a gunman to assassinate Lacerda but instead killed an air force major who was providing security for him. The attempt on Lacerda's life, coupled with the other misdeeds he had charged Vargas with, culminated in a national campaign to impeach or overthrow the president. This in turn precipitated a military coup in August that triggered the president's suicide. It was literally a contest of titans, a battle between the old and the young populists, and Lacerda led the winning side. Lacerda became known as the slayer of giants, adored by his followers but detested by Vargas's faithful.

Lacerda had been campaigning for a seat in Congress, which he won handily in October 1954, partly due to his fame. In fact, he received more votes than any other congressional candidate. He had adopted the lantern as his symbol, to shine light into the dark corners of government. His new office allowed him to scrutinize the entire federal government, which he did with his customary relish and fiery oratory.

Populism after Vargas

Adhemar had toyed with the idea of running for president in 1950, but he desisted when polls he commissioned showed Vargas far ahead. Instead, he made a deal to support Vargas in exchange for the latter's backing in 1955. Adhemar returned to São Paulo and prepared to run for the governorship in 1954.

At this point, Adhemar's flamboyant career was blocked by the meteoric Jânio Quadros, a thoroughgoing populist. Jânio had appeared out of nowhere to win a São Paulo city council seat in 1947. As he campaigned and agitated, Jânio gained a reputation as a bohemian, unpredictable, and quixotic figure. In 1950 he won a seat in the state legislature, where his notoriety grew due to his constant questioning of officials and demands for honesty and morality in public office. He adopted the broom as his campaign symbol, by which he implied he would sweep corruption out of government.[12]

In 1953, with the backing of influential Paulistanos, he ran for mayor on a platform that stressed cleaning up graft and curbing expenditures. His victory over veteran politicians attracted national attention, and the following year he took on Adhemar de Barros in the gubernatorial election. He used unorthodox appeals that won broad support from the working and middle classes. A surprise endorsement carried on television marked the first effective use of that new medium in Brazilian politics. Jânio's victory confirmed his reputation as a dragon slayer and quintessential populist.

Jânio and Adhemar both looked covetously at the presidency in 1955. Jânio ended up not running, however, and an indictment for corruption stalled Adhemar's campaign. Instead, the highest office went to another populist, Juscelino Kubitschek.

Juscelino had worked his way up the political ladder in Minas Gerais, Brazil's most populous state. Having reached the governorship, he believed he had a chance to win the presidency in 1955. He conferred with government party leaders and with Vargas himself and realized that it would be a wide-open race. Vargas's 1954 suicide made it even harder to predict the outcome.

Juscelino threw himself into the fray with an energy and determination rarely seen. He had already won a reputation for vigor: he traveled so much in Minas Gerais he was known as the "jet-propelled governor." His presidential campaign included several grueling trips in a specially equipped DC-3, in which he visited hundreds of towns and logged tens of thousands of miles. He used the radio extensively and even made some television spots to publicize his plan of action if elected. He left nothing to chance, even giving the vice presidential nomination to the PTB in order to win that party's support.[13]

Juscelino's hard work paid off with a plurality of votes in 1955. Unable to relax even as president, he threw himself into his job and pledged to produce "fifty years of progress in five." Among his accomplishments were a fledgling automobile industry, expansion of capital goods manufacturing, a new capital city in Brasília, improved highways, and a more vigorous foreign policy. Toward the end Juscelino also used his term to begin running for reelection in 1965.

Juscelino's running mate, João "Jango" Goulart, also made a career as a populist. A neighbor of Vargas during the latter's estrangement from politics in the 1940s, Goulart joined the PTB and soon became party chief in Rio Grande do Sul. Handsome, wealthy, and ambitious, Jango helped Vargas ride herd over the many PTB constituencies. In 1953, in fact, Vargas appointed him minister of labor, to handle an unexpected surge of strikes and labor disruptions. Jango's solution, doubling the general wage levels, so enraged employers and conservatives that they forced his resignation. Vargas nevertheless granted the wage increase and enhanced his and Jango's reputations as friends of labor.[14]

When Juscelino invited Jango to be his running mate, he hoped to restore a coalition that Vargas himself had envisioned in 1945, between working politicians who belonged to the PSD and newer labor and popular leaders in the PTB. Jango got out the votes and made sure that Juscelino won, but he himself received more votes than the president. Afterward, Jango occupied himself with labor and social policy, leaving economics and other initiatives to Juscelino. Their parties never coalesced, and each leader remained close to his original constituency. It was a workable arrangement but hardly ideal. Populists never found it easy to share power with others.

Adhemar, meanwhile, managed to win acquittal of the charges against him and staged a comeback by winning the São Paulo mayor's race in 1957. His personal wealth grew, and he invested heavily in campaign slogans, literature, polls, and public works. His life became an eternal election campaign.

From the moment of his election as governor in 1954, Jânio had turned his attention to the presidential succession. He used his potential candidacy in 1955 as leverage to gain influence and federal patronage. During his gubernatorial term, São Paulo prospered from business expansion and heavy investments in infrastructure. São Paulo surpassed Rio in population in the 1950s and became an industrial megalopolis.

In 1959 Jânio began campaigning for president, accepting the nomination of the UDN but definitely remaining an independent. His fresh image, unorthodox methods, and promises of national prosperity attracted a plurality of the voters, who also returned João Goulart to the vice presidency. As the first president inaugurated in the new capital of Brasília, Jânio made headlines in early 1961, pursuing an ambitious program of reforms while retaining his reputation for moralism and eccentricity. He pursued fiscal austerity, an activist foreign policy, morality in government, and industrial expansion.[15]

Soon, however, relations between the president and Congress soured, and in August Jânio abruptly resigned. He hoped to be called back by Congress and graced with extraordinary powers and glory. Instead, Congress accepted his resignation and left him out of a job. The next year he announced his candidacy for another term as governor of São Paulo, but in 1963 he was defeated by his old rival, Adhemar de Barros. Jânio's career seemed to have run its course.

Jânio's resignation as president in 1961, meanwhile, caused a crisis in Brasília. His vice president was none other than PTB chief Jango Goulart, who had quietly supported Jânio's ticket in 1960. Jango's leftist tendencies, plus the fact that he was leading a trade mission in communist China in mid-1961, led Jânio to believe that the army and conservatives would not accept a vice presidential succession. He was right about that: the army, with support from Congress and the other service chiefs, declared that Goulart could not become president. But neither did they call Jânio back.

At this point, another populist figure, Leonel Brizola, jumped into the limelight and virtually stole the show. Brizola had grown up poor in Rio Grande do Sul but managed to earn an engineering degree. He joined the PTB in 1945 and proved a skillful organizer, with a penchant for militant socialist rhetoric. Through marriage to Goulart's sister and hard work in the PTB, he became a leader in state politics. After holding several lesser posts, he won election as mayor of Porto Alegre in 1955 by promising to improve the lives of the workers. For three years he enhanced his reputation as an engineer with a social conscience, speaking on the radio, writing newspaper columns, meeting with civic groups, and supervising projects. He was definitely a comer.[16]

His success as mayor led to a victory in the 1958 gubernatorial election. His administration proved vigorous and constructive, marred only by the controversial nationalizations of the American-owned electric power and telephone companies.

When the army sought to prevent the succession of his brother-in-law, João Goulart, to the presidency in 1961, Brizola organized a revolt among civilian and military forces in Rio Grande. By threatening to divide the army, Brizola's challenge succeeded in forcing Goulart's accession to office. Brizola now had a national reputation for aggressive, confrontational politics.

A year later Brizola won more national prominence by being elected federal deputy from Guanabara (formerly Federal District of Rio de Janeiro) by the most votes ever cast. From his new political base he pressured Goulart and Congress to carry out major reforms, such as land distribution, rent control, and nationalization of utilities. While popular among workers, Brizola's platform alienated businessmen, the upper-middle class, the U.S. embassy, and the military. By polarizing issues, he helped bring on the crisis of 1964.

Another populist emerged on the scene in the late 1950s in the northeastern state of Pernambuco. Miguel Arraes was born into a rural middle-class family in the interior of Ceará. He eventually settled in Recife and graduated from law school in 1937. A government job and family connections led to his appointment as finance secretary of Pernambuco in 1947. By 1955 he joined the Frente do Recife, a reformist center-leftist coalition that reached out to rural workers. Arraes won election as mayor of Recife in 1960 and gained a reputation for courting poor voters with slum-improvement programs.[17]

In 1963 Arraes ran successfully for governor of the state of Pernambuco. His campaign was noteworthy for allying with peasant leagues and broadcasting radio messages to rural voters, recently able to receive them by transistor radio. Once in office, Arraes implemented a minimum wage for rural workers, expanded farm credit, and promoted unionization in the countryside. Land reform, too, became a potent rallying cry thanks to Arraes's leadership. Although he was not an ally of President Goulart, critics accused Arraes of radicalizing politics in the northeast and blamed him for successive waves of strikes and lockouts. For virtually the first time in history, a national-level leader promised to address grievances of the masses of rural poor. One U.S. observer referred to the ferment in the northeast as "the revolution that never was."

Carlos Lacerda finally gained the limelight in 1960 when he won election as governor of the newly created state of Guanabara. He found his calling, serving as executive for the first time in his career. Instead of the perennial critic, Lacerda proved a constructive, energetic, inspirational, and enormously successful administrator. He built schools, roads, low-cost housing, water and sewer systems, and virtually anything else the city of Rio needed. A true friend of the United States, Lacerda won special concessions from international donors. His 1961–65 term was unquestionably the high point of his career. His last day in office was transformed into a marathon media event to rally support for Lacerda and his movement, in the vain hope of launching him into the presidency.

The Fall of Populism

Between 1963 and 1966 populism was eradicated in Brazil. The single largest reason was the military's opposition to the open, expansive, increasingly radical politics that the populists waged. Military and communist strategists alike believed that revolution was possible and maybe imminent in Brazil. Fidel Castro had seized control of Cuba, and guerrilla warfare was breaking out everywhere in the world. The military authorities, charged with protecting the state, decided that the risk of revolution was too great to allow political experimentation to proceed. The leftists fought them but ultimately lost.

Most military officers focused their hatred on President Goulart, whose erratic and ineffectual administration had prompted major demonstrations and crises. The economy was in shambles, civil society was increasingly split by irreconcilable differences, and the international situation was becoming more menacing. Behind Goulart, however, they saw others equally or more dangerous. Brizola, thought to be manipulating the president, was a worse threat because he had divided the army once before in 1961. Arraes had assisted in the formation of peasant leagues, which could unleash banditry and rural warfare. Lacerda was a loose cannon who would bring down the government rather than cooperate with anyone else in power. And through it all, the PTB, which Vargas had founded two decades before, was within reach of a congressional majority. The state itself could lurch toward the left at any minute, necessitating military action.[18]

The military did not banish populism all by itself. It had ample support from some of the populists themselves as well as from most working politicians. The infighting among the populists became intense, bitter, and alarming by 1964. Goulart weighed the possibility of ordering military coups against Arraes and Lacerda in 1964. Adhemar de Barros put the full weight of São Paulo's government and state police behind the coup of 1964, and Lacerda did the same in Guanabara. Only Quadros and Kubitschek, out of office, remained on the sidelines.

Moreover, the great majority of working politicians in 1964 also supported the coup against Goulart. They saw the trends as prejudicial to their own careers—the growing strife and confrontation in politics, the huge costs of mobilizing voters and followers, the chance that the PTB would win control of Congress, and the increasingly divided polity that offered fewer opportunities for compromise. They mostly endorsed the military action of March 1964 in order to protect their own jobs.

Even after the coup, those populists still active tended to push the military into hard-line positions. Brizola's guerrilla activity in Uruguay confirmed the worst fears of the so-called *linha dura* officers. Carlos Lacerda, who might have compromised with the military to allow a return to civilian government, refused to do so and made the hard-line triumph almost inevitable. His Frente Ampla alliance with Kubitschek and Goulart between late 1966 and 1967, which they hoped would convince the military to turn over power, in fact backfired and

Figure 2.2. Miguel Arraes in a 1963 dock-workers' demonstration in Recife.
(Courtesy of Instituto Joaquim Nabuco, Recife)

brought on more dictatorial policies. Not only did the populists help trigger the military coup, they bore some responsibility for the severity and length of the subsequent dictatorship.[19]

During the worst years of repression, from the late 1960s until the late 1970s, some of the populists lost their political rights and never recovered them. Goulart retired to a ranch in Uruguay, where he died. Kubitschek perished in a highway accident in São Paulo. Lacerda died of a stroke in Rio de Janeiro. Adhemar passed away in Paris in 1968.

Democratization and the Return of Populism

The restoration of political rights and a general amnesty in the late 1970s allowed most of Brazil's exiles to return home, including the populists. The transition to democracy lasted a decade and proved slow, painful, and frustrating to the masses of citizens and most politicians. It was called by many names: decompression, *distensão, abertura* (the opening), and eventually just the transition. The army finally turned power over to civilians in 1985 on the condition that no officers could be tried for crimes committed during the dictatorship.[20]

Some former populists attempted to make comebacks in the 1980s, even before the restoration of civilian rule. Brizola founded the Democratic Labor Party (PDT), with which he won election as governor of Rio in 1982. He was notable for founding integrated school centers for children; curbing police abuses; and pressuring Congress to hold direct elections for president in 1984. After running unsuccessfully for president in 1989, he was elected governor of Rio de Janeiro the following year. He stood for president again in 1994 but lost. In 1998 he lost the race for vice president.

Jânio Quadros lost his bid to become governor of São Paulo in 1982 but then surprised critics by winning the mayoralty of São Paulo in 1985, over social scientist Fernando Henrique Cardoso. Jânio's decision not to run for president in 1989 marked the end of his active career; he died shortly afterward.

Miguel Arraes was jailed for a year following the 1964 coup, then spent most of the period 1965–79 in Algeria, representing petroleum exporters. He returned to Brazil in 1979 and three years later won election to Congress. Using his image as an elder statesman, he ran for governor in 1986 and took office the following year. He failed to make a large showing in the primaries for president in 1989 but was elected federal deputy that year. In 1994 he won election as governor of Pernambuco for the third time and showed no signs of retirement, but he lost in 1998.

Throughout the dictatorship, the military continued to hold elections for most public offices, attempting to keep a working majority in Congress and control over critical statehouses. In fact, voter turnouts rose even faster than they had before 1964, because suffrage was obligatory. General discontent with military government, moreover, led to creative electoral dissent: millions of voters cast blank or invalidated ballots in protest. Most observers believe this contributed to the military's decision to begin the transition back to democracy. Finally, systematic analysis of polls suggests that voters actually grew in sophistication during the dictatorship. By the 1990s political scientists described Brazil as a model of the "new democracy" sweeping the world.[21]

The long years of repression and controlled participation left parties and other structures disorganized and unable to mediate between governors and citizens. The new scenario of the late 1980s contained parties, to be sure, yet they were weak and amorphous. New forms of representation and participation arose to create what one analyst calls "direct democracy and state-led representation."[22]

The most innovative party to surface in these years was the Workers' Party (PT), a vigorous socialist-oriented political movement. Led by autoworkers union official Luiz Inácio "Lula" da Silva and leftist intellectuals, the PT grew rapidly in major cities, attracting many working-class, middle-class, and student voters. In 1989 Lula came within a few percentage points of winning the runoff for president against Fernando Collor de Melo. Lula returned even stronger in the 1994 elections.[23]

Fernando Collor de Melo (1990–92) was widely regarded as a neopopulist, due to his antipolitics stance and flamboyant use of the media. Offspring of a wealthy family from Alagoas, Collor was raised in Rio and Brasília, where his father served in Congress. His family, which owned television and radio chains in the northeast, was notorious for its rough-and-tumble approach to politics. Collor, with rich backers and unlimited media budgets, ran as an outsider without party connections. Young, athletic, and new on the scene, he convinced a majority of voters that he would conduct a thorough housecleaning and restore good government. He campaigned against the maharajas in backward regions who stole public money and denied democracy to the people. With brilliant use of slogans, sound bites, photo sessions, television debates, and press briefings, Collor convinced Brazilians that he would be an effective leader.

After little more than a year in office, however, evidence of his involvement in a huge bribery scheme began to surface, and within months he was impeached. He resigned from the presidency in disgrace. His little-known vice president, Itamar Franco, succeeded Collor for the remainder of the term.[24]

The 1994 election saw little evidence of populism. Brizola, the only old-timer who ran, fell behind in the polls, lost in the first round, and was again out of public office. Neither of the front-runners, Fernando Henrique Cardoso nor Lula, could even remotely be called populists. Lula's credentials as union leader and his party's platform located him squarely in the camp of democratic socialism. Neither of his campaigns contained elements of populism. Fernando Henrique, likewise, had been critical of populism for most of his academic career. His widely read book, *Dependency and Development in Latin America* (1979), coauthored with Enzo Faletto, devoted a chapter to showing how populists served the interests of the national bourgeoisie by keeping the masses in line.

Fernando Henrique, as Cardoso was known popularly, won the 1994 election in the first round, an accomplishment in any country. An experienced leader of the Senate, a seasoned negotiator, and president of the 1988 Constitutional Convention, he had strong credentials for the presidency. Moreover, he had become finance minister and was charged with carrying out an anti-inflation program in Franco's last year in office. A task fraught with dangers, the Plano Real worked and helped sweep him to victory. Even after the election and January 1995 inauguration, the president managed to keep inflation at bay. He continued to enjoy strong support in opinion polls and carried out a tough but fair program for privatizing public-sector enterprises and opening the country to international competition.[25] By 1997 his congressional supporters had amended the constitution in order to allow for reelection, something already done by Peru's Fujimori and Argentina's Menem. In exchange, though, he accepted a permanent reduction of the presidential term to four years.

By 1998, Miguel Arraes was the only mature populist still holding public office in Brazil. In fact, he did not like to be called a populist, preferring the image of a crusty, shrewd, and seasoned rural leader, steadfastly faithful to his peasant origins in the interior of Brazil's northeast. Still, Lula launched his bid again in 1998, this time buttressed by vice presidential candidate Leonel Brizola, always a big draw in Rio and Rio Grande do Sul. As the campaign heated up, some polls showed Cardoso and Lula neck and neck. In the end, though, Cardoso won in the first round. His last administration continued most of his policies from the first, and he left a strong positive legacy when he stepped down in January 2003.

Beyond Populism?

Lula ran for president yet again in 2002, his fourth and finally victorious attempt. Much of the campaign against him that year stoked fears that Lula would be a radical and would scare off foreign and even domestic capital with leftist policies. Once inaugurated, though, Lula surprised critics and angered supporters by extending many of Cardoso's economic policies. After several months of business continuity, foreign capital began to flow back in and the São Paulo stock exchange resumed its steady rise. To be sure, Lula launched his own version of antipoverty programs—Zero Hunger—and tied family subsidies to keeping children in school. His approval ratings remained high both at home and abroad.

The last two icons of populism from the mid-twentieth century, Brizola and Arraes, passed away in 2004 and 2005, leaving the country largely populist free. Gradually, however, Lula began to look more like a populist than the labor socialist he began his career as. His long struggle to win the presidency impressed people, as did his commitment to help the less fortunate among them. He championed causes like land reform that his predecessors paid only lip service to. And amazingly, the extreme concentration of income began to decrease with the family subsidy transfers. Added to that, his approval ratings remained high despite some withering financial and corruption scandals in his cabinet and party.

Analysts are divided about Lula's populist characteristics. Wendy Hunter and Tim Power agree that Lula seems to fit the traditional definition yet argue that his stunning reelection in 2006 was due rather to his extraordinary dedication to helping the poor. Basically he won with overwhelming support from the poorest voters, who had benefitted the most from his policies, especially in 2006. They conclude that "the main story of Lula's reelection can be told without reference to the concept of populism." Kirk Hawkins finds that Lula's speeches contain modest elements of populist discourse compared to other famous figures. Lula himself occasionally took populist stances that evoked predecessors like Getúlio Vargas.[26]

In the end, Lula became a populist, moving into that style of governance from his earlier union origins. His phenomenally successful two terms as president suggest that he chose well. He may, however, end up as Brazil's last populist: neither of the presidential candidates in the 2010 election displayed any populist characteristics, and the old guard is gone.

An Assessment

Because the populists discussed here dominated the middle and late years of the last century and set the tone for politics in general, they might be regarded as simply the most successful leaders of the era. They were, of course, but that is not what made them populists. Instead, they shared characteristics that set them far apart from the majority of Brazil's sitting politicians. By way of conclusion, this section highlights those attributes and differentiates populists from ordinary officials.

Almost all the populists were born in provincial towns and rural areas, far from the metropolises where they eventually made their careers. Many had fathers active in politics, but the sons usually rejected paternal influences and struck out on their own. They were not religious or inclined to the regimentation of military life. They threw themselves into politics early in life and never gave up trying to scale the heights of elective office, especially those with executive powers. They had extraordinary energy, drive, intelligence, and powers of communication. These qualities, when joined with the adulation of the followers, made them charismatic. They enjoyed and thrived on the campaign trail, the skirmishing, and the rhetorical fights, at which they were very good. They seemed to have been born for public life.[27]

The populists introduced new forms of opinion shaping and voting behavior, replacing old-fashioned clientelism and patronage with mass suffrage. Using radio and television, new means of transportation, polling services, public relations, efficient organization, and mass print media, they revolutionized the way politicians gained office. From the 1950s on, every aspiring office holder had to use these campaign techniques. Some adopted them reluctantly (Vargas preferred to rely on relatives and his own intuition), while others embraced them enthusiastically (for example, Adhemar and Lacerda). The result was mass politics in which complex and socio-psychological processes came to shape voters' decisions. The populists were in charge, to be sure, but even they did not fully understand the forces they had unleashed.[28]

The cost of the new politics rose astronomically after the advent of populism because of the need to reach masses of voters. Today national candidates spend tens of millions of dollars to get elected, with all the complications that high finances imply. Aspirants to high office buy books and take courses on "marketing político." Politics is no longer the domain of elder statesmen and gifted amateurs.

One of the most remarkable legacies of populism has been the enfranchisement of nearly the entire adult population and the creation of election procedures that ensure honest results. Between the hotly contested election of 1930 and that of 1994, the turnout for president rose from 2 to 94 million (see table I.1). The secret ballot became the most common way to select political leaders, as even the military came to realize in the 1970s, when their elaborate rigging of election rules failed to guarantee victories.

Populists helped to destroy thousands of localized political redoubts by incorporating them into the national arena. From Vargas's and Juscelino's DC-3 visits to small towns, to Collor's and Brizola's television ads bounced off satellites, national politics have invaded even the most remote and isolated locales. A few television networks, a dozen radio chains, several polling services, and a score of newspapers dominate the communications industry. The populists had a great deal to do with this expansion and consolidation. Adhemar bought radio stations and newspapers and owned an airplane for his campaigns. Vargas financed the first mass circulation daily, *Última Hora,* with a government loan. Today, politicians, pollsters, and media moguls work hand in hand. By the same token no local official can ignore national issues because of their penetration into every nook and cranny of the country.

The thousands of traditional politicians active in midcentury politics did not have the skills or charisma of the populists. They served in elective and appointive posts at the municipal, state, and federal levels. They got into politics at a later age and came from families with urban roots. They favored preservation of a limited, controlled electorate rather than a growing, volatile one. They grudgingly accepted the advent of mass politics yet resented the successes of the newcomers.[29] That is why most supported the 1964 coup that temporarily sidelined populism.

Put in a temporal perspective, Brazil's populist era lasted only a brief time. Populists occupied the presidency a scant thirteen years (1951–64). They controlled statehouses longer: São Paulo about fifteen years; Rio Grande do Sul and Guanabara five each; and Pernambuco three. At the municipal level, populists governed about two dozen years total. In this light, the Populist Republic was an impermanent episode preceded and followed by authoritarian and socially conservative regimes. After the fall of military government, populism resurfaced (as neopopulism) for just a few years.

Populism in Brazil did not have as profound an impact as it did in Uruguay or Argentina, where Batllismo and Peronismo remain powerful influences. On the other hand, as the other chapters in the book make clear, Brazil's populists made more of a difference than those of Mexico, Chile, Peru, and Venezuela. For better or worse, the conduct of national politics in Brazil has been permanently changed by the populist experiments of the 1930s, 1940s, 1950s, and 1960s.

Notes

1. For a general introduction to the subject, see Francisco Weffort, *O populismo na política brasileira* (Rio: Paz e Terra, 1978) and Michael L. Conniff, "The Populists of Brazil, 1945–1966," *Review of Latin American Studies* 4, no. 1 (1991): 44–65.

2. Michael L. Conniff, *Urban Politics in Brazil: The Rise of Populism, 1925–1945* (Pittsburgh: University of Pittsburgh Press, 1981), ch. 4.

3. Jordan M. Young, *The Brazilian Revolution of 1930 and the Aftermath* (New Brunswick, N.J.: Rutgers University Press, 1967).

4. Michael L. Conniff, "The Tenentes in Power: New Perspectives on the Brazilian Revolution of 1930," *Journal of Latin American Studies* 10 (1978): 61–82.

5. Conniff, *Urban Politics,* ch. 6. A number of studies about Pedro Ernesto have appeared recently, among them João Roberto Oliveira Nunes, "A administração Pedro Ernesto e a questão educacional" (master's thesis, IUPRJ, 2001); Carlos Eduardo Sarmento, *O Rio na era Pedro Ernesto* (Rio: FGV, 2001); Thiago Cavaliere Mourelle, *O trabalhismo de Pedro Ernesto* (Rio: Editora Juruá, 2010); Alexandre Elias da Silva, "Política e populismo no Rio de Janeiro, 1931–1936" (master's thesis, Universidade Federal Fluminense, 2006).

6. Regina Sampaio, *Adhemar de Barros e o PSP* (São Paulo: Global Editora, 1982), 39–48.

7. John W. F. Dulles, *Vargas of Brazil: A Political Biography* (Austin: University of Texas Press, 1967), 250–80.

8. Sampaio, *Adhemar;* John French, "Workers and the Rise of Adhemarista Populism in São Paulo, Brazil, 1945–1947," *Hispanic American Historical Review* 68, no. 1 (1988): 10–33.

9. Dulles, *Vargas,* 290–96; interview with Alzira Vargas do Amaral Peixoto and her 1950 correspondence with Getúlio Vargas.

10. Dulles, *Vargas,* 305–35; Thomas E. Skidmore, *Politics in Brazil: An Experiment in Democracy, 1930–1964* (New York: Oxford University Press, 1967).

11. John W. F. Dulles, *Carlos Lacerda, Brazilian Crusader,* vol. 1 (Austin: University of Texas Press, 1991).

12. Maria Victória de Mesquita Benevides, *O governo Jânio Quadros* (São Paulo: Editora Brasiliense, 1981).

13. Edward Anthony Reidinger, *Como se faz um presidente: A campanha de J. K.* (Rio: Nova Fronteira, 1988).

14. Luís Alberto Moniz Bandeira, *O governo João Goulart: As lutas sociais no Brasil (1961–1964)* (Rio: Civilização Brasileira, 1977).

15. Thomas E. Skidmore, "A Case Study in Comparative Public Policy: The Economic Dimensions of Populism in Argentina and Brazil," *New Scholar* 7, no. 2 (1978).

16. Luís Alberto Moniz Bandeira, *Brizola e o trabalhismo* (Rio: Civilização Brasileira, 1979).

17. José Arlindo Soares, *A frente do Recife e o governo do Arraes: Nacionalismo em crise, 1955–1964* (Rio: Paz e Terra, 1982) and Joseph A. Page, *The Revolution That Never Was, Northeast Brazil, 1955–1964* (New York: Grossman, 1972).

18. Skidmore, *Democracy.* Several of Weffort's early interpretations of the 1960s, focusing on the later populist period and military coup, are gathered in *O populismo.*

19. Dulles, *Carlos Lacerda,* vol. 2 (Austin: University of Texas Press, 1996). For the antipopulist nature of the 1964 coup, see Octavio Ianni, *Crisis in Brazil* (New York: Columbia University Press, 1970), originally published as *O colapso do populismo no Brasil.*

20. The most important sources in English are Alfred Stepan, ed., *Democratizing Brazil: Problems of Transition and Consolidation* (New York: Oxford University Press, 1989); Thomas E. Skidmore, *The Politics of Military Rule in Brazil, 1964–1985* (New York: Oxford University Press, 1988); and Wayne Selcher, ed., *Political Liberalization in Brazil* (Boulder: Westview, 1986).

21. The best treatment of voter behavior during the transition is Kurt von Mettenheim, *The Brazilian Voter: Mass Politics in Democratic Transition, 1974–1986* (Pittsburgh: University of Pittsburgh Press, 1995). On the restoration of representative government, see Francisco C. Weffort, "What Is a 'New Democracy'?" *International Social Science Journal* 136 (May 1993): 245–56. Scott Mainwaring assesses the long-term impact of activism in "Urban Popular Movements, Identity, and Democratization in Brazil," *Comparative Political Studies* 20, no. 2 (July 1987): 131–59.

22. Mettenheim, *The Brazilian Voter.*

23. Margaret E. Keck, *The Workers' Party and Democratization in Brazil* (New Haven: Yale University Press, 1992).

24. Collor's election is analyzed by Venício A. de Lima, "Brazilian Television in the 1989 Presidential Campaign: Constructing a President," in *Television, Politics, and the Transition to Democracy in Latin America,* ed. Thomas E. Skidmore (Washington: Woodrow Wilson Center Press, 1993), 97–117, and André Singer, "Collor na periferia: Ä volta por cima do populismo?" in *De Geisel a Collor: O balanço da transição,* ed. Bolívar Lamounier (São Paulo: CNDCT, 1990), 135–52; his administration by Ronald Schneider, *Brazil: Culture and Politics in a New Industrial Powerhouse* (Boulder: Westview, 1996), ch. 5.

25. Gamaliel Perruci, "Neopopulism in Brazil's Democratic Consolidation: A Comparative Analysis," *Journal für Entwicklungspolitik* 11, no. 1 (1995): 29–50.

26. Wendy Hunter and Timothy J. Power, "Rewarding Lula: Executive Power, Social Policy, and the Brazilian Elections of 2006," *Latin American Politics and Society,* 49, no. 1 (Spring 2007): 21; Kirk A. Hawkins, "Is Chávez Populist? Measuring Populist Discourse in Comparative Perspective," *Comparative Political Studies,* 42, no. 8 (August 2009): 1056.

27. See the results of a random sample analyzed in "The National Elite," *Modern Brazil: Elites and Masses in Historical Perspective,* ed. Michael L. Conniff and Frank D. McCann (Lincoln: University of Nebraska Press, 1989), 24–29.

28. Mettenheim, *Brazilian Voter.*

29. The populists' collective biographies are analyzed in Conniff, "The Populists."

3
Chile's Populism Reconsidered, 1920s–1990s

Paul W. Drake

When Chile returned to democracy at the end of the 1980s, some politicians and social scientists feared that populism would be unleashed. They were apprehensive that it might bring destabilizing and inflationary campaigns for mass mobilization and redistribution. Despite their worries, populism failed to capture center stage, reflecting its historic weakness in Chile. This essay will examine why standard, classic, full-blown Latin American populism never took hold in Chile and why lesser varieties of populism assumed different forms there.

In general, Latin American populism has exhibited three interconnected features. First, it has been dominated by paternalistic, personalistic, often charismatic leadership and mobilization from the top down. Second, it has involved multiclass incorporation of the masses, especially urban workers but also middle sectors. Third, populists have emphasized integrationist, reformist, nationalist development programs for the state to promote simultaneously redistributive measures for populist supporters and, in most cases, import substitution industrialization.[1]

Populism has been most common in Latin America where competitive party systems have been weak and military interventions frequent, as in Peru, Argentina, Ecuador, and Brazil. In those countries, populists have filled the vacuum created by the weakness of civilian political institutions. By contrast, populism has been uncommon in nations with strong party systems and relatively noninterventionist militaries, including Costa Rica, Colombia, Venezuela (after 1958), Uruguay, and, in many respects, Chile, which has never been ruled by a mesmerizing leader of a multiclass urban movement committed to rapid elevation of the workers and hothouse industrialization. Charismatic figures have rarely been successful in Chile because of the highly Europeanized, institutionalized, and durable political parties. Those organizations filled the ideological spectrum, left little room for personalistic mass mobilization or independent adventures, and withstood seventeen years of Gen. Augusto Pinochet Ugarte's draconian efforts to eradicate their influence. Moreover, two Marxist parties—the Socialists and Communists—preempted any nonideological populist bid to the working class. Rather than being ushered onto the political stage abruptly by some firebrand, Chilean workers were gradually integrated into the established order through multiparty, electoral politics. In comparative terms, industrialization also evolved fairly incrementally, from the late nineteenth century through the 1960s. And military takeovers were extremely rare before the 1973 coup d'etat.[2]

Nevertheless, some scholars have detected elements of populism in Chilean political development. They have nominated six candidates for a populist pantheon. In all these instances, some form of populism only took off when the regular party system lost support and broke down (1920, 1932, 1952, and 1989) or when populism was channeled within that system (1938). Even when populism did surface, it usually did so only in partial form, as a leadership style, as a multiclass coalition, or as a redistributive program.

First, Arturo Alessandri Palma has been depicted as a populist precursor in 1920 because he pioneered a demagogic campaign style promising redemption to the urban masses. Second, the Chilean Socialists have been identified as a populist party that entered government in a multiparty coalition in 1938 along with nonpopulist parties, mainly the Radicals and Communists. Third, the Popular Front coalition, although not headed by some spellbinding orator, resembled Latin American populist movements in its social base (mainly the urban middle and working classes) and its program (simultaneous promotion of national industry and the welfare state). Fourth, some scholars tagged Carlos Ibáñez del Campo as a populist when he ran against all the major political parties and won the presidency in 1952 on a personalistic platform promising to "sweep out the rascals." Fifth, although dedicated to the Chilean road to socialism, the Popular Unity government (1970–73) of Salvador Allende Gossens has been painted as partially populist. Critics have pointed to its initial Keynesian pumping up of demand that resulted in runaway inflation, calls for austerity, and a military coup d'état to restore order. Sixth, during the return to democracy at the end of the 1980s, Chilean leaders feared populism as a turbulent force and strove to avoid its appearance. It only surfaced briefly with the unorthodox campaign of a renegade businessman. This chapter will assess those six claimants to the populist label in the context of Chilean party politics.

A Populist Precursor: Arturo Alessandri

Alessandri pioneered populist pyrotechnics in his 1915 campaign for senator from the Liberal Party. Although he never really pushed a fervent program of industrialization and redistribution, his personal resonance with the masses made him a populist precursor. He broke with the aristocratic custom of relying on deals among elites, parties, and local electoral *caciques*. Instead, Alessandri appealed directly to the middle and working classes with florid oratory, claiming to represent his "beloved rabble" against the "gilded scoundrels."[3]

Thereafter Alessandri ran for president in 1920 as the paladin of a center-left multiparty coalition known as the Liberal Alliance. It relied on dissident elites (particularly in the outlying provinces), urban middle-class groups, and organized labor represented by the Liberal, Radical, and Democrat parties. Student leaders helped knit together the middle and working classes by providing politicized education in night courses for laborers.

The essential element, however, was Alessandri's personal appeal to the downtrodden. In extreme cases of adulation, workers knelt to kiss his hand and brought sick children to be cured by his touch. He denounced standard party politics in the Parliamentary Republic (1891–1925) for squabbling over spoils while ignoring the nation's needs for economic development and social justice. He campaigned as a reformer, promising to defuse class conflict through evolutionary changes, warning that the choices were "Either Alessandri as President or the Revolution."

Alessandri mainly sought to open up the political system to the middle sectors, not to launch major projects for industrialization or social welfare. Like many populists in Latin America, he assured landowners that benefits for organized labor would be confined to the cities. Although his narrow victory—the famous "revolt of the electorate"—inspired high hopes among his followers for significant reforms for the middle and lower classes, the conservative Congress blocked most of his initiatives.[4]

Ousting the ineffectual Alessandri in 1924, the military dominated national politics thereafter, either directly or from behind the scenes, until the Great Depression. For most of those years, army strongman Carlos Ibáñez was the power behind or on the throne (1927–31). He repressed political parties and labor organizations. When Ibáñez fell in 1931, populism reemerged, this time propelled by the agony of the economic catastrophe and the disarray of the party system. Now populism was led by self-proclaimed Socialists.[5]

A Populist Movement: Chilean Socialism

Out of the political chaos spawned by the depression in 1931–32 emerged a new national movement: indigenous Chilean socialism. The Socialist Party's (PS) official birth in 1933 resulted from the so-called Socialist Republic, a junta that held power for twelve tumultuous days in 1932. The most flamboyant leader of that junta was Air Force Commander Marmaduke Grove Vallejo, who was hailed by the Socialists as their man on horseback. "The race loves Grove . . . by instinct, intuitively, subconsciously, the nation divines the heroic quality, religiously heroic, the mythical quality of . . . Grove, caudillo of the Chilean Left."[6]

In their leadership, composition, platforms, and international connections, the Chilean Socialists fit a populist mold in the 1930s. They relied heavily on the charisma of Grove, whom they described as the patron and savior of the working class. Beneath the maximum leader, other Socialists were also highly magnetic and personalistic, which not only galvanized voters but also tore the party asunder. Caudillism, clientelism, and factionalism became permanent features of the PS.

Although attracting numerous followers from working-class ranks, the Socialists also enrolled, especially as leaders, many recruits from the middle strata. Like the American Popular Revolutionary Alliance (APRA) and other populist movements, they targeted both "manual and intellectual workers," both wage and salary earners. The PS hoped to become an all-encompassing party of the masses, like the APRA in Peru or the PRI in Mexico. It failed to reach such magnitude because it faced stiff competition for blue-collar votes from the Communists and for white-collar votes from the Radicals. Although unable to establish a monopoly over the masses, the Socialists prospered by being more personalistic and middle class than the Communists, more Marxist and lower class than the Radicals. Thus they grew quickly to become the largest single party of workers in the 1930s.

Mixing socialism with populism, the PS appealed to the common people with personalism, with class solidarity against the oligarchs, with nationalism against the imperialists, and with Marxist symbols, jargon, and ideology. Officially, their ultimate aim was to create Marxian socialism, but they also promoted industrialization and welfarism for the urban underprivileged, most notably when they shared power with the Radical Party. They were always committed to nationalism and anti-imperialism. They hoped to achieve the "second national independence" by promoting import substitution industrialization and by nationalizing foreign enterprises. Although more ideological and union based than some populist parties in Latin America, the PS exhibited the philosophical eclecticism typical of populists in the hemisphere.

Outside Chile, the Socialists shunned any formal international affiliations.

They wove the closest bonds with APRA, the quintessential populist movement in Latin America. Other parties of similar ilk with which the PS identified included the Democratic Action (AD) of Venezuela, the ruling Revolutionary Party (PRI) of Mexico, and the Socialists of Argentina.[7]

The Chilean Socialists engaged in highly populist campaign techniques, social alliances, and program proposals on their own in the 1930s. They also joined multiparty, polyclass coalitions that pursued populist development programs through the 1940s. Those interparty efforts took wing with the Popular Front, forged in 1936.

Populism in Government: The Popular Front

As in some other countries in Latin America, populist policies responded logically to the challenges of the 1930s and 1940s in Chile. That integrationist strategy provided a nonrevolutionary response to the need for inward-looking economic development, for incorporation of the working class, and for relegitimation of the state in the wake of the Great Depression. Tandem support for industrialization and the welfare state satisfied, for a time, manufacturers with protection and credit, agriculturalists with expanding urban markets and restraints on peasant organization, the middle classes and the military with state growth and nationalism, and the more skilled urban workers with social security, consumer, and union benefits superior to those accorded to other lower-class groups. In Chile, that winning formula was known as the Popular Front.

The Popular Front united the Radical, Socialist, and Communist parties, comprising mainly the middle and working classes, behind a nationalistic program to expand industrialization and the welfare state. Since Grove lost the presidential nomination to a mild-mannered, right-wing Radical, Pedro Aguirre Cerda, the coalition lacked a charismatic leader at the top. Aguirre Cerda himself observed that he was "neither a caudillo nor a messiah."[8] Although Grove provided some fireworks as a tireless campaigner for the nominee, it was mainly in terms of composition and program that the Popular Front served as a Chilean form of populism. It also reflected European multiparty patterns of the era, especially in Spain and France.

Chileans as well as Peruvians realized that the Popular Front resembled APRA. Chilean Socialist leaders argued that the APRA in Peru and the National Revolutionary Party in Mexico were already internal "popular fronts." The main difference was that the Chilean one was a multiparty vehicle allowed to reach power, while the Peruvian version was a single party banned from participation.

APRA, the PS, and the Popular Front all enjoyed multiclass support from the outlying regions and urban masses. They all emphasized democracy, nationalism, and state intervention to promote industry and welfare. The anti-Fascism and anti-Communism of APRA and the PS drew them closer to the United States during World War II and the early years of the Cold War. Through participation in the Popular Front, the Socialists toned down their Marxian tendencies and became more of a social democratic labor party in the 1940s.[9]

In office, the Popular Front (1938–41) and its successor Radical presidents (1942–52) stressed state-guided industrialization more than redistribution to the workers. Even the mild social reforms that were implemented were restricted to the cities, thus placating the landowning elites. The front's influence over workers maintained social peace during the acceleration of industrialization. Multiclass movements incorporating urban labor became the accepted, legitimate social base of government.

The socialist and populist elements that had erupted to challenge the status quo during the Great Depression were now assimilated into the multiparty system and national government. The Chilean left channeled the populist mobilization of the lower classes into a Marxist framework but also into the established network of political participation and bargaining. The economic, social, and political crisis of the early thirties now found resolution through integration of the left and labor, plus the urban middle and lower classes, into national governing institutions.[10]

For most of the 1940s, populist mobilization and programs lost momentum, especially as Chile tightened its belt during and after World War II. The Radical Party, through myriad coalitions which frequently included the Marxist parties, continued to govern the country, but not with the reformist zeal exhibited in 1938. The workers gained little and became disillusioned with popular front politics. The Socialists disintegrated, lost electoral strength, and then tried to recuperate by turning in a more Marxist direction.[11]

By the 1950s, the possibilities for populist governments dimmed. Import substitution industrialization passed the relatively easy stage of replacing consumer goods from abroad and began encountering bottlenecks. Stagflation beset the Chilean economy. Political competition moved toward a zero-sum game as the number of demand-makers multiplied beyond the capacity of the economy and the central government to satisfy. In particular, peasants and rural-urban migrants added their voices to the chorus of demands. Although a populist campaign style resurfaced at times, the broad coalitions and accommodating programs of the 1930s and 1940s became less sustainable.

A Populist Campaigner: Carlos Ibáñez

A political chameleon, former 1920s dictator Carlos Ibáñez tried to return to power in 1938 in league with the Chilean Nazis (National Socialist Movement), in 1942 as the standard-bearer of the traditional right (Conservative and Liberal parties), and in 1952 as an independent reformer. The only consistent threads were his opposition to the coalitions headed by the centrist Radical Party and his posture as a nationalistic, personalistic, paternalistic strongman above everyday party politics. He triumphed in 1952 when voters were disillusioned with four-teen years of coalition government under the Radicals.

In the 1952 presidential campaign, Ibáñez ran as a putative populist leader, but one without an organized movement or program. Although not charismatic, he appealed with promises of personal authority to those fatigued with multi-party coalitions, compromises, quarreling, and corruption. His only significant organized base came from the tiny Agrarian Labor Party. Ibáñez drew support from all political and social camps, including remarkable numbers among the middle sectors and rural workers. His backers formed an ideological melange stretching from quasi-fascist right-wingers to semi-socialist left-wingers.

Brandishing the symbol of a broom, the General of Victory criticized the Radicals for having sold out to the United States and for having created stag-flation in the economy. But his own platform and promises were exceedingly vague. The antiparty style of Ibáñez, more than any clear-cut social coalition or reformist program, made him appear like a populist, as did his admiration for Argentina's Juan Perón. He won with 47 percent of the votes in the multican-didate election.[12]

Even some Socialists backed Ibáñez briefly in hopes of forging a labor move-ment similar to Peronism and avoiding the alienation from the workers suffered by their namesakes in Argentina. Once again, they were flirting with a populist option. Other Socialists, along with many outlawed Communists, supported the token candidacy of Salvador Allende to stake out an independent Marxist strategy for the future. They were soon joined in opposition to President Ibáñez by the rest of the Socialists and Communists when it became evident that he had no intention of carrying out his promises of economic redistribution and nationalism.

Ibáñez's populist trappings were thin, and Ibañismo proved to be a very ephem-eral political phenomenon. The first two years of Ibáñez's presidency (1952–58) witnessed populistic expansionist policies that raised wages, demands, and in-flation. Thereafter he mainly concentrated on the conservative tasks of reining in inflation through orthodox stabilization measures and of striking a generous deal with U.S. copper companies to encourage new investments. Like the Rad-icals before him, Ibáñez entered office as a reformer governing with leftist par-ties and departed as a conservative surrounded by rightist groups. The lower-class support he had enjoyed drained away to the Christian Democrats and Marxists.[13]

After turning against Ibáñez, the Socialists rejected populism and multiclass coalitions behind centrist reformers. Instead, they stressed their devotion to Marxism, the working class, and collectivist programs for massive nationalization and redistribution of power, profits, and property. They switched from popular-front politics to worker-front politics, from class collaboration to class conflict, from compromise to confrontation. The PS shifted from identification with APRA to identification with Fidel Castro's Cuban Revolution. The Socialists and Communists thus built an alliance that eventually carried Salvador Allende to the presidency in 1970.[14]

From Populism to Socialism: The Popular Unity

The Popular Unity (UP) government was preceded by centrist reformers from the Christian Democrat Party (1964–70). Their leader, Eduardo Frei Montalva, had great personal appeal. The Christian Democrats represented a multiclass amalgam concentrated among the middle classes, women, peasants, and urban squatters. They promised and carried out redistribution of land and income while continuing to protect domestic industry. Despite such populist inclinations (especially in certain factions of the party), the Christian Democrats and their "revolution in liberty" have not been stamped as populist by most scholars or politicians. They relied very little on charisma; their social coalition was far more middle class and far less working class than most populist movements. Moreover, their economic policies were more moderate, more technocratic, and less inflationary than those of most populist governments.[15]

By the late sixties, both the right and left in Chile scorned populist options. Rightists assailed populists as demagogic agitators who spurred excessive mass expectations, fueled inflation, frightened domestic and foreign capital, and engendered political instability. Even worse in their eyes were the Marxist parties. At the same time, leftists lashed populists and centrists as charlatans who duped the masses into supporting palliative reforms that subtly preserved the hierarchy of power and privilege.

Both the right and the left came to believe that Chile needed drastic remedies to break out of the economic, social, and political stalemate produced by decades of populistic coalitions and policies. Both denounced "the compromise state" that accommodated capitalists as well as workers but produced little growth or change. While the left called for a socialist transformation, the right preferred more unrestrained capitalism. First Allende from the left and then Pinochet from the right disdained any populist leadership style, tore apart any populist coalition between industrialists and workers, and discarded and destroyed reformist populist policies.[16]

President Salvador Allende (1970–73) led a socialist, not a populist, movement and government. Indeed, the leaders of Popular Unity vowed explicitly not to repeat the reformist experience of the Popular Front or other populist types in Latin America. On the eve of their 1970 victory, the Socialists officially adhered to Marxism-Leninism and declared that "revolutionary violence is inevitable and legitimate." During Allende's presidency, the PS slogan became "Advance without Compromise." They shared the leadership of the Popular Unity with the Communists, towing behind them the shrunken Radicals and other minor parties.[17]

Although a moderate Socialist, Allende had stayed further left over the decades than populist contemporaries and friends like Víctor Raúl Haya de la Torre of APRA and Rómulo Betancourt of AD. As a leader, Allende spurned the populist motif: "The process in Chile is neither paternalistic nor charismatic. . . . I am not a Messiah, nor am I a caudillo."[18] He was the steward of an extremely intricate and structured multiparty coalition, not the personalistic champion of unorganized masses. His followers came disproportionately from the working class, not a broad blend with significant middle-class participation. During his administration, class and ideological conflict escalated as Chile polarized into two irreconcilable camps.

President Allende employed some populistic wage, price, and spending policies to redistribute income to workers and peasants in his first year. He used essentially Keynesian mechanisms to increase the purchasing power of consumers in the working class. The goal, however, was to propel the country toward socialism, not just to reform the capitalist system to include the workers. Moreover, Allende redistributed not only income but also property and wealth, both foreign and domestic. The Popular Unity set out to expropriate, not foment, national industry. Unlike populists in Latin America, Allende tolerated direct action by workers and peasants to seize factories, housing spaces, and farmlands. These mobilizations from below went far beyond any populist reforms and particularly frightened the middle and upper classes.

Like populist experiments elsewhere, the buoyant first year of the Allende government was followed by two disastrous years in which demand outpaced supply, deficits ballooned, inflation skyrocketed, foreign exchange dried up, and workers' gains shrank. Opposition calls for stabilization and a military takeover escalated in 1973. The fight was not just between conservatives and populists, however. It was between polarized social and ideological visions of Chile's future, between capitalism and socialism. On every dimension, the Allende experiment, though not an armed revolution, was far more radical than any populist episode in Latin American history. Indeed, it was the most leftist, revolutionary government ever seen in South America.[19]

Allende was followed by one of the most rightist, reactionary governments ever seen in South America, the bureaucratic authoritarian regime of General Augusto Pinochet (1973–90). After destroying socialism and democracy, he not only opposed any whiff of populism but also undermined any basis for its rebirth in the future. Pinochet lambasted all politicians as corrupt demagogues. He outlawed or suspended all party activities. By crushing the labor movement and removing most protection for industry, he undid the accomplishments of past populistic coalitions and reduced the likelihood of their resurgence.

Pinochet also undercut and foiled populist policies by reducing the role of the state in the economy and social welfare, redistributing income to the upper class, privatizing many government operations and functions, welcoming foreign investment, and installing a free-market model oriented toward export promotion. By 1988, the success of that model at producing economic growth obliterated any nostalgia within the opposition for statist policies. Except for a slightly greater emphasis on equitable distribution, Pinochet's opponents vowed to maintain his economic system.[20]

Redemocratization without Socialism or Populism

Populism did not disrupt the transition back to democracy or occupy center stage.[21] The reasons for populism's weakness were several. The need to follow a private-enterprise free-market model, honor the foreign debt, husband foreign exchange, attract foreign capital, restrain the size and cost of government, and hold down inflation rendered any massive income redistribution or any induced reindustrialization out of the question. As a result of the neoliberal economic transformations under Pinochet, the chief nemeses of populism—capitalist and export elites—had gained strength, while the main supporters of populism—organized and unorganized urban workers—had been weakened and chastened.

Centrist and leftist politicians did not want populism to upset the new democracy any more than they wanted it to disturb macroeconomic equilibrium. Moreover, the examples of political disorder and economic distress caused by populism in neighbors like Peru and Argentina chilled any thoughts of populist appeals. Instead, the opposition's standard-bearer, Christian Democrat Patricio Aylwin, and most other politicians tried to lower working-class expectations, which had already been repressed by Pinochet and by the depression of the early eighties. Aylwin explicitly ran against populist policies.

Aylwin was also backed by the Socialist Party. Under Pinochet, it had been divided between those leaning toward Marxism-Leninism and those more attracted to European social democracy. In an agonizing self-reappraisal in the 1980s, the Socialists resurrected their democratic and reformist traditions from the 1930s and 1940s, but they did not revive any populist tendencies. As the more moderate "renovated" Socialists came to dominate the party, it discarded hopes of rejuvenating the Allende experiment. Instead, the PS concentrated its efforts on assembling and maintaining a broad, pragmatic, center-left coalition with the Christian Democrats. Their goal was to restore democracy without capsizing the economy.[22]

The December 1989 election won by Aylwin included a minority candidate with some so-called "right-wing populist" features. A maverick, wealthy businessman, Francisco Javier Errázuriz claimed to represent the "center-center" of Chilean politics. He spurned all major parties, praised the free-market system, and promised social justice. Like Ibáñez in 1952, Errázuriz appealed to the same antiparty undercurrent with the same type of vaguely nationalistic, reformist, anticorruption, antipolitician platform aimed at the same broad segments of the middle classes and unorganized workers. This personalistic effort fetched only 15 percent of the votes. Nevertheless, it demonstrated at least a small constituency for very moderate populist appeals, especially when parties were weakened after so many years underground. Errázuriz apparently siphoned off mainly right-wing votes from the middle class, but not many ballots from the center-left coalition of Aylwin. The Errázuriz movement lost strength in the 1990s.[23]

The victorious Aylwin coalition was not personalistic or populistic in any way, even though it represented an alliance of the center and the left of the middle and working classes. Aylwin captained a highly organized movement of very disciplined political parties. Although rusty from their hibernation under Pinochet, those machines turned out 55 percent of the votes in the 1988 plebiscite to deny the dictator's continuation and delivered 55 percent again in the 1989 presidential election for Aylwin. Once in office in 1990, they were determined to preserve political and economic stability. Therefore they steered far away from any populist adventures. With its vaunted free-market economic model, Chile became the paragon of antipopulism at the beginning of the 1990s. That cautious, centrist technocratic approach continued under Aylwin's successor, Christian Democrat Eduardo Frei Ruíz-Tagle (1994–2000), an engineer elected president by the same multiparty coalition.[24]

Conclusion

The pure, full-fledged, classic populism seen in Argentina, Brazil, and Peru never took hold in Chile. That country's sturdy multiparty system usually blocked, blunted, or absorbed populist initiatives. Building on some precursors, populist impulses were strongest in the 1930s and 1940s, coursing through the Socialist Party and the Popular Front. Populism did not prosper thereafter in Chile, and it did not flourish in the 1990s, when multiparty democracy reasserted its hegemony.

In the future, as in the past, keeping populism at bay will likely depend on the ability of the parties to recapture their traditional strength, to reincorporate the masses into political participation, and to redress the grievances of those working-class Chileans neglected by the dictatorship. Through 2009, that same alliance of the center and the left of the middle class retained power behind two Socialist presidents, Ricardo Lagos (2000–2006) and Michelle Bachelet (2006–2010). Although they placed a greater emphasis on poverty reduction, they continued a social democratic, free-market approach devoid of populism.

Notes

I wish to thank Eduardo Silva for his comments on this essay.

1. My treatment of Latin American populism relies heavily on Michael L. Conniff, ed., *Latin American Populism in Comparative Perspective* (Albuquerque: University of New Mexico Press, 1982), especially the essays by John D. Wirth, foreword, ix–xiii; Michael L. Conniff, "Introduction: Toward a Comparative Definition of Populism," 3–30; and Paul W. Drake, "Conclusion: Requiem for Populism?" 217–45. It also draws upon Paul W. Drake, *Socialism and Populism in Chile, 1932–52* (Urbana: University of Illinois Press, 1978), particularly for the 1930s and 1940s.

2. For a similar argument on the ability of firmly established parties to inhibit or dilute populist challenges, see Miguel Urrutia, "On the Absence of Economic Populism in Colombia," in *The Macroeconomics of Populism in Latin America,* ed. Rudiger Dornbusch and Sebastian Edwards (Chicago: University of Illinois Press, 1991), 369–87. A variation on this argument about party systems can be found in Robert R. Kaufman and Barbara Stallings, "The Political Economy of Latin American Populism," *Macroeconomics of Populism,* 15–34. See also Ruth Berins Collier and David Collier, *Shaping the Political Arena* (Princeton: Princeton University Press, 1991).

3. Claudio de Alas, *Arturo Alessandri* (Santiago: n.p., 1915); Robert J. Alexander, *Arturo Alessandri: A Biography* (Ann Arbor: University Microfilms International, 1977).

4. Arturo Alessandri Palma, *Recuerdos de gobierno,* 3 vols. (Santiago: Nascimiento, 1952), 1:25–57; Millar Carvacho Ren, *La elección presidencial de 1920* (Santiago: Editorial Universitaria, 1981); Claudio Orrego V. et al., *7 ensayos sobre Arturo Alessandri Palma* (Santiago: ICHEH, 1979); Ricardo Donoso, *Alessandri, agitador y demoledor,* 2 vols. (Mexico and Buenos Aires: Tierra Firme, 1952, 1954), 1:245–50; C. H. Haring, "Chilean Politics, 1920–1928," *Hispanic American Historical Review* 11, no. 1 (February 1931): 1–26.

5. Frederick M. Nunn, *Chilean Politics, 1920–1931* (Albuquerque: University of New Mexico Press, 1970); Carlos Vicuña Fuentes, *La tiranía en Chile,* 2 vols. (Santiago: Imprenta O'Higgins, 1938).

6. *La Opinión,* September 30, 1932; Jack Ray Thomas, "The Socialist Republic of Chile," *Journal of Inter-American Studies* 6, no. 2 (April 1964): 203–20; "Marmaduke Grove and the Chilean National Election of 1932," *Historian* 29, no. 1 (November 1966): 22–33; "The Evolution of a Chilean Socialist: Marmaduke Grove," *Hispanic American Historical Review* 47, no. 1 (February 1967): 22–37; Carlos Charlín O., *Del avión rojo a la república socialista* (Santiago: Quimantu, 1972); Manuel Dinamarca, *La república socialista chilena* (Santiago: Ediciones Documentas, 1987).

7. Alejandro Chelén Rojas, *Trayectoria del socialismo* (Buenos Aires: n.p., 1967); Julio César Jobet, *El Partido Socialista de Chile,* 2 vols. (Santiago: Prensa Latinoamericana, 1971); Salomón Corbalán González, *Partido Socialista* (Santiago: n.p., 1957); Ernst Halperín, *Nationalism and Communism in Chile* (Cambridge: Massachusetts Institute of Technology Press, 1965); Fernando Casanueva Valencia and Manuel Fernández Canque, *El Partido Socialista y la lucha de clases en Chile* (Santiago: Quimantu, 1973); Ignacio Walker, *Socialismo y democracia: Chile y Europa en perspectiva comparada* (Santiago: CIEPLAN, 1990), 117–244; Miriam Ruth Hochwald, "Imagery in Politics: A Study of the Ideology of the Chilean Socialist Party" (PhD diss., University of California, Los Angeles, 1971); Juan Manuel Reveco del Villar, "Los influjos del APRA en el Partido Socialista de Chile" (unpublished thesis, FLACSO, Santiago, 1989).

8. Alberto Cabero, *Recuerdos de Don Pedro Aguirre Cerda* (Santiago: Editorial Universitaria, 1948), 170–75.

9. John Reese Stevenson, *The Chilean Popular Front* (Philadelphia: Temple, 1942); Marta Infante Barros, *Testigos del treinta y ocho* (Santiago: Editorial Andres Bello, 1972); Boris Yopo H., "El Partido Socialista Chileno y Estados Unidos: 1933–1946," *Documento de Trabajo FLACSO* 224 (October 1984); Partido Socialista, *Primer congreso de los partidos democráticos de latinoamérica* (Santiago, 1940).

10. Marcelo Cavarozzi, "The Government and the Industrial Bourgeoisie in Chile, 1930–64" (PhD diss., University of California, Berkeley, 1975); Brian Loveman, *Struggle in the Countryside* (Bloomington: Indiana University Press, 1976), 67–189.

11. Halperín, *Nationalism and Communism in Chile,* 59–61, 117–62, 229; Paul W. Drake, "The Chilean Socialist Party and Coalition Politics, 1932–1946," *Hispanic American Historical Review* 53, no. 4 (November 1973): 619–43; Julio Faúndez, *Marxism and Democracy in Chile: From 1932 to the Fall of Allende* (New Haven: Yale University Press, 1988).

12. Carlos Ibáñez del Campo, *Programa presidencial* (Santiago, 1938), *Lo que haremos por Chile* (Santiago: n.p., 1952); Ernesto Wurth Rojas, *Ibáñez, caudillo enigmático* (Santiago: n.p., 1958); Federico G. Gil, *The Political System of Chile* (Boston:

Houghton Mifflin, 1966), 73–80; H. E. Bicheno, "Anti-Parliamentary Themes in Chilean History: 1920–70," *Government and Opposition* 7, no. 3 (Summer 1972): 351–88; Donald W. Bray, "Chilean Politics during the Second Ibáñez Government" (PhD diss., Stanford University, 1961); Jean Grugel, "Populism, Nationalism, and Liberalism in Chile: The Second Administration of Carlos Ibáñez, 1952–58" (PhD diss., University of Liverpool, 1986); Robert H. Dix, "Populism: Authoritarian and Democratic," *Latin American Research Review* 20, no. 2 (1985): 29–52; Faúndez, *Marxism and Democracy in Chile,* 103–10.

13. Ricardo French-Davis, *Políticas económicas en Chile: 1952–70* (Santiago: CIEPLAN, 1973).

14. Halperín, *Nationalism and Communism in Chile,* 57–58, 128–42, 192–201; Hochwald, "Imagery in Politics," 68–73, 117–232; Alan Angell, *Politics and the Labour Movement in Chile* (London: Oxford University Press, 1972), 174–82.

15. One author who refers to fractions of the Christian Democrats as populist or corporatist is James Petras, *Politics and Social Forces in Chilean Development* (Berkeley: University of California Press, 1969), 198–250; however, his conceptualization—mainly referring to mobilization and incorporation of the masses from the bottom up ("populist") versus the top down ("corporatist")—is far different from the terminology used in this volume. Cf. Michael Fleet, *The Rise and Fall of Chilean Christian Democracy* (Princeton: Princeton University Press, 1985).

16. Manuel Antonio Garretón, *The Chilean Political Process* (Boulder: Westview Press, 1989).

17. Jobet, *El Partido Socialista,* 2:128–49, 172–77; Halperín, *Nationalism and Communism in Chile,* 39–40, 135–76; La Unidad Popular, *Programa básico de gobierno de la Unidad Popular* (Santiago, 1970).

18. Regis Debray, *The Chilean Revolution* (New York: Vintage Books, 1971), 94–123.

19. On the Allende experiment see Felipe Larraín and Patricio Meller, "The Socialist-Populist Chilean Experience, 1970–73," in *Macroeconomics of Populism,* 175–214; Kaufman and Stallings, "The Political Economy of Latin American Populism," 15–34; Paul W. Drake, "Comment," in *Macroeconomics of Populism,* 35–40; Eliana Cardoso and Ann Helwege, "Populism, Profligacy, and Redistribution," in *Macroeconomics of Populism,* 45–70; Edy Kaufman, *Crisis in Allende's Chile* (New York: Praeger, 1988); Stefan de Vylder, *Allende's Chile: The Political Economy of the Rise and Fall of the Unidad Popular* (London: Cambridge University Press, 1974); Barbara Stallings, *Class Conflict and Economic Development in Chile, 1958–1973* (Stanford: Stanford University Press, 1978); Paul E. Sigmund, *The Overthrow of Allende and the Politics of Chile, 1964–1976* (Pittsburgh: University of Pittsburgh Press, 1977); Arturo Valenzuela, *The Breakdown of Democratic Regimes: Chile* (Baltimore: Johns Hopkins University Press, 1978); Arturo Valenzuela and J. Samuel

Valenzuela, *Chile: Politics and Society* (New Brunswick: Transaction Books, 1976); Ian Roxborough, Philip O'Brien, and Jackie Roddick, *Chile: The State and Revolution* (New York: Holmes and Meier, 1977); Peter Winn, *Weavers of Revolution* (New York: Oxford University Press, 1986).

20. On the Pinochet years, consult Pamela Constable and Arturo Valenzuela, *A Nation of Enemies: Chile under Pinochet* (New York: Norton, 1991); J. Samuel Valenzuela and Arturo Valenzuela, *Military Rule in Chile: Dictatorship and Oppositions* (Baltimore: Johns Hopkins University Press, 1986); Paul W. Drake and Iván Jaksic, *The Struggle for Democracy in Chile, 1982–90* (Lincoln: University of Nebraska Press, 1991).

21. On the return to democracy, see Drake and Jaksic, *The Struggle for Democracy in Chile, 1982–90.* Also useful is Joseph S. Tulchin and Augusto Varas, *From Dictatorship to Democracy: Rebuilding Political Consensus in Chile* (Boulder: Westview Press, 1991).

22. *La renovación socialista: Balance y perspectivas de un proceso vigente* (Santiago: Ediciones Valentin Letelier, 1987); Ricardo Lagos, *Hacia la democracia* (Santiago: Ediciones Documentas, 1987); Manuel Antonio Garretón, "The Political Opposition and the Party System under the Military Regime," in *The Struggle for Democracy in Chile, 1982–90,* 211–50.

23. On the 1989 campaign in Chile, see Alan Angell and Benny Pollack, "The Chilean Elections of 1989 and the Politics of the Transition to Democracy," *Bulletin of Latin American Research* 9, no. 1 (1990): 1–23; César N. Caviedes, *Elections in Chile: The Road toward Redemocratization* (Boulder: Lynne Rienner, 1991), 55–78; Concertación de Partidos por la Democracia, *Programa de gobierno* (Santiago: n.p., 1989).

24. On the general turn against populism in Latin America at the start of the 1990s, see Laurence Whitehead, "The Perils of Populism?" *Hemisfile* 2, no. 1 (January 1991): 1, 2, 12.

4

Populism in Mexico

From Cárdenas to López Obrador

Jorge Basurto

At its very core, Mexican populism addressed the needs of the people, mainly the poorest classes. Populist policies made the masses winners in the political game, rather than losers. Populists provided more opportunities for the masses to improve their lives. Unlike the neoliberals who govern Mexico today, populists spoke for government action to achieve a more equitable distribution of wealth. Populism in Mexico resembled European social democracy and the U.S. concept of the welfare state.

Mexican populism also contained nationalism and corporatism. The former meant promoting economic development using mainly Mexican capital. The latter entailed efforts by the government to build up labor, farmer, middle-class, and even business associations and to integrate them into the state itself, or rather to be intermediary between the rank and file and the leaders.

Mexico's most celebrated populists were Gen. Lázaro Cárdenas and Luis Echeverría (presidents, respectively, 1934–40 and 1970–76). If we take into account the positive aspects of populism, Cárdenas's son Cuauhtémoc, leader of the opposition and twice a presidential candidate, might be regarded a neopopulist in contemporary Mexico.

Cardenismo

Lázaro Cárdenas, Mexico's leading populist, was born in 1895 in a small town in Michoacán into a middle-class family. Cárdenas was a man with an active, versatile mind. He finished primary school and then worked at odd jobs. In 1910–11 he edited a newspaper that supported the presidential candidacy of Francisco

I. Madero. Because he sympathized with the revolutionaries, he joined Emiliano Zapata's army in 1913 at the age of eighteen. Later he transferred to other units, ending up under the command of future president Plutarco Elias Calles (1924–28). Cárdenas remained loyal to Calles during the so-called Maximato (after Calles's title of Jefe Máximo) of the early 1930s, when the latter ruled through puppet presidents.

Cárdenas's loyalty earned him an appointment as candidate and afterward governor of his native state (1928), and then he served as head of the revolutionary party and minister of interior. In 1933 he became war minister, the top post to which a general could aspire. He was clearly a rising power and good politician with civilian instincts and an inclination toward leftist programs.

Cárdenas handled the 1934 succession expertly, winning the official nomination without serious challenge and forcing Calles to give his blessings as well. Cárdenas had cultivated the support of peasant farmer associations and had allied with organized labor. He had also earned the backing of junior officers and army troops. Calles accepted Cárdenas, secure in the belief that he would continue to rule Mexico from behind the scenes.

Cárdenas convened party delegates in early 1934 in order to work up a platform for the campaign. Taking his cue from the multiyear Soviet planners, Cárdenas orchestrated passage of the six-year plan (Plan Sexenal). His program stressed labor and land, and he was assured of Calles's support and that of the official party. Using the election campaign to build a mass following, Cárdenas traveled sixteen thousand miles and visited all the states. Everywhere he went he spoke with the local chieftain, met the army garrison commander, and held audiences with the townspeople. He regularly held hours in town plazas, where peasants and workers could sit on park benches and speak with him.

Because he always protected and helped Indians, they gave him the nickname "Tata Lázaro," or Father Lázaro in Michoacán. His victory in 1934 was one of the most peaceful in years. He was a very popular man when he assumed the presidential sash in December 1934. Even after his election he continued to tour the country to meet with the people.

Cárdenas gradually signaled that he would not serve as a puppet under Calles. He ordered the federal police to crack down on gambling and prostitution, which hurt some prominent generals. He reduced his own salary by half and refused to live in the Chapultepec presidential palace.

From the very beginning, Cárdenas announced his intention of carrying out the land and labor reforms of the party's Plan Sexenal. He also said he would lend official backing to agrarian and workers unions in view of his need to support his whole reform program. Cárdenas openly associated with well-known leftists Francisco Múgica and Vicente Lombardo Toledano. This raised the level of political tension because right-wing groups, like the fascistic Gold Shirts, often clashed in the streets with their leftist counterparts.

Calles, who was in Los Angeles for medical treatment, returned to Mexico in May 1935 and denounced Cárdenas's initiatives, which he termed a "marathon of radicalism." The president had anticipated such a reaction, however, and had cultivated support among army officers and soldiers. He forced Calles into exile and then systematically fired hundreds of conspirators from the ranks of government and the army; they were defeated and banned from the political scene.

Cárdenas had become enormously popular for standing up to Calles and championing land and labor reforms. With the political threat of a coup removed, Cárdenas proceeded to make good his promises. During his term he distributed fifty million acres of land to some eight hundred thousand peasant families, more than all of his predecessors combined. He even furnished peasants with rifles in order to protect the newly acquired land from the ancient owners and caciques. The new owners were not always as efficient as the old ones, however, and they tended to consume more at home, signaling the virtual demise of the traditional power of the landowning class and the weakening of the hacienda system.

To replace the failing system, Cárdenas stimulated the spread of farms, called *ejidos,* some of which were worked by the community as a whole. To demonstrate how this collective farming would work, he transformed a huge expropriated hacienda on the Coahuila-Durango border into a model communal farm system, called La Laguna. Some thirty-five thousand persons, gathered into 226 *ejidos,* raised cotton, cereals, and other crops. Cárdenas invested a great deal of money in agricultural extension while also supporting social programs like education, rural electrification, and health. He expected the *ejidatarios* to begin selling their harvests in the marketplace, thereby relieving the need to import farm staples. Having the peasants enter the market economy was the main goal of the land reform.

In the beginning, La Laguna was a commercial success, but President Miguel Alemán (1946–52) considered collective *ejidos* socialistic, so he took away all support for this system, which resulted in a decline in farm production.

Organized labor became a solid ally of Cárdenas. Vicente Lombardo Toledano organized the Mexican Workers' and Farmers' General Confederation (CGOCM) in 1933 and enjoyed strong backing from Cárdenas. By 1935 they were close associates. In February 1936, he founded the Mexican Workers' Confederation (CTM), which claimed a million members by then and was a de facto government ally. Lombardo was a strong-willed Socialist as well as a pragmatic politician. He was incorruptible and always kept the workers' interests in mind. He knew he could count on Cárdenas to help his unions win better contracts.

Cárdenas also promoted educational expansion and reform. He favored education for the masses, based on the principle of the common good prevailing over individual advancement. Even with meager federal revenues, Cárdenas managed to increase the share that education received. He was able to build three thousand new schools and train some one hundred thousand new teachers, mostly recruited from the cities. Public school enrollment rose from 1.7 to 2.2 million during Cárdenas's term. Meanwhile, the president charged teachers with carrying out rural reforms and adult education, even in the face of much opposition in little communities across the nation. Despite these advances, the number of illiterates in Mexico actually rose due to the extremely high birthrates in rural areas.

One of the most remarkable episodes of Mexican populism occurred in 1938 when Cárdenas nationalized most of the petroleum industry. Two years before, oil field workers unions federated and joined Lombardo Toledano's CTM. Although these workers earned more than average, they suffered hardships connected with living in camps away from families and had to buy provisions in company stores. The oil companies, dominated by British and U.S. firms, refused to bargain with the unions over wages and conditions. The federation called a strike in 1937, which was sanctioned by the CTM.

After a mandatory six-month cooling off period, government mediation kicked in. The Department of Labor found in favor of the laborers, but the companies refused to settle and appealed the case to the Supreme Court. Cárdenas and other officials were already irritated with the oil companies for having shifted their plants away from Mexico in the 1920s and 1930s, largely to Venezuela. Exports had fallen from 193 to only 41 million barrels since 1921.

In early 1938 the Supreme Court reached a judgment in favor of the unions. At that point, seventeen companies (mostly foreign) wrote to Cárdenas refusing to comply with the decision. Exasperated, Cárdenas interpreted their refusal as defiance of Mexican sovereignty and immediately expropriated the companies. He put them under a state company formed earlier to administer government-owned oil lands and contracts, Petróleos Mexicanos (PEMEX).

Expecting the U.S. government to support them against the Mexican government, the companies submitted claims of $450 million dollars, representing both existing and potential production. Cárdenas countered with an offer of $10 million, his estimate of actual capital investment. During the next two years, the companies waged a vicious campaign against Mexico and even threatened invasion. The firms boycotted Mexican crude, putting severe pressure on balance of payments. The petroleum lobby in Congress as well as the British government unsuccessfully pressured the White House to invade Mexico or boycott trade.

U.S. ambassador Josephus Daniels believed the companies had committed a grievous error in defying the Mexican Supreme Court decision. He convinced U.S. president Franklin Roosevelt to resist the pressure. Finally, when hemispheric defense planning in 1940 required Mexican cooperation, the Roosevelt administration set up arbitration commissions to settle the oil compensation conflict. The U.S. companies ended up receiving $24 million in 1941. Settlement with British companies took until August 1947.[1]

Late in 1938 Cárdenas decided to restructure the official party in anticipation of a presidential succession. Renamed the Party of the Mexican Revolution, the new organization formally comprised four sectors: labor unions (the CTM), the National Peasants' Confederation (CNC), the army, and a miscellaneous sector made up mostly of public employees' associations, which in fact were the basis for populist corporatism. The newly reformed party represented a considerable share of the politically active population. The CNC counted 2.5 million members, CTM claimed 1.25 million, and the military and government unions had about 55,000 each. That year soldiers were given the right to vote, which gave considerable power to junior officers who could get their recruits into voting booths.

These hierarchical units within the party ostensibly channeled information and popular demands up, but, in fact, they mostly passed orders down. No one doubted that Cárdenas commanded the party from above. He chose to support his minister of defense, Manuel Avila Camacho, a desk officer and administrator rather than field commander, for the next presidential term.

By then the president had taken sufficient measures to assure the army's loyalty, and he soundly defeated a brief rebellion. In fact, this proved that Cárdenas had succeeded in depoliticizing the army. Academy-trained young officers who had not fought in the revolution were reaching command positions now and were loyal to Cárdenas and his program. The president trimmed the army's share of the federal budget from 25 to 19 percent between 1934–38. He also passed a military reorganization bill in 1939 that attempted to replace the spirit of caste among officers with a desire to serve the nation. Finally, the Military Service Law of 1939 helped diminish the gap between officers, troops, and the civilian population.

The presidential succession of 1940 proved tense but did not explode. The party delivered the votes necessary to elect Avila Camacho for the 1940–46 term. Cárdenas continued to play a role in politics until his death; he became an unofficial voice of the past, a reminder of what the revolution had been fought for.[2]

The Stabilizing Development

Cárdenas's administration led to the strengthening of Mexico's business elite, even while producing important structural reforms. After Cárdenas stepped down in 1940, the government placed a higher priority on economic growth, regardless of which sectors of the society owned capital and accumulated profits. Therefore, the process of capital accumulation and profit concentration accelerated greatly, along with the penetration of foreign capital in industry and commerce. Meanwhile, public ownership in the economy also grew rapidly, eventually accounting for about half the capital stock (especially in petroleum and electric power), yet these enterprises produced only 3 percent of manufacturing output. In effect, shortages of private funds were made up for by the government, which provided infrastructure and even low-cost inputs for private businesses, mainly petroleum. This was essentially the structure of the mixed economy that the Mexican government shaped after 1940, and it was clearly different from a purely capitalist economy.

At the same time, inequality of income distribution between labor and capital reached unusual levels in comparison with other Latin American countries.[3] This was due to the control government exercised over the workers through bureaucratic leaders more responsive to the government than to their constituents. During the period of stabilizing development, a middle class emerged that politically received little attention, and its standards of living, although not completely satisfactory, were much better than those of the agrarian sector, especially *ejidatarios,* which languished.

By the mid-1960s the stabilizing development model had exhausted its potential. Members of the middle and lower strata were frustrated and protested during the student movement in 1968, which was violently repressed by the government of President Gustavo Díaz Ordaz. This constituted a crisis and opened up latent divisions within the "revolutionary family," as the government elite was called.

In 1970, Luis Echeverría, presidential candidate for the official Institutional Revolutionary Party (PRI), ran on a reform platform clearly borrowed directly from Lázaro Cárdenas—that is, populist and highly nationalist—that promised a more equitable distribution of income and a political system more responsive to the masses. With regard to capital formation, Echeverría favored domestic sources, which would reduce Mexico's reliance on foreign capital. He was not, however, hostile to outside investment. With respect to public investment, such investment would be sufficiently strong to direct the overall course of economic growth. Thus Echeverría promised to restore to the state its traditional role of guiding the development process.

Putting this program into practice necessarily encroached on vested interests and required political classes' mobilization in Echeverría's favor. In particular he needed to build up a popular base with which to sustain his administration because the preceding presidents had destroyed the old alliance between PRI and the popular sectors. He attempted to mobilize the working class through the traditional unions and to recruit several union federations headed by dis-contented leaders. He also tried to rekindle in the peasantry the hope of a to-tal agrarian reform. Finally, he sought to incorporate into the Mexican political system the middle classes, which politically had been largely forgotten since the 1940s. On another front, Echeverría envisioned general political reforms, in-cluding the democratization of the PRI, whose image had become completely discredited.

The nationalist-populist reforms of Luis Echeverría failed largely because they were founded on false premises. The chief executive believed that the presi-dential system conferred omnipotence on him and that this authority could be further reinforced by mass mobilization. He was especially hopeful that he could win over the financial elite and the more conservative elements of the bureaucracy. This had been the successful formula of Cárdenas in the 1930s. Thirty years of stabilizing development, however, had shifted the balance of power away from the presidency. In fact, economic and bureaucratic power had grown so much by 1970 that the state had lost its autonomy. The political system had become so corrupt that most politicians were simultaneously major businessmen and millionaires.

Economy and Crisis

In the beginning of the 1970s signs of weakness in the economy began to ap-pear faintly. By 1972 the Mexican peso, previously a bastion of stability, began to fall in international financial markets. Echeverría's economic advisers did not wish to allow its devaluation, however, and sustained it at artificially high levels that led to an intense flight of capital and serious internal unrest. This policy encouraged imports and discouraged exports. Finally, in August 1976, it forced the first of a seemingly endless series of devaluations.

The domestic economy had other flaws, many government induced, that inhibited robust profits and high employment. Mexico's industrial plant and capital stock were obsolete and inefficient. Low productivity increased costs and turned out products incapable of competing on the international market. The foreign debt mushroomed, as did the domestic budget deficit.

In August 1982, in the last months of José López Portillo's administration

(1976–82), the finance secretary announced that Mexico did not have sufficient hard currency to pay service on its foreign debt and declared a moratorium for three months. The following month he announced the nationalization of all banks and adoption of exchange controls.[4] Various factors brought about the crisis of confidence. One was the dramatic rise of international interest rates, which reached a high of 22 percent. Another was a decline in prices for raw materials Mexico exported. Together they pushed Mexico into temporary bankruptcy.

Miguel de la Madrid, who took over the presidency in December 1982, had to devote himself to practicing the politics of economic reorganization, as well as industrial conversion and moral renovation. He gave his highest priority to fulfilling international obligations, especially the foreign debt. He ordered punctual payment of both interest and capital, giving rise to accusations that he had knuckled under to the International Monetary Fund, a multilateral watchdog. Prompt debt service, however, made it impossible to maintain a high domestic savings rate, so the economy plunged into recession. De la Madrid had to promote exports of nonpetroleum products, even at the cost of internal consumption, in order to generate foreign exchange with which to service the debt. He also ended currency stabilization and let the peso float, which temporarily stimulated exports and discouraged imports.

As the 1980s wore on, the administration began to develop a neoliberal model that encompassed not only emergency financial recovery measures but also a broad effort to stimulate private enterprise, both national and foreign. This required the state to give up ownership of major public-sector businesses, which numbered nearly 1,155 in 1982. Privatization over the next six years reduced this number to only 502.[5]

A powerful case was made for privatizing the public-owned businesses, which were in disastrous shape in the mid-1980s. Part of them operated at huge losses, which had to be covered out of government revenues or loans. This was due partly to setting their prices below cost so as to subsidize private industry and consumers, but they were maintained as a way of keeping jobs running. In addition, they were managed by dishonest and inefficient party hacks who routinely diverted resources into graft that could benefit the PRI. The beneficiaries of this favoritism fought tooth and nail to protect their privileges because they were the very basis of their political power.

De la Madrid viewed inflation as an unwelcome byproduct of excessive demand. To combat it required slashing public spending, especially on such things as government jobs, education, and consumer subsidy programs. He managed to reduce public expenditures by 44 percent in his first four years. In addition, he attacked inflation by holding down salaries and wages, leading to a dramatic decrease in the general standard of living for the masses. These policies had as side effects massive numbers of bankruptcies of small- and medium-sized businesses and wide-spread unemployment.

De la Madrid's drastic economic policies violated the basic principles of the old populist alliance between government and the working class. The weight of the economic recovery crisis fell almost totally on the shoulders of the working and middle classes. The Mexican Workers' Confederation and the National Peasants' Confederation, central pillars of the PRI since the 1930s, were now relegated to subordinate positions in the government. They took orders from above and maintained discipline among the rank and file, without sharing in the rewards they had customarily enjoyed.

The nationalization of banking led to the founding of exchange houses as substitutes for banks. Foreign currency speculation, in turn, caused a market crash in 1987 in which small and medium savers lost their profits and capital. Speculators used this capital to negotiate the purchase of the once-nationalized banks whose owners had been generously indemnified. Eventually, the government used investors' confiscated assets to pay off shareholders of the nationalized banks, a move which would have been unthinkable under the terms of classic populism.

De la Madrid clearly distanced himself from the populist measures and rhetoric of the past. The only echoes of populism heard were empty promises of responsible stewardship of the economy and general improvements in the standard of living. The actual results were minimal. The business sector did not respond to the unlimited confidence placed in them, and investments never reached earlier levels. Exports did grow rapidly, especially manufactured goods, which rose 30 percent annually between 1982 and 1985. But most of the increase was a result of decreasing export prices, which was due to the devaluation of Mexican currency, and to worker overtime, which was caused by factory owners not investing more in plant and machinery. Indeed the profits earned by manufacturers depended mostly on reducing real salary levels. By the late 1980s Mexican workers earned only half the wages of their counterparts in Singapore and two-thirds those of Korean workers. Salaries fell from 45 percent of national income in 1982 to 34 percent in 1986.

Another negative factor in the 1980s was the continuous drop in petroleum prices on the international market, causing a loss of eight billion dollars in 1986, as compared with 1982 prices. This sum, equal to about 6 percent of GDP, meant less foreign reserves available for domestic savings. Internal borrowing on the order of 16 percent of GDP made up the difference.

In sum, the presidency of Miguel de la Madrid did not produce positive results in the economy, and therefore the general situation of the country deteriorated enormously. The middle class suffered declines in living standards, but the poor, of course, bore the brunt of the recession. Conditions were ripe, therefore, for the surge in reform sentiment that would drive neo-Cardenismo.

Neo-Cardenismo

The economic crisis of the 1980s and de la Madrid's abandonment of the classical alliance with the workers' and farmers' confederations brought into the open a latent split that had always existed in the PRI. Within the party, traditionalists led by Cuauhtémoc Cárdenas and the Porfirio Muñoz-Ledo (PML) proclaimed that the popular-national-revolutionary model was still valid and should guide the party. They claimed the mantle of Mexico's most revered president, Gen. Lázaro Cárdenas. For this reason, their movement can be termed neo-Cardenismo. Reformists, on the other hand, claimed that a neoliberal model was needed to keep up with current trends of globalization.

Neo-Cardenistas held up two principles. First, they argued for adherence to the principles of the 1910 revolution, the 1917 Constitution, and Lázaro Cárdenas.[6] Accordingly, they criticized the economic program adopted in the 1980s as a betrayal of the revolution. Second, they called for overhauling the PRI, which had been altered but never seriously reformed since its formation in 1929. Frozen in place during the late 1940s, the PRI had become a rigid and increasingly inflexible system of power holding. By the 1990s it was regarded as the most serious obstacle to the development of Western-style democracy in Mexico.

As enunciated by Cuauhtémoc, neo-Cardenismo drew heavily on the ideas and actions of Mexican populism as envisioned by his father. Lázaro Cárdenas had his own conceptions concerning the guiding role of the state in the economy. He firmly believed that the state should play a determinant role as entrepreneur and planner of the economy in order to get the necessary strength to control and direct investment and therefore a more equal distribution of income. Such a strength should be used as well for the defense of self-determination, nationalism, and popular interests. He proclaimed that the problems of the country should never be left solely to the anonymous operations of the marketplace. Instead, the state should regulate them because only it "has a general interest and, for this reason, only it has a global vision."[7] Accordingly, state intervention needed to be even greater and directed by the sociopolitical goals of the revolution.

Luis Echeverría and López Portillo upheld this interventionist position in the 1970s and early 1980s. It must be taken into account that the aim of this policy was to make up for insufficient investment by the private sector and at the same time create or save jobs. But it led to bloated government payrolls, gross mismanagement of state-owned industries, ill-advised rescues of bankrupt businesses, and fiscal negligence and graft. In 1973 state enterprises absorbed 54 percent of federal revenues; by 1979 their share reached 70 percent.[8]

Neo-Cardenistas agree with this policy; they think the state should provide services to the population by managing public utilities and basic industries in order to justify its strength and thereby its autonomy. This would also allow the state to exercise a stabilizing influence in the economy and uphold employment levels.

Finally, Cuauhtémoc believed that the strength of the state, as an embodiment of the nation, could only be preserved by a strong president around whom all political affairs revolved. Therefore, he favored enhancing the president's authority in order to defend "a harassed country" against impositions by more powerful nations, in spite of the fact that enormous power concentrated into the hands of one person is widely criticized.[9]

Neo-Cardenistas revived the revolutionary nationalism of the 1930s with its emphasis on self-determination and sovereignty. They denounced heavy reliance on foreign credit as a surrender by the government of its independence. Cuauhtémoc himself argued that "behind the sources of credit stand vested political and economic interests that, in addition to mere financial profits, sought to transform a commercial relationship into one of political dependency. Negotiations concerning our debt are dominated by our imperialistic neighbor, whose government has been dangerously aggressive and uses strength as an instrument to resolve its problems."[10]

Neo-Cardenistas criticized the government of Miguel de la Madrid for giving its highest priority to repaying the nation's foreign debt—which amounted to 70 percent of GDP—at a time when unemployment was high and domestic savings low, instead of trying to stimulate the economy and putting the Mexican people's interests ahead of those of foreign bankers. To better understand their point of view, it is useful to remember that the enormous external debt of the Latin American countries was partly the result of the oil crisis of the 1970s. Vast profits accruing to the exporting countries, called petro-dollars, were deposited in international financial institutions. These, in turn, began a lending frenzy so that their assets would produce dividends. Soon, interest rates soared to as high as 22 percent, while prices for raw materials dropped sharply. A high official of Mexico's leading development bank, Nacional Financiera, recounted later that agents for the banks used to stand in line to offer loans according to the conditions stated above.

Neo-Cardenistas, therefore, argued that the government should not rush to negotiate the terms of foreign debt, which in truth was the responsibility of both debtors and creditors. When the latter knowingly made loans that exceeded the countries' capacity to pay, they actually meant to make the countries more vulnerable to external pressures. Therefore, they argued, creditors should be required to offer better terms, such as extension of repayment periods, lower interest, debt forgiveness, and limits on the size of remittances relative to exports and GDP.[11]

The neo-Cardenistas did not call for a simple debt moratorium, however, but rather strenuous negotiations to limit capital outflow. They would place a lower priority on debt payment in favor of investing in economic development that would benefit the nation and all its people. This would also improve the general standard of living and create new jobs.[12]

De la Madrid had counted on petroleum exports to supply all the foreign currency needed to service the debts. In fact, knowledge of Mexico's huge oil reserves had induced international bankers to make loans in the first place. When oil prices retreated in the 1980s, however, de la Madrid found he had to authorize even higher exports. Neo-Cardenistas criticized this move because according to the experts the world reserves would be exhausted in twenty to thirty years. Given this fact, Mexico should have limited production to cover domestic needs only. Otherwise overexploitation would jeopardize the future of the country.

Beyond the estimates of future world prices, the whole issue of Mexico's petroleum was extremely sensitive. Lázaro Cárdenas had to confront the great powers when he expropriated the oil properties of foreign companies in 1938. North American and, above all, British interests threatened intervention for a time.[13] Cárdenas enjoyed special reverence for this move, which permitted Mexico to make enormous economic progress during and after World War II. For this reason neo-Cardenistas distrusted the motives of policymakers who pushed for greater exports. Cuauhtémoc believed U.S. strategic planners "want to use our reserves today in order to conserve their own; they consider our reserves as part of their strategic resources."[14]

Neo-Cardenismo also defended the independence of the country with respect to foreign capital, above all that of the United States. General Cárdenas, upon the termination of his presidential term in 1940, wrote to his successor, Gen. Manuel Avila Camacho, exhorting him to give preference to domestic over foreign investors in order to avoid decapitalizing Mexico. This was the political ideal and thesis of neo-Cardenismo, and the basis for criticism of PRI. It was also the foundation for the alliances of several progressive parties, especially those supporting Cuauhtémoc for president in 1988.

The Democratic Current

On the basis of these ideas and principles, in mid-1985 Cuauhtémoc Cárdenas started talks with other politicians within his own party, the PRI, particularly one of the leading ideologues of the Mexican revolutionary nationalism, Porfirio Muñoz Ledo. The former was nearing completion of his term as governor of Michoacán, and the latter was finishing his tour as Mexico's ambassador to the United Nations. Over the next year they built a progressive coalition within the PRI called the Democratic Current. The public announcement of their alliance in August 1986 caused great consternation in political circles. Some PRI stalwarts leaned toward joining the Democratic Current, but few actually did. The president of PRI moved quickly to negotiate a truce with them. He requested that the dissidents refrain from attacking the government's economic policies and PRI's undemocratic internal procedures. The Democratic Current leaders could not, however, accept such restrictions since these positions were central to their movement. Other efforts were made to tone down the dispute, but it was clear that major policy differences undermined traditional PRI unity.[15]

Less than a year later, Cuauhtémoc demanded that during the PRI convention they poll local leaders throughout the country in order to select the next presidential candidate and determine planks for their platform. Such consultations, amounting to a primary system, would have replaced the hoary tradition of the "tapado," the custom of the president designating his successor. The PRI leadership rejected the proposal, despite the fact that article 147 of the party bylaws actually called for open primaries. Because of these attacks on party procedure, the PRI leaders abandoned their efforts at conciliation, and the split between them and the Democratic Current widened. On March 10, 1987, the party expelled Cuauhtémoc, and Muñoz Ledo resigned shortly after.

The Democratic Current then became an independent movement, since its populist-revolutionary traditions had been rejected and it was barred from coming to power through the PRI. Its leaders proclaimed that the PRI had lost its way due to the apathy and inertia of its leaders. PRI only survived, they said, by means of election fraud that discouraged the participation of progressive members. The Democratic Current held that it must press for democratization within its ranks so that the party could become an agent of free and popular elections among the general population. A second major theme was "to improve living conditions for the masses through an economic recovery along popular nationalist lines."[16]

Economic nationalism formed a cornerstone of the Democratic Current program. This included restrictions on foreign ownership of manufacturing firms, protection of natural resources, and capture of business profits for the good of the nation itself.[17] It also highlighted the need for international cooperation to proceed on the basis of parity among nations. On the domestic political scene, the Democratic Current stressed the desirability of restoring "the national alliances that protected the sovereignty, progress, and stability of the nation"—that is, the Cardenist coalition of the 1930s of associations participating in decisions made at various levels of the state in a certain way, which makes it possible to speak of modern corporatism.[18]

Once the Democratic Current had broken definitively with PRI, the way was clear for Cuauhtémoc Cárdenas to run for president as an independent. His candidacy, announced in July 1987, won the immediate support of the Authentic Party of the Mexican Revolution, which had languished in the shadow of the PRI for thirty-five years.

Cuauhtémoc's candidacy was soon supported by splinter parties from the left, including the Mexican Socialist (formerly Communist) Party. This electoral coalition was called the Democratic Front. The residual popularity of Lázaro Cárdenas certainly added to Cuauhtémoc's appeal, but his own personality, along with his "sad dog" visage, also attracted support. Finally, the serious depression and unemployment undoubtedly boosted his following.

The results of the August 1988 election were clouded by claims of fraud, but as usual the official party candidate, Carlos Salinas de Gortari, was declared the victor. His margin, however, was unusually narrow: Salinas 53 percent; Cárdenas 31 percent; and Manuel Clouthier, the conservative candidate of the Party of National Action (PAN), 17 percent. In the 1988 congressional election, PRI won only 51 percent of the seats, compared to 29 percent and 18 percent, respectively, for the other two. The victory of Salinas de Gortari was actually a wake-up call for the entire political system.[19]

Rejection of Populism

During the next few years the global situation underwent more changes. Neoliberal economics, favored by Great Britain and the United States, won more converts. It prescribed total surrender of the economy to market forces and elimination of state intervention. The International Monetary Fund (IMF) was a conspicuous advocate of neoliberalism, and some of the countries that adopted it, the so-called newly industrialized countries, made considerable progress.

President Salinas, who was the primary architect of de la Madrid's economic program, also adopted the neoliberal model and explicitly rejected populism. He blamed populism for the country's crisis but failed to mention the role played by incompetent and corrupt governors. Like de la Madrid, he repudiated state guidance of the economy and continued to privatize the public-sector enterprises. He dropped all pretenses of economic nationalism and stressed the acceptance of foreign investors, especially those from the United States. To the extent possible, his administration favored returns to capital over those to labor. Employment and workers' well-being became mere dependent variables of the economy. Productivity and profitability became the overriding goals of the government. Finally, all of this should be regulated only by the law of supply and demand; that is, a return to nineteenth-century laissez-faire.

In rural areas, meanwhile, property ownership patterns underwent profound transformations, almost the opposite of those brought about by classical populism. The agrarian reform law was amended to permit the sale of *ejidos*. Moreover, domestic and foreign investors could purchase *ejidos* land. Finally, formerly sanctioned social ownership of the land was eliminated in favor of private ownership.

Under the neoliberal regime, the popular organizations representing labor and farmers were relegated to carrying out decisions made in the planning ministries. Efforts to raise salaries met with rigid opposition, so that labor leaders became mere spectators and executors of higher policy. They could not prevent the general redistribution of income from labor to capital and were forced to issue humiliating statements of solidarity with the government agencies. Rank and file, denied both electoral influence and genuine union representation, could only take their grievances to the streets in protest.

Even more remarkably, PRI's platform had become so conservative that it approximated that of its traditional rival, the PAN. Still, President Salinas held on to some of the traits of populism, such as formulating a general program of government that, if implemented, would benefit labor, farmers, and the middle class. This holdover was no more than window dressing, however, for employers and business managers refused to accept it. He sustained as well the traits of corporatism.

To stimulate economic growth, meanwhile, President Salinas implemented a vigorous program of infrastructure investment, called the Program of National Solidarity (PRONASOL), which absorbed a third of public expenditures. Much of this money came from the sale of public enterprises. The highly publicized successes of PRONASOL were popular and boosted the PRI's turnout in the off-year elections of 1991. Prior to the voting, television spots praising the virtues of PRONASOL were repeated every five to six minutes over virtually every station. To capitalize more, the emblem of PRONASOL was almost identical to that of the PRI.

Perhaps even more important to Salinas's success than PRONASOL was the beginning of economic recovery prior to the elections. The growth cycle affected not only legitimate businesses but the tens of thousands of so-called informal businesses that operated on the margins of the legal system, paying no taxes, social security, or other levies. This huge but little-studied sector accounted for between 20 and 30 percent of the economic activity of the country. Likewise, the informal sector employed a fifth of the workforce, some 5.7 million people, including many thousands of children working in the streets around the country, mostly as vendors. Their teenage and adult counterparts worked in artisan shops, peddled wares from pushcarts, washed windshields at traffic intersections, and found other casual work. Even if the government had wished to halt this informal entrepreneurial activity it could not have. And some economists believed that a significant share of the recovery in the 1990s was due to the informal sector. Such spontaneous economic growth seemed to avoid the kinds of violence and social problems that assailed other Latin American cities, like São Paulo and Caracas.[20]

The results of the neoliberal economic recovery in the mid-1990s were important. Economic growth resumed, inflation diminished, and new money flowed into direct investment. Capital returned from abroad. The GDP began growing at rates of 4–5 percent a year. Still, according to the Economic Commission for Latin America, income inequalities were growing worse. Half the population was poor and 22 percent lived in conditions of extreme poverty.[21] As we will see, since the neoliberal economic strategy could not overcome this situation, it could hardly have been regarded as a success.

The shift from populist politics to neoliberal ones seemed the result of the influence of the International Monetary Fund (IMF). It meant abandoning the dream of turning Mexico into a developed country using its own resources and capital while guaranteeing a fair distribution of wages among all the social classes. The neoliberal state was incapable of doing such things.

Salinas's political record, meanwhile, was tarnished by the persistence of traditional autocratic behavior in the executive branch. He refused to dismantle the corporative state. Working directly and through the PRI, the government controlled all state agencies. PRI could not survive without the patronage it reaped from government jobs, and the government could not survive without PRI's ability to mobilize voters at election time and, when necessary, commit fraud. This created a great tension, for Salinas experienced considerable pressure from below and abroad to democratize the regime.

Few signs suggested that political reform was imminent under Salinas. The PRI victories in the August 1991 elections were full of irregularities; PRI used all the state financial resources to win. Moreover, the Mexican Institute of Public Opinion estimated that PRI accounted for 97 percent of political advertising on television, 86 percent on the radio, and 72 percent in the print media. The remainder was divided among the other nine parties.

The Discrediting of Neoliberalism

Carlos Salinas finished his term with an aura of triumph. Unfortunately, the glow masked failures and deep divisions. As reported by the Economic Commission for Latin America, Salinas ignored nearly half the population—that is, the masses who lived in extreme poverty and who erupted in violent protest. On January 1, 1994, the day that NAFTA took effect, the Indians of Chiapas rose up in revolt to demand that the government desist from the dispossessions and exploitation they had been subjected to for five hundred years. Neoliberal policies had driven down standards of living, which among the Indians were already so low they were pushed over the edge of violence. The leaders of this revolt claimed to be the heirs of Emiliano Zapata, and their armed movement adopted the name Zapatista Army for National Liberation (EZLN).[22]

The conflict had interesting ramifications. In its wake arose powerful social forces that once had a marginal action—in a word, the civil society. Immediately, myriad nongovernmental organizations came to the defense of the Zapatistas and obliged the regime to declare a general amnesty and to hold talks with the rebels. The negotiations gained worldwide attention because they were held in the cathedral of San Cristóbal de las Casas, capital of the state of Chiapas, under the auspices of Bishop Samuel Ruiz as mediator and under the watchful eyes of thousands of unarmed onlookers. This attention prevented an attack by rural bosses and landowners who believed that their properties were threatened, properties they had often acquired through expropriation from the Indians or maintained illegally with the complicity of the authorities.

The talks failed, and from that moment on, Salinas stopped efforts at reaching an understanding. The rebels remained on the scene, a problem left for the next administration.

The neo-Cárdenas movement felt great sympathy with the Zapatista rebels, and their only hesitation had to do with the rebels' military approach. The neo-Cardenistas and the newly founded Party of the Democratic Revolution (PRD), heir to the Democratic Front, gained strength even though they did not establish direct links to the Zapatistas.

The year 1994 was critical in the political realm, even though it was tinged with blood. PRI presidential candidate Luis Donaldo Colosio was assassinated, as was Sen. Francisco Ruiz Massieu, general secretary for the PRI. Fingers immediately pointed to the party itself and to the government.

The struggle for democracy within the PRI led to deep divisions and signs of dissolution. The progressive wing led by Cuauhtémoc and Muñoz Ledo persisted in the form of a new group called Democracy 2000.

State-level elections also affected the struggle of the PRD and neo-Cardenistas, especially where fraud marked the results and the reformers protested. In some of these same cases, the conservative PAN also protested, and in those instances President Salinas ordered the results thrown out and PAN candidates were sworn in. In this struggle for democracy, the PRD waged the battle and PAN reaped the rewards.

Triumph of Democracy: The Zedillo Years

President Ernesto Zedillo, accidental successor to the presidency in 1994, owed his election to the PRI, yet he also inherited massive problems from Carlos Salinas that plagued his administration. In a way, he paid back the PRI for these problems with a steady march toward more democratic elections in 1997 and 2000, a march that led to the defeat of PRI in the latter year. Zedillo's electoral reforms opened the door for the PAN opposition to win the presidency, but they also allowed populism to persist and eventually to thrive in the country's capital, the Federal District.

From the standpoint of populist analysis, even though he was not a populist himself, Zedillo pursued a populist agenda of improving and expanding voters' access to the polls and ensuring free contests among candidates. His reforms included making the electoral tribunal independent, overhauling the Supreme Court, limiting campaign expenses, and making press coverage more transparent. Virtually all populist movements in the region have made improving and expanding the efficacy of elections priority goals. Zedillo also made the Federal District mayoralty elective, as well as the legislative assembly, thereby converting Mexico City into an autonomous and more self-governing entity. Such a move marked the beginning of populism in Brazil in 1934 (see chapter 2). As we will see, this allowed first Cuauhtémoc Cardenas and then Andrés Manuel López Obrador to win the mayoralty and use it as a springboard to presidential elections.

López Obrador had challenged Priísta Roberto Madrazo in the Tabasco gubernatorial election of 1995 and had seemingly managed to win. Still, Madrazo, a strong-willed and powerful figure in the PRI, had broken nearly all the elections rules and blatantly stolen the election. Zedillo took López Obrador's side and proposed a graceful exit for Madrazo, which the latter refused. Instead, he seized the governor's palace and took the office by force. López Obrador would surface in 2000 as a candidate in the Federal District mayoral election.

Meanwhile, Cuauhtémoc Cárdenas, who had run for president unsuccessfully in 1988 and 1994, took advantage of the new status of the Federal District to run in its first mayoral election ever in 1997, on the PRD ticket. He managed to win decisively, with 48 percent of the votes, compared to 26 for the PRI and 16 for PAN. Still, he failed as mayor due partly to sabotage by the PRI and to his own fairly austere and diffident behavior in office. He did not build his popularity in such a way that it could have helped his eventual run for the presidency in 2000. His poor performance was due in part to his focus on national issues and the coming presidential election, to the exclusion of local problems that plagued residents of the city. He served only twenty-one months as mayor.[23]

Cuauhtémoc Cárdenas did run for president in 2000, but he again lost, coming in third behind Vicente Fox and Francisco Labastida Ochoa, with slightly over 16 percent of the national vote. Fox's victory may well have been helped by the disillusionment of voters in Mexico City, who rallied to Fox's promise to be the "president of change." This pretty well marked the end of Cárdenas's career: now sixty-six years old, he had failed three times to win the presidency. Cárdenas never achieved the appeal nor authority of his father and could not be classified as a populist. With the PAN in the presidency, Cárdenas passed into the background to serve as a pundit and moral voice on the Mexican left.

Although Cárdenas was not a populist, his capture of the Federal District mayoralty opened the way for a true populist to win that office, Andrés Manuel López Obrador. Cárdenas also paved the way for his successor by developing a party platform that closely resembled those of his father and of the classic populists of the mid-twentieth century. The PRD supported private enterprise but reserved an important role for the state as owner of critical industries (electricity and petroleum, for example) and as regulator and protector of domestic manufacturing. It vehemently opposed the neoliberal policies of the PRI during the 1980s and 1990s. It also pledged the government would protect the less fortunate and provide jobs and social services so that the working poor could lead dignified lives. As already noted, it pushed for electoral reform, expansion of the electorate, and more democratic representation. López Obrador's ideology borrowed heavily from Cárdenas's. His innovation, however, was to employ these appeals in what became a populist movement, inviting participation, crowd-pleasing meetings, an aggressive media campaign, and daring challenges to the establishment. For example, under the banner "the streets are for everyone," he sponsored outdoor entertainment throughout the city.

López Obrador was born in Tabasco and studied political science at the Universidad Nacional Autónoma de México in Mexico City, the nation's foremost incubator of politicians. He belonged to the PRI until 1988, when he bolted to the Democratic Current, led by Cárdenas and Muñoz Ledo. He gained fame by denouncing corruption in the PRI, especially its relations with PEMEX and the oil workers' union, which were central to Tabasco's economy.

López Obrador assumed the presidency of the PRD in 1996 and achieved a number of important advances for the party. In 1997 the PRD supplanted PAN as the main opposition party in Congress and won three more governorships, in addition to the Federal District. López Obrador was definitely a force on the rise in the late 1990s.[24]

Populism Reborn—The Fox Years

The year 2000 will undoubtedly go down in Mexican history as a crucial turning point, the year in which Vicente Fox of the PAN defeated the PRI candidate and ended seventy-two years of PRI control of the federal government. Fox derived some popularity and charisma from his cowboy appearance and unorthodox career. He was not a populist, however, because his program did not stress national interests nor did he appeal to the lower and middle classes. On the contrary, he said his government would be by businessmen for businessmen. His main attraction was not being from the PRI. On the other hand, López Obrador, the mayor of Mexico City, emerged in these years as a populist in the classic mold and nearly captured the presidency six years later.

López Obrador won the election for mayor with 37 percent of the vote, defeating the PAN candidate, who received 34 percent, and the PRI candidate, with 23 percent. It was not the huge victory that Cárdenas won in 1997 but a respectable outcome in the year Fox captured the presidency. With five years in office (he would have to resign in 2005 to run for president), López Obrador could stretch out and devote much more attention to the affairs of the Federal District and to building his image as a defender of the people and promoter of the nation.

The López Obrador mayoralty has been judged a major success by Mexican and foreign observers, and it certainly launched his bid for the presidency. He proved imaginative, agile, energetic, and persistent in his pursuit of a well-run city and a satisfied electorate. He placed second in an evaluation of four hundred mayors of big cities around the world. His overarching goal was to provide services to the poor, in the form of subsidized transport, food, and utilities, while maintaining a working relationship with the nation's economic elite. As one observer put it, "his strategy is interesting: first, he consolidates his popularity with the poor, then he takes care of the rich, and finally he looks to the forgotten middle class." It was an approach that resembled those of Vargas, Perón, and even Lázaro Cárdenas himself.

The mayor's programs were audacious, bold, and flamboyant. He seemed bigger than life, trying to satisfy the overwhelming needs of a huge Third World city. He used the city as a stage to entertain the entire country, sometimes even the world. He was helped in this by the dense radio, television, and newspaper coverage he received. *New York Times* reporters were mesmerized: Ginger Thompson noted how he managed to work with pro-U.S. businessmen to rebuild the historic city center, to bring Rudy Giuliani in to consult on zero tolerance crime policies, and to lead the charge against the neoliberal economics that had prevailed since the 1980s. She cited a Mexican journalist who wrote that the mayor wrote his speeches with his left hand and governed with his right. Tim Weiner, also of the *Times*, called him an innovator who came from the left yet governed in the center. His popularity with the poor and middle class grew to the extent that he was able to distribute favors and services to the population. This was all the more pronounced because President Fox did little to help the working classes.

López Obrador had good organization and follow-through skills, allowing him to achieve visible results in many different areas. On the public works front, he improved mass transit with a new articulated bus system, an elevated peripheral highway, and a thirty-five kilometer expressway. He built sixteen new schools and a university, all in poor districts of the city. He added to the network of public hospitals and expanded low-cost housing. Yet he struck a pose as a fiscal watchdog, reducing his own and many city employees' salaries. He drove an old car to prove his austerity credentials. Some of his programs were later imitated at the national level by President Calderón.

2006: The Demise of Populism

No one doubted that López Obrador had kept the presidency clearly in view as he built his popularity in the capital. And he seemed destined to succeed, as he entered the campaign with a substantial lead over the other contenders in opinion polls. His basic strategy was to extend to the national scene the policies and programs he had enacted in Mexico City. He even insisted on making campaign tours in buses and modest cars. Unfortunately for him, he emerged in 2005 as the candidate to beat, and all the other candidates ganged up on him mercilessly. Fox used the huge resources of the presidency to harass and distract him, including several judicial indictments that nearly disqualified him. PAN hired expert electioneers to undermine the mayor in the media. PRI piled on, hoping to make a comeback. Among the most damaging attacks were the assertions that López Obrador was a danger to Mexico and that he would emulate Hugo Chávez if he came to power. Gradually the media shifted to attack mode, likely due to the huge amounts of campaign money the PAN and PRI deployed.

Even Cuauhtémoc, vainly believing that he could resurrect his career and run again, refused to give López Obrador his full support and later cut a demeaning deal with Fox to chair a major commission. This deeply eroded the effectiveness of the PRD. Most of these attacks on López Obrador were baseless and intended to inflict maximum damage. One writer called it a dirty war.

López Obrador committed mistakes of his own that also undercut his campaign. He declined to take part in the first televised debate, leading commentators to call him arrogant and aloof. He refused to employ campaign and media experts who might have helped deflect the negative attacks on him, instead trusting to his own defensive instincts. In one case this hurt him deeply, as he was obliged to apologize to Fox for intemperate remarks he had made. Yet even as his commanding lead in the polls dwindled, he believed that he would win.

When the election results revealed a contest too close to call, the Federal Electoral Institute reviewed the returns for a long period before declaring Calderón the victor, with a miniscule lead of 0.58 percent of the national votes. The public and international observers viewed the outcome with skepticism, yet there were no overwhelming signs of fraud, and the institute had gained much credibility in the preceding decade. The continuation of the PAN in power seemed inevitable.

López Obrador then compounded the mistakes he had made by declaring a strike to protest the election results. He mounted a rump government, with ministers and department chiefs, promising to continue the protest until he was declared the rightful winner. His party faithful occupied the central part of the capital for over a month, bringing traffic and ordinary business to a halt. The inconvenience this caused deeply damaged his reputation, making him appear a poor loser and a spoiler. When the strike finally ended, he could no longer contemplate a future in national politics. His career was over. For his part, Calderón was elected legally but not legitimately. He never achieved the authority that Fox had enjoyed. His call for reconciliation with the PRD could never happen, because of the deep wounds and humiliation inflicted on López Obrador.

Conclusion

The crash of López Obrador's career was reminiscent of those of other populists: Vargas in 1954, Perón in 1955, and Alan García in 1990, for example. Their falls were all the more tragic because of the successes they had achieved previously. History has shown populists to be resilient and able to virtually "return from the dead," so we should not count López Obrador out forever. Yet it is difficult to imagine a path by which he could return and run for high office. He was succeeded to the mayoralty of the Federal District by a more moderate PRD leader, Marcelo Ebrard, who seemed determined to seek the presidency by avoiding the excesses of his predecessor.

The outburst of populism in Mexico City after 2000, certainly a fresh and innovative episode after twenty years of neoliberalism and uninspired national leadership, may have been foredoomed. Big city populist mayors traditionally have a hard time emerging on the national scene. Their lives and politics are closely scrutinized in the national press, and their parties lack the structure needed for national campaigns. López Obrador thus swam against the stream of history.

The emergence of populism in Mexico, embedded in the guts of the revolution and brought to power by Lázaro Cárdenas, remains one of the most exciting elements in Mexican history. Suppressed for decades by undeserving successors to Cárdenas, populism returned in the form of pressure to improve the lives of the masses during the catastrophic decade of the 1980s. Fittingly, a quasi-populist movement led by his son Cuauhtémoc and dissident labor leaders split the PRI and led to a progressive rival, the PRD. Where the son lacked the stamina and fire to mount a true populist government in Mexico City, his successor from Tabasco, López Obrador, did so with remarkable courage and ability. His eventual demise owes most to the still-powerful forces of conservatism and elitism in Mexican society.

Notes

1. Jorge Basurto, *El conflicto internacional en torno al petróleo de México* (Mexico: Siglo XXI, 1976).

2. Jorge Basurto, *Cárdenas y el poder sindical* (Mexico: Ediciones ERA, 1983).

3. Carlos Tello, "Sobre la desigualdad en México," in *México a fines del siglo,* ed. José Joaquín Blanco and José Woldenberg (Mexico: Fondo de Cultura Económica, 1993).

4. David Colmenares, Luis Angeles, and Carlos Ramírez, *La nacionalización de la banca* (Mexico: Terra Nova, 1982).

5. Sergio de la Peña, "La política económica de la crisis," in *Primer informe sobre la democracia: México, 1988,* ed. Pablo González Casanova and Jorge Cadena (México: Siglo XXI, 1988).

6. Lázaro Cárdenas, *Ideario político* (Mexico: Ediciones ERA, 1972).

7. Speech by General Lázaro Cárdenas, November 30, 1934, in *Los presidentes de ante la nación* (Mexico: Chamber of Deputies, 1966), 4:11 ff.

8. Armando Labra, "El estado y la economía," in *El Estado mexicano,* ed. Jorge Alonso (Mexico: Ed. Nueva Imagen, 1982), 5. The most important were Petróleos Mexicanos (PEMEX), Federal Electricity Commission, Federal Railroads, National Food Bank (Conasupo), the principal Social Security Institutes (IMSS and ISSSTE), Aeroméxico, National Commission on Foreign Trade, and the development bank, Nacional Financiera. To these were added a huge number of banks nationalized in 1986.

9. Corriente Democrática, "Documento de Trabajo número dos," *Estudios políticos* 7 (April–June 1988).

10. Speech in Monterrey, in Jorge Laso de la Vega, *La Corriente Democrática. Hablan los protagonistas* (Mexico: Editorial Posada, México, 1987), 308.

11. Ibid., 43–44, 309–10.

12. Speech at the UNAM Medical School, June 23, 1987, in *Estudios políticos* 7, no. 3 (July–September 1988).

13. Basurto, *El conflicto internacional.*

14. Speech in Monterrey, Laso de la Vega, *La Corriente Democrática,* 310.

15. María Xelhuantzi, "La Corriente Democrática: De la legitimidad y de alianzas," *Estudios políticos* 7 (April–June 1988).

16. Corriente Democrática, "Documento de Trabajo número dos," *Estudios políticos* 7 (April–June 1988).

17. Ibid.

18. Philippe C. Schmitter, "Corporatism (Corporativism)," in *The International Encyclopedia of the Social Sciences* (New York: Macmillan, 1968–1991).

19. Lorenzo Meyer, *El liberalismo autoritario* (Mexico: Océano, 1995).

20. The Mexico City Chamber of Commerce calculated that street vendors had annual sales of some two billion pesos a year (U.S. $667 million) and that they failed to pay 600 million pesos in taxes (U.S. $200 million). Rosalba Carrasco and Francisco Hernández, "El cercano mundo de la economía informal," *La Jornada,* July 15, 1991.

21. *La Jornada,* September 24, 1991.

22. Carlos Montemayor, *Chiapas: La rebelión indígena de México* (Mexico: Joaquín Mortiz, 1997).

23. Cuauhtémoc Cárdenas, *La esperanza en marcha* (Mexico, D.F.: Ideario Político/ Editorial Océano, 1998).

24. Andrés Manuel López Obrador, *Un proyecto alternativo de nación* (México, D.F.: Editorial Grijalbo, 2004).

5

The Paths to Populism in Peru

Steve Stein

Populism arose in Peru in the 1930s to fill a need for a more modern, inclusive politics for the masses. The old regime could no longer respond to the powerful social and economic changes brought on by urbanization after World War I. This was especially true in and around the capital of Lima. The old political elite was morally and politically bankrupt.[1]

The early 1930s witnessed the rise of two strong populist movements, the Alianza Popular Revolucionaria Americana (APRA) party led by Víctor Raúl Haya de la Torre and the electoral machine of Luis M. Sánchez Cerro. These two competing campaigns ushered in a new era, yet the populists were shut down by mid-decade by the army and the forces of reaction.

Five decades later, Peru experienced a populist resurgence with the Aprista government of Alan García (1985–90) followed by the two-term presidency of neopopulist Alberto Fujimori (1990–2000). García had replaced two other regimes with populist tendencies, the Revolutionary Government of the Armed Forces, which had discredited itself by the late 1970s, and the second presidency of Fernando Belaúnde Terry (1980–85), who ended up presiding over a failed center-right technocracy.

This chapter begins by examining the dynamics of the country's early populist movements in the 1920s and 1930s. Next, it moves to the populist features of the Odría government (1948–55), the first Belaúnde Terry administration (1963–68), and the Velasco Alvarado period of military rule (1968–75). It concludes with a discussion of populism in the 1980s and 1990s, which stresses the economic, social, and political changes that led to the reemergence of populism under Alan García and its resurrection as neopopulism by Alberto Fujimori (1990–2000).

The Birth of Populism, 1919–33

The 1920s were a tumultuous time marked by the explosive growth of Lima and by the first effects of the Great Depression. The eleven-year rule of President Augusto B. Leguía came to an abrupt end with a military coup in 1930. The leader of the coup, forty-one-year-old army major Luis M. Sánchez Cerro, created one of the country's first populist movements. An important sign that a new era had begun was a marked and visible increase in political activity by the popular sectors of Lima. From the very day of Leguía's downfall, working-class mobs staged demonstrations and riots that destroyed his residence and those of some prominent supporters. During subsequent months the popular sectors dominated the urban political scene. The terms *pueblo, masas,* and *elementos populares,* which had in previous years been largely absent from the political vocabulary, became prominent in the public statements and writings of nearly all public figures in the early 1930s.

Many upper-class Peruvians lamented the disturbing rise of mass politics, coupled with the economic turmoil of the Depression. "Although it is painful for us to confirm it," wrote army general and future president Oscar Benavides, "unfortunately it appears as if a streak of ignorance, of madness, has invaded us, wresting from us our most innermost feelings of nationality." The climate of fear and despair was so intense that many actually predicted Peru's extinction as a nation-state. Conservative pundit and politician Víctor Andrés Belaúnde lamented that "the very bases of civilized life threaten to disappear."[2]

The political crisis feared by both Benavides and Belaúnde was a major factor in the rise of populist movements in Peru. It was the result, in great measure, of the disintegration of the so-called República Aristocrática, the elite-controlled political system in power from 1895 through the 1920s. That system epitomized those "dignified traditions" that the elites remembered with such reverence after 1930. Its collapse left a major political vacuum. Most of those who had been prominent in past years literally abandoned the political field.

In addition, in the decades prior to 1930 Lima's politics had been undergoing a process of massification. This resulted from the profound social and economic changes accompanying the growth of urban population in Peru. Beginning roughly around 1900 and picking up pace during World War I, the surge in Lima's inhabitants, the product of Peru's first major wave of rural-urban migration, became particularly visible during the Leguía government. In those eleven years, the capital's population jumped 68 percent, from 224,000 to 376,000.

As Lima grew during the 1920s, its mass population expanded to unprecedented numbers. The city's occupational structure reflected this change. Construction workers engaged in building a modern capital became the largest single segment of the male working class. Following them in importance were large numbers of semi- and unskilled laborers. These included peddlers who went from door to door selling foods or cheap consumer goods, vendors in the various open markets of the city, sellers of lottery tickets, gardeners, waiters, delivery-men, and simply unskilled manual laborers, who gathered at the train station to get whatever day work they could find.

In all, approximately 110,000 individuals held working-class-type jobs in 1931, nearly double the number tabulated in the census of 1920. In propor-tional terms, the city's popular sectors had grown in those years from 58 to 68 percent of the total population.

During these same years, Lima also experienced a substantial growth of the middle sectors. Middle groups had begun to emerge since the mid-nineteenth century. Most held jobs created when Lima diversified from a largely bureau-cratic and commercial center to manufacturing and services. The middle sec-tors included most government and commercial employees, students and edu-cators at all levels, independent merchants, and military officers. Also, increasing numbers of lawyers, doctors, engineers, and storekeepers swelled the ranks of this stratum. Employment in all these areas was the product of the economic boom of the Leguía years and the attendant growth of public expenditures, which nearly tripled between 1917 and 1929.

The urban masses and middle sectors made their formal entry into poli-tics in August 1930, following the downfall of Leguía. They joined the two populist movements that rallied voters for the election of 1931, those led by Sánchez Cerro and Haya de la Torre. Despite differences in rhetoric and style, these two movements proved to be remarkably similar. Both Sánchezcerrismo and Aprismo were vertical, patrimonial movements united by relationships of personal loyalty between leaders and followers. Both cut across class and status lines to include individuals with potentially conflicting priorities from various levels of Peruvian society.

APRA did expound a detailed platform, in contrast to Sánchez Cerro who did not have one, but specific issues or ideology were not crucial to the appeal of either movement. One vital difference between the two movements, how-ever, was that APRA's verticality was usually expressed in ties to institutional-ized social groups—such as unions or professional and employee associations. Sánchez Cerro, on the other hand, generally avoided references to recognized occupational or social categories, emphasizing instead his one-to-one commit-ment to each and every Peruvian.

A political unknown before August 1930, Sánchez Cerro, the army major who had commanded the overthrow of President Leguía, ascended immedi-ately after the coup to the presidency of Peru, only to be overthrown six months later by an alliance of civilians and military officers unhappy with his actions as chief executive. He subsequently formed a political movement in early 1931 to support his presidential bid in the upcoming October election. In the ensuing electoral campaign, Sánchez Cerro—seemingly overnight—became the country's most successful and popular politician.

The most distinguishing feature of his spectacular campaign was its projection of identity between the leader and his working-class followers. Sánchez Cerro was able to use his ethnic identity—he was a dark-skinned mestizo—to emphasize his common origins with the masses. Numerous times during the campaign his working-class supporters could be heard boasting that "he's a *cholo* [mestizo] like us." While many upper-class Peruvians were scandalized that a man of mixed racial origins could dominate a political stage previously occupied almost exclusively by members of the white aristocracy, the urban poor saw him as one of their own who had scaled the political heights.[3]

The specifically racial content of Sánchez Cerro's politics was a distinctive element of this and later populist movements. Since racial identity and racism have historically had a strong effect on Peru's social, political, and economic relations, his personification of the racial outsider became a powerful tool for gaining working-class support. "He was of our race," reflected one of his working-class followers, "and because of that all us working people supported him." The masses' identification with the cholo candidate, in turn, helped convey a fundamental theme of his campaign: potential supporters could approach Sánchez Cerro personally to ask for individual favors. Daily, his campaign headquarters filled up with poor voters seeking audiences with the candidate. His accessibility created the notion that he was a generous figure. When approached directly by his followers, Sánchez Cerro responded sympathetically. He patted his "humble supplicants" on the back, wrote down their names, and sometimes gave them money from his pocket or some article of clothing. Always speaking to followers in simple language, using the familiar *tú* form, he would say, "*Toma hijo, toma hija. Hijito, hijita, sí, ya vamos a ver*" (Take this son, take that daughter. My little son, my little daughter, yes, we'll look into that).

The words of a song popular during the campaign suggested to admirers what could be expected of Sánchez Cerro once in office:

Cuando suba Sánchez Cerro   When Sánchez Cerro is in power,
no vamos a trabajá   we won't have to work
pue nos va a llové todito   because every little thing's going
como del cielo el maná.   to rain on us like manna from heaven.[4]

A critic of Sánchez Cerro, writing to a friend about the candidate's relationship with the masses, implicitly revealed how the elite perceived the populist leader:

Sánchez Cerro has offered to pull the mob out of its present situation, as is evident in cases like these. My aunt's family has gone downhill socially and economically. When she decided to sell her possessions in order to go to England, the native country of her husband, she received the following offer from her butler: "Don't sell anything, don't go to England. Wait for a short while until Luis takes power, he is my friend. I will get a job in the post office and I'll get a job for the *patrón*." You can laugh about that offer. A vegetable seller in the market says to a client of hers: "As a vegetable seller I have trouble finding good husbands for my daughters, but now we can start looking for better candidates, because when Luis Miguel is in power, I will be the head of the state shops, my daughter who's a midwife will have a good job, and my other daughter will be an accountant in a ministry." Such cases number in the hundreds.[5]

Even more telling than the words of Sánchez Cerro's political enemies were those of his political friends. They provided vivid testimony on the success of his personalistic and paternalistic style. A seemingly endless stream of letters, speeches, and proclamations written by members of Sánchezcerrista clubs attested to the nature of the candidate's influence on working-class voters. Their content reflected an unquestioning faith in a man who, by virtue of his innate superiority, could single-handedly solve Peru's and their problems. Variously referred to as a *patrón* or a *padre protector* (protective father), he was seen as capable of providing the daily bread for his children and tending to their other needs. According to his working-class supporters, he was a man who, guided by his particularly strong sense of *fé, cariño y amor* (faith, affection, and love), would save the country from all present and future dangers.

Sánchez Cerro appealed especially to the most deprived members of the working classes. Lower-class Sánchezcerristas were typically humble vendors in markets and on the streets, construction workers, street cleaners, and laborers in small artisan industries. A sizable proportion of them were recent migrants to the city, some of whom continued to dress in traditional Indian clothes. This group on the whole was very poor, had unstable jobs, and did not belong to unions. Often barely able to read and write, some wrote letters to Sánchez Cerro filled with misspelled words and incoherent sentences.

Víctor Raúl Haya de la Torre, Sánchez Cerro's major opponent in the 1931 election, also appealed to large segments of working-class voters. In the long run he would become Peru's leading populist of the twentieth century. Haya's following, however, was drawn mainly from the upper reaches of the working class—those more organized and unionized—as well as from the ranks of middle-class voters. Not only was there a clear distinction between Sánchezcerrista and Aprista voters, but also the two movements followed very different evolutions.

Whereas Sánchezcerrismo appeared almost overnight on the political scene, the APRA party rose to prominence gradually over a decade of personal contact between its leader and members of Peru's small industrial proletariat.

Beginning in 1919, when he gained attention as a student leader of workers on strike for the eight-hour day, Haya strove diligently to forge bonds of political clientelism between himself and Lima's workers. He did this by staying in contact with leaders of organized labor, by organizing dramatic protests, and by launching and administering the Popular University, where well-to-do students taught evening and weekend classes to workers. All these efforts produced strong bonds of friendship and personal loyalty that became the foundation of the Aprista Party. In the classrooms of the Popular University, for example, professors from middle and upper social strata and their worker-students bridged the social gap. The remarkable solidarity that emerged between these two groups—made up of reciprocal trust—grew out of their experiences as teachers and pupils. The *frente de trabajadores manuales e intelectuales* (alliance of manual and intellectual workers), Haya's favorite title for the Aprista movement, was the offspring of these workers' schools he formed beginning in 1921.

The Popular University conclusively launched Haya de la Torre's political career. One labor leader recalled, "My case is a clear example. In the poverty and harsh conditions of my *callejón* home, my educational fortune consisted of a third grade education. . . . Since I was lost in this nebulous ignorance, the Popular University was for me a guide toward wider horizons." The university student-instructors were invariably singled out for special praise. They were seen as a "bunch of good and disinterested fellows from the University," leading a new crusade to bring "the rays of learning to our dark minds."[6]

The kind of dependent relationship implied by these avowals became a central feature of the party that Haya launched formally in October 1930. And the same kind of dependent relationship extended into the Aprista campaign for the 1931 election. Like Sánchez Cerro, Haya de la Torre adopted the role of father figure toward his working-class followers. In the 1920s, he had styled himself "the father of the workers," while in the 1931 campaign he became "father of APRA." Evidently his "children" had grown in numbers far beyond a small group of union leaders, and they became the cornerstone to win the high stakes in the election.

During the 1931 campaign numerous observers remarked on Haya's extraordinary personal warmth, his contagious smile, his generally pleasing disposition, and his prodigious memory for people and events of the past. Many of his person-to-person conversations with the Aprista faithful revolved around the in-

Figure 5.1. Víctor Raúl Haya de la Torre, campaigning in 1931. (Courtesy of Haya de la Torre personal collection, given to author)

timate problems of their daily lives. Haya always seemed ready with sympathetic understanding and pertinent advice. Even his most avowed enemies could not help but envy the benefits Haya gained from the paternalistic concern he projected. In the words of Communist leader Eudocio Ravines: "He possessed an ingenious and friendly loquacity that gave people the physical sensation of being loved, set apart individually from among the rest. He was acute at discovering and focusing on the immediate and small problems of the people and treating them with a captivating friendliness, verbally showing interest in them."[7]

Haya's personal warmth took the form of long handshakes, pats on the back, and fond embraces in individual encounters. His inclination for physical expression became an integral part of his style. In the proud words of the APRA newspaper *La Tribuna*, the six million people that made up the Peruvian population in 1931 could feel embraced by the affectionate and forgiving arms of Haya de la Torre: "Proletarian Peru: Rise to your feet! Your guide has arrived: Víctor Raúl Haya de la Torre! His arms! . . . Those gigantic arms that have never closed return open with the hunger of holding yours."[8]

Notwithstanding the presence of the term in its very title, the APRA (Alianza Popular Revolucionaria Americana) was in many respects far from revolutionary. The party undertook to preserve the social structure of the country by representing the various strata within its ranks. In fact, its organization and day-today operation reflected the hierarchy of society as a whole. It was led by middle- and upper-class veterans of the Popular University. The former students, largely members of the organized industrial labor force, made up the rank and file. The nexus between these different strata of Peruvian society was the person of Víctor Raúl Haya de la Torre, who had established the alliance in the first place.

The political confluence of *la juventud del brazo y del cerebro* (the youth of muscle and the youth of brains), as Haya referred to the party, was necessary, according to the Apristas, because of "the ignorance that predominates in our working classes." Aprista leaders reasoned that since workers lacked the consciousness and skills for independent political action, the direction of the party, and eventually the nation, should be entrusted to middle- and upper-class intellectuals. They would be the specialists, the political technicians who would manage the state with the interests of the masses in mind.

APRA's doctrine of a vertical division of power won acceptance by and even applause from workers in the party. APRA's most prominent labor leader, Arturo Sabroso, described the workers' view of party and national leadership:

> A government totally made up of people from the proletariat was never considered a possibility. Precisely when we became convinced of this, a few fellow workers said, fine, we will join the party, but fifty percent workers and fifty percent intellectuals in everything: deputies, senators, everything. Others of us reasoned that, no, it's impossible to have half workers. In a parliamentary bloc you have professional men, technicians, doctors, engineers, economists, lawyers, professors, workers, and employees. For study and consultation on so many problems, you need experts in their fields. This will assure that all the studies can be more effectively carried out. It is not a question of demagoguery. This is being realistic.[9]

Haya de la Torre perched at the top of this hierarchical framework. With the title of *jefe máximo* (highest chief), he served as supreme interpreter and director—in the words of an official Aprista publication—of the "vague and imprecise desires of the multitude." The Aprista masses recognized his right to lead for having been "the creator of the doctrine and its principal instrument . . . [and he deserved to lead] for having done what he has done."[10]

Haya's dominant relationship with his party closely paralleled Sánchez Cerro's omnipotence within his political movement. Moreover, Apristas considered themselves members of a single large family in which the parents were to be respected and emulated by their children. As one party flier urged, "Aprista: your party is a great family in which whoever knows teaches, and whoever does not know learns."[11]

In a 1970 interview, Haya outlined the nature and origins of his paternalism by comparing, in ideal terms, the leader-follower relationship in Aprismo to the social relations that characterized the traditional *casa grande* or seigniorial house in his native city of Trujillo:

> In Trujillo there existed the very highest nobility . . . These ties are very strange because they come from the family. Aristocratic ties were conserved in Trujillo . . . I was nurtured in this aristocratic tradition . . . One inherited this like a kind of code of conduct. This aristocracy was closer to the people. It was an old tradition. They treated the people very well. In Trujillo good treatment of the servants is traditional. The families that lived in what were called the *casas grandes* obeyed this rule. That the children wait on the servants on their birthdays, that they do all these things; be the godfather of their marriages, all this sort of thing . . . And you have to go up to each one of the servants and greet them and kiss them . . . It is a different spirit. And we who come from the North, for example, with the blacks, very affectionate, and everything. At the same time there was always something very cordial with the people. That is APRA! The Aprista masses have seen in their leaders people who had come from the aristocracy . . . We were educated in that school . . . People who do not know the inner workings of the party do not understand these things . . . We were born of this stock . . . In a country which was not an industrialized or a bourgeois country, still a patriarchal country, these ties meant much. And APRA owes its success in its first years to this fact.[12]

As these descriptions of Sánchezcerrismo and Aprismo indicate, the formation of the two movements, their campaign styles, their rhetoric—their very reasons for existence—revolved around the presence of a charismatic and dominant leader who provided cohesion. Central to the mass recruitment carried out by both parties was the glorification of the special personal qualities of their respective leaders.

Despite the obvious differences between a military caudillo and a teacher caudillo, both Sánchez Cerro and Haya embodied qualities familiar and appealing to the electorate. Accounts of past accomplishments, testimonials to present capabilities, and the personal appearances of the candidates ended in the projection of a similar image: that of a big-hearted, affectionate, and protective father possessed of an extraordinary ability both to understand the intimate needs of his followers and to reward the faithful.

Poor people particularly valued the real or imagined access to their leaders in times of adversity or crisis. Since even in ordinary times they had few resources with which to solve problems, they desperately sought protective bonds from politicians when emergencies arose. The Great Depression was just such a crisis in Peru. The public's enthusiastic responses to these two populist movements owed much to the deepening impoverishment of the workers, who saw Sánchez Cerro and Haya de la Torre as generous figures who could protect them. Hence, far from radicalizing the Peruvian working classes, the Depression drew them toward populist alternatives as the most faithful political embodiment of traditional patrimonial social relations.

The initial surge of populism was cut short by the suppression of Haya de la Torre and his Aprista Party by the military after 1932 and by the assassination of Sánchez Cerro in 1933. In July 1932 an Aprista revolt broke out in the northern city of Trujillo. In the course of taking over the city, activists captured and executed thirty-four army officers. The revolt was eventually put down, after which the army executed an estimated one thousand Apristas by firing squads. The Trujillo revolt became a mortal sin in the eyes of an unforgiving military, and for over a decade the movement was banned from politics. Following the death of Sánchez Cerro, members of the traditional oligarchy returned to power and restored elite government.

Populism at Midcentury

The political behavior and values that featured in the early 1930s populist campaigns persisted and reappeared as ingredients of later movements. The substantial popularity garnered by President Manuel Odría in the 1950s, for example, and by the Revolutionary Military Government, led by President Juan Velasco Alvarado in the 1970s, had populist overtones. Even though neither Odría nor Velasco took office by electoral means—a key feature of populism—they relied on populist appeals to generate support for their regimes. In doing so, often quite effectively, they fit within the populist sphere.

The regimes of both Odría and Velasco arose during periods of social and political crisis similar to those of the early 1930s. In the case of Odría, the crisis had political roots stemming from APRA's attempt to reassert itself in national politics after years of clandestine existence.

APRA had won back its legal status in 1945 and participated in the elections of that year. Although Haya did not run, the party played a major role in the victorious Frente Democrático Nacional (National Democratic Front—FDN) coalition that captured the presidency, and the party won a majority of seats in Congress. The FDN had difficulty governing the country, however, due to increasing strife between Apristas and the president. The deteriorating climate of disorder led to widespread political violence. Both Apristas and military leaders attempted several times to take over the government until Gen. Manuel Odría finally succeeded in October 1948.

Odría governed Peru for the next eight years, relying on a political style that was strongly reminiscent of Sánchez Cerro's. He constructed his recruitment efforts around the creation of a variety of "political charities" directed at the highly visible and growing urban poor. Most effective were frequent, highly publicized visits of his wife, María Delgado de Odría, to the Lima slums, bearing gifts of food and money. The elite disdained these forays as blatant imitations of Eva Perón, yet la Señora María succeeded in winning favor for her husband. Government publications describing her "good works for the people" bear striking resemblance to the accolades directed at Sánchez Cerro and Haya de la Torre in the 1931 presidential campaign:

> Her hands, open, sincere, friendly, extend toward the suffering poor of Lima, toward the afflicted of all the Peruvian provinces, toward every place where there is a need for a spontaneous and understanding heart that holds back nothing. Her magnificent and tender figure radiates that contagious cheer that makes the poor of the nation so happy, cheer given without limits to the young, the old, the sick, all that expect everything from her. To the poor of the nation she has given shelter, medicine, food, advice, and above all, love and more love. She has become the guide of the needy, who will soon call her Protector of the Humble. [13]

Odría himself acted paternalistically when he ordered the legalization of squatter settlements to house Lima's growing lower-class population. Often naming their settlements after the president or his wife, impressive numbers of the capital's popular masses paid homage to the first family. They also filled out the ranks of pro-government demonstrators in the largest plazas of the city. Acting reciprocally, they repaid the man who had benevolently looked after their needs.

In 1956, the year that Odría reluctantly turned over the Government Palace to elected President Manuel Prado, another of Peru's twentieth-century populists made his debut in politics. Fernando Belaúnde Terry, the youthful dean of the nation's leading school of architecture, launched himself as a candidate in that year's presidential race. Even though he campaigned little, he garnered a surprising 36 percent of the vote.[14]

During the following six years, Belaúnde fashioned a political persona and an organization, Acción Popular (AP), in preparation for the election of 1962. When the results of that contest were overturned by the military, Belaúnde mounted a new and successful bid for the presidency, which he won the following year.

The term *populist* has stuck to Belaúnde more than to any other Peruvian leader. In view of his oddly reluctant brand of campaigning, however, that label had as much to do with the name of his party as with his populist style. Belaúnde did, however, share one important characteristic with the other populists. He repeatedly used the "grand gesture" to gain attention and attract support. The architect-politician successfully coupled highly visible and dramatic actions with speeches full of heady rhetoric. He managed to create the image of a leader who was tremendously energetic and, at the same time, very much in touch with the real concerns of the people.

Belaúnde's first "grand gesture" occurred during the 1956 presidential race. Backed by students, intellectuals, and professionals, he founded the Frente Nacional de Juventudes Democráticas (National Front of Democratic Youth—FNJD) to make his run for the presidency. Responding to doubts from the National Elections Board about whether he had enough followers to qualify for the ballot, Belaúnde convoked a massive demonstration in Lima's main square as proof of his eligibility. When the police showed up in force and shot water cannons to disperse the demonstrators, he wrapped himself in the Peruvian flag and, despite being hit directly with a violent torrent of water, boldly faced down his assailants. He subsequently portrayed his 1956 presidential bid as a political battle in which he stood side by side with "the youth" on the front lines.

The use of dramatic symbolism, in word and in action, became the hallmark of Belaúnde's campaign. During the period leading up to the 1962 election, the aspiring candidate burnished his public image with a series of well-publicized trips through the Peruvian hinterlands designed to put him in contact with "the whole of the Peruvian population *pueblo por pueblo,*" town by town, as he so effectively put it.

> We have traveled from Huanuco to Ancash [two towns in the Peruvian Andes] by the Inca Highway, and in the cold of the highlands I once again donned with pride my Huaraz poncho, with the same solemnity as a priest would don his sacred vestments to recite a prayer for the past, present and future of Peru. . . . I go to seek out the pueblos, to hear their needs, and to gather their hopes.[15]

Belaúnde also used the scenario of his travels to develop one of the most effective themes of his populist rhetoric, the importance of popular participation for the advancement of the nation.

> Every time that I come upon, from the heights, a Peruvian village, I ask the same question and receive the same inspiring answer. As I look upon the humble village with its picturesque bell tower, I ask my guide: "Who built the church?" And the guide tells me, "The people did it." Turning to him again, I ask: "Who built the school?" And once again he answers: "The people did it." As I follow the winding road between the peaks, I ask him one more time: "Who opened this road?" And once again, resound-

ing in my ears like the verse of a triumphal march, I hear in this expressive and eloquent phrase which contains the whole history of the Peru of yesterday and today, and the prophesy of tomorrow: "The people did it."[16]

Despite his evocative words promising a preeminent role for "the people," Belaúnde's actions as president showed that he was unwilling to move beyond rhetoric and to create real participation in governmental decisions and programs. One of the best examples of this reluctance was Cooperación Popular, the agency he trumpeted as the government's daring effort to institutionalize popular action. While publicists for Cooperación Popular continually stressed the spirit of mutual aid and collaboration, it in fact never became more than an agency by which the government distributed top-down technical aid. When at one point it appeared that Cooperación Popular might actually transform itself into an enduring peasant or worker organization, Belaúnde ended up withdrawing support from his own brainchild. Similarly, Acción Popular never developed into an organic party with strong grassroots support, in large part because its leader was not ready to accept the kind of popular input he so energetically stressed in his powerful rhetoric.

In other areas of governmental policy the Belaúnde avid in words became a Belaúnde reluctant in actions. When launching his highly visible agrarian reform project, for example, he declared that all lands would be affected. But almost in the same breath he exempted properties "dedicated to the industrial transformation of agricultural products." In effect, nearly all the country's land that had significant value, such as coastal sugar and cotton plantations, would not be touched by the redistribution program.

A similar gap between campaign rhetoric and government action arose when Belaúnde tabled his promise to resolve Peru's long-standing claims against a Standard Oil subsidiary. Then, after five years of inaction, he decided to nationalize the foreign holdings with compensation. The settlement was so unfavorable, however, that widespread repudiation of the agreement precipitated a coup by the military before it could be enacted.

With the failures of Cooperación Popular, agrarian reform, and his petroleum policy, the public became increasingly disillusioned by Belaúnde's inability or unwillingness to make good his grand rhetorical gestures. With his support severely undermined, virtually no one protested when he was unceremoniously ousted from the Government Palace in October 1968. Belaúnde would return as president in the years 1980–85, but his second administration was neither effective from the standpoint of generating stability and growth nor successful as a populist mobilization. He completed his term in 1985 under a cloud of failure.

While Belaúnde's leadership failures clearly motivated the military officers who overthrew him in 1968, early pronouncements by the new Revolutionary Military Government revealed even greater concern with threats to social and political order in the nation. Throughout Latin America, guerrilla activity had erupted in the wake of the Cuban Revolution. In the Peru of the 1960s, apocalyptic visions of insurrection raised fears of a communist takeover. Massive waves of rural migrants spawned vast squatter settlements around cities. Both rural and urban land invasions threatened public order and the sanctity of private property. Strikes and student demonstrations were becoming more and more frequent. Rural guerrilla movements had broken out in various parts of the interior, and urban guerrilla bands began to operate in Lima. Debates about the possibility of violent revolution became more and more widespread.

Leaders of the Revolutionary Military Government of 1968 insisted that they could ameliorate social conflict, real and potential, by building an efficient government and a more equitable Peru. They declared that their political-military bureaucracy would naturally serve the interests of the entire population. They resurrected the populist pledges to overcome class conflict through inspired leadership. The regime of Juan Velasco Alvarado (1968–75) took government patrimonialism to a new level by forming clientelistic institutions designed to bond working-class citizens to a tutelary state. The foremost of these was the Sistema Nacional de Apoyo a la Movilización Social (National System for the Support of Social Mobilization—SINAMOS). SINAMOS regularized clientelism in various ways. All public and private welfare programs operated under its supervision. It became a formal broker between individuals, working-class associations, and the state. And it took primary responsibility for mass political mobilization.

In its treatment of Lima's squatter settlements, for example, SINAMOS substituted government bureaucrats for populist politicians in the performance of face-to-face clientelistic relations. The agency's offices were routinely packed with poor people seeking help for their marginal settlements or recognition of their land titles. Harkening back to the scenes of supplicants requesting help from Sánchez Cerro some forty years earlier, each of these activities bore the same stamp of politics of dependence that had been launched by the populists of the 1930s.

Although the Government of the Armed Forces regularized populist favors somewhat, it was not above reviving the personalist forms of paternalism that characterized earlier years. In some instances, blatant political charity may have even surpassed that of the government's predecessors. At massive political meetings in Lima's main square, for example, President Velasco Alvarado threw packages of cigarettes to his scrambling supporters. Not to be outdone, the regime's popular minister of the interior, Armando Artola, flew over various Lima squatter settlements in a helicopter during the Christmas season and dropped holiday cakes *(panetones)* to the people gathered below.

La Crisis and the Crisis of Populism

All of the foregoing populist movements, from Sánchez Cerro to Velasco Alvarado, were built on the hopes of rank-and-file followers that they would benefit materially from their candidate becoming president and continuing in office. Such hopes rested on two populist assumptions: the man in power both could and would exercise his personal benevolence in their favor. Yet the decline of people's faith in those beliefs during the 1980s led to political failure for latter-day populist Alan García and to serious doubts about the survival of populism in the future.

Alan García had moved to the head of the APRA party following Haya's death in 1981. Throughout the second administration of Belaúnde, García campaigned on a platform of Aprismo and finally reached the presidency. Elected in 1985 with just under 50 percent of the vote, he initially appeared to be the great hope for restoring national unity and even populism. In the months following his inauguration, the young and dashing president increased his approval rating to 85 percent.

García's initial popularity resulted from masterful use of traditional populist stratagems. Especially important were his *balconazos*, impromptu appearances on the balcony of the Government Palace, microphone in hand, to make announcements and to conduct face-to-face dialogues with "the people." He also made frequent unannounced appearances at various sites around the country to hear about and discuss the problems of everyday citizens and even to pitch in on community projects, disaster relief, house repair, and the like. Populism certainly appeared to be alive and well under García as he maintained a high degree of support for most of the first two years of his presidency. Nevertheless, by the end of his term of office in 1990, the Aprista leader had not only been rejected by the majority of Peruvians but also by most members of his own party. What had happened to reduce the support of the president from 85 percent to less than 5 percent in the space of three short years?

In fact, the major threat to populist politics began to emerge at the end of the 1970s, years before García had risen to prominence. That threat, dubbed by its contemporaries "La Crisis," was the most serious economic and social upheaval in Peru's modern history. It would seriously undermine the two cornerstones of populism: faith in benefits from above and improvements in a system governed by a populist leader.

The early populists, Sánchez Cerro and Haya de la Torre, had taken advantage of the economic downturn of the Depression to consolidate their popular followings, something that Alan García might have done also. For Peruvians, however, the crisis of the early 1980s was more severe than the troubles of the 1930s. At the same time it created cruel hardships for most citizens, it caused a profound questioning of all of the nation's formal institutions and of the very values that had held society together since colonial times.

La Crisis hit Peruvians in all spheres of their daily lives. The deterioration of employment conditions over the 1980s was particularly acute. At the beginning of the decade some 60 percent of the economically active population were fully employed, 30 percent were underemployed, and 10 percent were unemployed. Ten years later, only 10 to 15 percent of the economically active population was considered fully employed, 70 to 75 percent were partially employed, and 15 percent were unemployed. The inversion of full and partial employment sectors promoted the explosive growth of Peru's well-known "informal sectors," made up of persons obliged to work outside of the formal economy. Not surprisingly major reductions in real income accompanied employment decline. In 1984 the minimum wage in Peru was 46 percent of what people had received ten years earlier; by 1990 it was estimated that real incomes of many had fallen to 20 percent of the levels achieved ten years earlier.

With jobs and incomes threatened, Peruvians suffered a sharp decline in health. Between 1975 and 1985, poverty-sensitive infectious diseases such as typhoid, dysentery, and hepatitis increased 400 percent. Malnutrition helped the spread of these diseases and increased levels of infant mortality.

La Crisis was accompanied by a surge of migration into the squatter settlements of Lima, the result of increasing poverty in provincial areas and of the dramatic upsurge of rural violence from the growing civil war between the Shining Path guerilla movement and the state. In earlier decades, people had migrated from the provinces to Lima in hope of improving their lives. Many occupied small pieces of land on the edge of the city and managed to build homes for themselves. The government helped many of these new settlers with credit, construction materials, and technical advice. It had been possible, through long and hard work over years, for the poor to transform shacks of woven reed mats into solid houses. Many felt they had fulfilled their dreams of a better life in the city. The change in designation of these settlements from *barriadas* (shanty towns) to *pueblos jóvenes* (young towns) symbolized their standing as a "positive" aspect of urban growth in Peru.

La Crisis, however, brought this process to a grinding halt, prompting disastrous overcrowding among the urban poor. By the mid-1980s, Lima's housing stock had begun to deteriorate badly. The resulting shortage forced new migrants and the grown children of earlier settlers to rent rooms in subdivided dwellings. The original inhabitants, meanwhile, had to find additional earnings to survive. The same squatter settlements that had been transformed from a series of precarious shacks into respectable neighborhoods over the previous twenty years were returned to the condition of overcrowded and unsanitary slums.

At the same time that most Peruvians suffered a marked decline in their material well-being, every day seemed to bring more economic insecurity as the country began suffering through one of the world's historically highest rates of hyperinflation. The result of economic policies that emphasized growth at all costs, in this case the massive printing of currency, inflation rates of up to 2,000 percent per year meant that people felt extremely vulnerable, not knowing what their income would purchase from week to week.

Alan García's style of *personalismo* had worked well for him in the early years of his presidency when the public appreciated his vigorous activity and applauded the results he obtained. But in the face of precipitous economic decline and acute uncertainty, people quickly lost confidence in the ability of their political *patrón* to deliver the protection and rewards expected of an effective populist leader. Gacía's rapid political decline was exacerbated by his refusal, from day one of his presidency, to work with any political organizations, even his own party, and his exclusion of any groups outside of his personal radius—unions, peasant federations, employers' associations—from the political process.

This exclusivist exercise of power represented a new expression of a tendency present in nearly all of his populist predecessors. The earlier movements had thrived on the violent rejection of political enemies: Sánchez Cerro was the anti-Aprista; APRA was the in-group "sect"; Odría was once again the anti-Aprista; and the Revolutionary Military Government was the anti-civilian. The extreme hardships of La Crisis weakened the public's belief in a president that attributed all public initiatives solely to his person; by association, the state itself began to appear useless. As people increasingly doubted in the ability of García and his government to distribute even hope, they simultaneously rejected formal political structures in Peru.

In the words of one working-class Limeño:

> They're all a bunch of crooks. They do whatever they want. Everything is rotten, nobody can save this country . . . Just look at what's happening with rice, sugar, all the prices are up in the clouds, there's just not enough money . . . And what do the politicians do? They just fight and fool around. The Apristas, the Populistas, the Comunistas . . . They're all the same. They all want to hold office, act important, make money, but as far as the people go . . . they're not interested![17]

The structure and performance of populism under Alan García contributed to an atmosphere of distrust that, in its most extreme manifestations, led to open aggression and violence all over the country. By the late 1980s and early 1990s, violence had become one of the most common forms of interaction between the different sectors of Peruvian society. Its most dramatic expressions ranged from an enormous jump in crime on the individual level to the massive collective violence of the Shining Path extremists. Social and political violence, along with declining living standards for the majority of the population, became the dominant fact of Peruvian life during this period.

The words of those most affected expressed eloquently the extraordinary levels of political bankruptcy and social polarization that lowered traditional inhibitions to violence for many Peruvians. As a loyal Lima maid explained to the author:

There is so much poverty. In contrast, there are others that receive more and have more. The rich are richer. You can see this because the poor people, there they are, with just the same. The rich just climb higher and higher, higher and higher. In contrast, the poor never climb above the place they are at, and instead of progressing, they move lower, so much that they get desperate and they rob or kill or anything like that. A person who makes a mistake ends up out of work. And then, that person looks for work elsewhere, and they can't find another job, and since they can't find one, they get desperate. And their kids, their wife, I don't know. All this begins to make them desperate. What's left for them? To beg for money, or they change totally and they start robbing.[18]

Even more direct and nihilistic were the lyrics of a song popular among the urban poor during the late 1980s:

This world, this land, is out of control.
There's no solution, there's no cure anymore.
Everything is rancor, fathers die, children die,
Mothers die, nobody knows, nobody speaks, total silence.
The conscience is dead, it exists no more.
It's men that have changed, they're all like beasts.[19]

Fujimori

In the atmosphere of mistrust and despair that prevailed in 1990, Alberto Fujimori arose out of nowhere to win the Peruvian presidency. A political unknown with no formal party organization and virtually no campaign staff, Fujimori cultivated an image of himself as an outsider and an "antipolitician."

He was indeed an outsider in more ways than one. Previous to the election, he had never aspired to political office. His campaign experience was limited to a successful bid to become rector of Peru's Universidad Nacional Agraria and later president of the National Commission of Peruvian University Rectors. Even more crucial to his outsider identity was his Japanese extraction. Fujimori reveled in his origins, and he enthusiastically accepted the nickname "El Chino," a term traditionally applied disdainfully to Peru's Asian population, and in the campaign he was able to turn the negative connotations of that epithet to his advantage.

The contrast between Fujimori and his upper-middle-class contender, famed author Mario Vargas Llosa, could not have been sharper when, in the final stages of the campaign, Vargas Llosa's supporters loudly proclaimed: "*Ningún Chino será presidente del Perú!*" (No Chinaman will be president of Peru). The clear racist connotations of the "white" candidate's supporters were not lost on the majority of the country's population that had, as had Fujimori, traditionally suffered political and social discrimination. As political and social outsiders, they found even more reason to identify with and support the outsider candidate whose campaign slogan was "A President Like You."

Once elected, Fujimori made stabilization of the economy and the fight against the Shining Path the hallmarks of his first term. During the campaign he had continually distinguished himself as the "anti-shock" candidate in contrast to Vargas Llosa, who argued that the country's hyperinflation could be ended only by the application of radical structural adjustment. But within two weeks of his inauguration, the new president implemented a shock program more radical than anything his electoral contender had proposed. In an effort to stabilize prices, the government eliminated all subsidies and price controls. As a result, from one day to the next the prices of basic necessities like bread and milk tripled while the price of gas for cooking increased twenty-five-fold, leading to an immediate jump in the number of Peruvians living in poverty.

For the popular and middle sectors, the typical bulwarks of populism who had been the real and symbolic beneficiaries of distribution politics, the shock would appear to seriously call into doubt Fujimori's classification as a populist. Nevertheless, by abruptly decreasing inflation by over 7,000 percent, the regime eliminated the out-of-control price increases that had caused the great economic insecurity of the later García years. For many, even a palpable decrease in living standards was an acceptable tradeoff for the day-by-day uncertainty of hyperinflation. La Crisis had truly lowered Peruvians' expectations, and a semblance of stability was a very welcome change.

To bolster his image with the poor, Fujimori cunningly enacted a series of high-visibility programs that targeted some of Peru's most impoverished populations in both rural and urban areas. Whether presiding over the opening of a school in a remote peasant village or handing out small gas stoves to shantytown dwellers on the outskirts of Lima, the president portrayed himself as personally responsive to the plight of the needy while building clientelistic connections in focused areas of Peru.

With these frequent appearances around the country—often dressed in regional garb—and his numerous impromptu public speeches, Fujimori's political style exhibited some important parallels with that of his failed predecessor, Alan García. Like García, Fujimori insisted on taking personal control of all decision making and brooked no questioning of his judgment. To this end, he concentrated government power in the ministry of the presidency, to the exclusion not only of other politicians, but even of his own cabinet appointees. He even nixed attempts by his closest supporters to build a permanent party, instead shutting down immediately after elections the four Fujimorista organizations—Cambio 90, Nueva Mayoría Perú 2000, and Vamos Vecino—that supported his presidential bids. Fujimori was clearly continuing down the exclusivist road trod by other Latin American populists.

The clearest instance of this antipolitical conduct was the *autogolpe*, or self-coup, in April 1992, when he dissolved Congress and the judiciary and ruled with quasi-dictatorial powers. To justify this action, Fujimori railed against nearly all political and civilian institutions. The great hardships of La Crisis had spawned fundamental doubts about existing political institutions, clearly indicated by the fact that a paltry 10 percent of Peruvians expressed any confidence in political parties, congress, and the judiciary. The very value of democratic practices and politics in general was being severely questioned. This attitude underlay statements like, "What has democracy done for us anyway?" and "It doesn't matter who wins, I still have to find a way to eat." Fujimori managed to address the mood of alienation and rejection of "politics as usual" among the electorate. In that context, his aggressive acts and declarations actually boosted the president's popularity among Peruvians disenchanted with the status quo who saw Fujimori as a bulwark against chaos.[20]

During the early years of his first term, the growing presence of the extremist Shining Path guerilla movement further buttressed the public's questioning of democratic norms and spurred the acceptance of authoritarian actions by the state. When four months after the *autogolpe* Shining Path's leader, Abimael Guzmán was captured by elements of the National Counterterrorism Division of the National Police, Fujimori used the occasion to further legitimize his authoritarian course. He reaffirmed the wisdom of suspending the nation's constitutionally defined branches of government, intensified his attack on traditional political institutions and politicians in general, and strengthened the power of his highly secretive Servicio de Inteligencia Nacional (National Intelligence Service—SIN) to which he falsely attributed Guzmán's capture. Subsequently, Fujimori increasingly utilized the growing power of the SIN, under the leadership of his shadowy presidential advisor Vladimiro Montesinos, to undermine any political opposition. The result was a further weakening of the whole of the nation's political institutions, a process earlier fomented by his populist predecessor Alan García. With both Fujimori and García, the failure of the populist leader equated to the failure of the very state itself.

Alberto Fujimori eventually served two full terms and was four months into his third term when in November of 2000 he resigned the presidency via fax from Tokyo, becoming the first chief executive in the history of Latin America to present a faxed resignation. He stepped down amidst plummeting popularity stoked by explosive revelations of government abuse and massive corruption. The most damaging of these was the appearance of the infamous "Vladivideo" that showed presidential advisor Vladimiro Montesinos holding out an increasingly large wad of bills to bribe a congressman-elect in exchange for his political support.

Fujimori remained in Japan in self-imposed exile for five years. Meanwhile, in Peru a growing number of accusations emerged linking him directly to grave human rights abuses during his presidency. Despite his questionable popularity and the serious charges against him, Fujimori flew to Chile in 2005, expressing his desire to run for the presidency once again in the 2006 election. He did end up in Peru in 2006, not as an electoral candidate, but extradited from Chile to stand trial for crimes against humanity. At this writing, he is serving a twenty-five-year prison term, the maximum allowed. In a surprising denouement, Fujimori's daughter Keiko, a member of Congress, ran for president against the revitalized Alan García in 2011. García won and has governed as a moderate in a markedly improved economic climate.

Notes

1. The analysis of the origins and dynamics of Sánchezcerrismo and Aprismo is based on the author's *Populism in Peru: The Emergence of the Masses and the Politics of Social Control* (Madison: University of Wisconsin Press, 1980). An alternative view of the emergence of APRA is Peter Klarén, *Modernization, Dislocation, and Aprismo: The Origins of the Peruvian Aprista Party* (Austin: University of Texas Press, 1973).

2. Benavides and Belaúnde quoted by Stein, *Populism in Peru*, 19.

3. Ibid., 103.

4. *Cancionero popular* (December 1931[?]), 4.

5. Stein, *Populism in Peru*, 105.

6. Ibid., 141.

7. Ibid., 181.

8. Ibid.

9. Interview with the author, January 29, 1971.

10. Stein, *Populism in Peru*, 155.

11. Ibid.

12. Interview with author, January 29, 1971; Stein, *Populism in Peru*, 156.

13. Percy MacLean y Estenós, *Historia de una revolución* (Buenos Aires: Editorial, E.A.P.A.L., 1953), 205–7.

14. For an analysis of populist politics as practiced by Manuel Odría, see David Collier, *Squatters and Oligarchs: Authoritarian Rule and Policy Change in Peru* (Baltimore: Johns Hopkins University Press, 1976). An insightful analysis of Belaúnde's populism was made by French political sociologist Francois Bourricaud in his classic examination of Peruvian politics, *Power and Society in Contemporary Peru* (New York: Praeger Publishers, 1970). For information on the period of Velasco Alvarado, consult Abraham Lowenthal, ed., *The Peruvian Experiment: Continuity and Change under Military Rule* (Princeton: Princeton University Press, 1975). A particularly acute analysis of the military government's mobilization of the urban masses is contained in Henry Dietz, *Poverty and Political Participation under Authoritarian Rule: The Urban Poor in Lima, Peru* (Austin: University of Texas Press, 1979).

15. Fernando Belaúnde Terry, *Pueblo por pueblo* (Ediciones Tawantinsuyo, 1960), 87.

16. Ibid., 15.

17. Raúl Gonzales, "Sucede en el Perú," *QueHacer* (Lima) 24 (1983): 15.

18. Vicki quoted in Steve Stein and Carlos Monge, *La crisis del estado patrimonial en el Perú* (Lima: Instituto de Estudios Peruanos and Coral Gables, FL: University of Florida, 1988), 109.

19. Ibid., 154–55.

20. These tendencies are discussed in "The 1995 Electoral Process in Peru: A Delegation Report of the Latin American Studies Association," Latin American Studies Association/North-South Center, 1995.

6

The Heyday of Radical Populism in Venezuela and Its Reappearance

Steve Ellner

The story of populism in Venezuela centers on one movement and to a certain extent on one man, Rómulo Betancourt, the maximum leader of the party called Acción Democrática (Democratic Action—AD) for many decades. The party's precursor organizations began among exiled students during the dictatorial regime of Juan Vicente Gómez in the 1930s. At first heavily Marxist in orientation, they shifted their public stands after Gómez's death in 1935 and deemphasized ideological formulations. Nevertheless, many of Betancourt's followers expected that when AD eventually came into office, it would reveal the extent of its socialist leanings. Yet by the time it finally did accede to power in 1945 by means of a coup d'etat, AD shared many of the prominent features of other postwar Latin American populist parties.

Following the coup, Betancourt and AD swept into power in the country's first direct, secret, and honest elections ever. These peak years of Venezuelan populism have become known as the Trienio, a heroic period of far-reaching reforms and organizational inroads for workers, peasants, and students. Before they completed their term, however, AD leaders were overthrown by the military in 1948.

Betancourt and his followers returned to power in 1958, and in subsequent years Venezuela enjoyed a long succession of elected governments. AD's principal rival, the Christian Democratic Party or Comité de Organización Política Electoral Independiente (COPEI), managed to win several presidential elections, thus establishing a periodic alternation between the two parties. Political observers generally admired Venezuela as one of the most democratic nations

Figure 6.1. Rómulo Betancourt speaks to radio audiences in 1960 during his second presidency. He suffered burns on his hand during a terrorist attempt on his life. (Courtesy of *El Tiempo de Puerto La Cruz*)

in the region in the 1970s and 1980s. Thus the legacy of populism was generally seen as positive,[1] but more recently it has come under heavy attack.

Some Venezuelan historians have compared AD and its predecessor parties with the Peruvian Alianza Popular Revolucionaria Americana (American Popular Democratic Alliance—APRA) during the heyday of Latin American populism in the 1930s and 1940s.[2] Nevertheless, there is little evidence of direct contact between the two movements during their formative years. The main founders of both parties initiated their political careers in the struggle against repressive dictatorial regimes in the 1920s. Subsequently, AD leaders drifted in a rightist direction, at least on certain issues, as did those of APRA. Both parties entered the government in the immediate postwar years when, in response to the initiation of the Cold War, they drew close to the U.S. camp. Finally, the charismatic leadership of Betancourt and Peru's Haya de la Torre and their frequent utilization of popular symbols have led historians to label both organizations populist.

A second area of contention is the characterization of Rómulo Betancourt as a social democrat prior to the founding of AD in 1941. Social democratic movements emphasize reform programs and fail to link them to socialism and other long-term goals relegated to the distant future. The case for labeling the young Betancourt a social democrat is based on his insistence in the 1930s that fellow leftists embrace a "minimum program" without publicly identifying with more ambitious, far-reaching changes.

Although there are important points of comparison between AD on the one hand, and APRA and social democracy on the other, the unique characteristics of the Venezuelan populists are worthy of special analysis. In order to determine differences and similarities, it is necessary to go beyond a mere discussion of the positions and policies pursued by AD. These stands in themselves were never that far reaching and thus cannot explain the vehemence of the conservative reaction to AD's control of the government during the Trienio (1945–48).

This essay will examine AD's potential for far-reaching change and the unannounced revolutionary strategy adhered to by many party leaders, which had its origins in the early thinking of Betancourt. A second, related topic is AD's internal structure, which was to a certain degree the logical consequence of this strategy. Populism's legacy and its influence in contemporary Venezuelan politics will also be examined, as well as the reemergence of certain basic features of populism led by Hugo Chávez in recent years.

The Origins of Venezuelan Populism

In the 1920s, Betancourt and other AD leaders had little access to radical ideas from abroad but were inspired by the vanguardist movements in art and literature in Venezuela, which were tolerated by the dictatorial regime of Juan Vicente Gómez (1908–35).[3] Betancourt and other members of the "Generation of 1928" participated in student protests in that year against the Gómez government. Their actions set off labor strikes and even a coup attempt by military cadets. The subsequent experience of jail and lengthy exile had a radicalizing influence on them. At first Betancourt and his followers, intent on returning to their native land as soon as possible, backed several invasion schemes led by Gómez's adversaries, whose commitment to democracy was less pronounced. A turning point occurred in 1932, when Betancourt conditioned his support for a group of anti-gomecistas—which included writer José Rafael Pocaterra—on the clear definition of the invasion's political objectives, the arming of a band of combatants led by two of his associates, and the acceptance of the right of his political companions to agitate in Venezuela in favor of their own program.

Betancourt's thoroughgoing identification with the Generation of 1928 led him into conflict with the communist movement, whose Marxist class analysis had no place for such a category which privileged the importance of age. Shortly after going into exile, Betancourt reacted harshly to an editorial in the newspaper of the anti-gomecista Partido Revolucionario Venezolano (Venezuelan Revolutionary Party—PRV), which he had recently joined. The author of the piece, the pro-Communist Salvador de la Plaza, called the Venezuelan student exiles "petty-bourgeois" and predicted that they would abandon revolutionary struggle once they achieved their only political objective: the downfall of the Gómez dictatorship. Betancourt, defending the students who had participated in the 1928 protests as revolutionaries, resigned from the PRV in protest, bitterly recalling the incident for years to come. Subsequently, Betancourt would consciously set aside this generational orientation and instead harp on the need to build a political party. Indeed, his visionary faith in AD, and in the lofty changes it promised to achieve for Venezuela, would supplant generational ties.

Both in his style and political outlook, Betancourt displayed a keen sense of the need to reach people at their own level, rather than imposing advanced concepts which few could grasp. In 1931, Betancourt drew up the Plan de Barranquilla, which called for a civilian-run government with democratic liberties, confiscation of gomecista property, revision of the terms of the contracts signed with foreign oil companies, and convocation of a constitutional assembly. While Betancourt criticized the Communists for failing to put forward short-term objectives, the pro-Communist, future novelist Miguel Otero Silva wrote him calling the Plan de Barranquilla excessively moderate. In his response, Betancourt defended the plan as appropriate for a citizenry that had never demanded more than modest improvements in their living standards. He went on to quote Lenin on the need to "determine in *cold blood* the real state of consciousness and preparation of the entire class and not just its Communist vanguard."[4]

One historian has maintained that Betancourt purposefully refrained from including a "maximum program" of far-reaching goals in the Plan de Barranquila, even though it was the founding document of the Agrupación Revolucionaria de Izquierda (Revolutionary Leftist Group—ARDI), which he led.[5] Indeed, Betancourt urged ARDI members to masquerade as liberal democrats in order to win over the backward masses and warned against publicizing their ultimate objectives of abolition of private property and formation of a soviet-style government.

Only during the years 1932–35, when Betancourt veered to the left, did he accept efforts to link the minimum program to long-term objectives. Betancourt's radicalization was related to several developments. First, he moved left due to the criticism from his followers that he had fallen under the influence of the APRA model of a multiclass party under the hegemony of the middle class, which tended to be less revolutionary than the working class (see chapter 5). Second, Betancourt found international communism more amenable after the Comintern abandoned sectarian policies and began promoting broad-based "popular fronts" in 1935. Finally, during his stay in Costa Rica (1931–35), the only important leftist organization was the Partido Comunista de Costa Rica (Communist Party—PCCR). Betancourt joined it, despite initial differences with its secretary general, who also accused him of being pro-Aprista.

Betancourt's scholarly sympathizers as well as several of his leftist detractors play down his adhesion to international communism as a result of his membership in the PCCR. His supporters emphasize the PCCR's heterodoxy and its independence from Moscow. Leftists point to Betancourt's failure to assimilate Marxist-Leninist aims and strategy.[6] Nevertheless, Betancourt during these years, far from being a social democrat who minimized long-term socioeconomic objectives, was a revolutionary socialist. The 1932–35 period was the only time in which Betancourt did not lash out sharply at the Communists, and, in fact, he left open the possibility of constituting an independent faction within the Partido Comunista de Venezuela (Venezuelan Communist Party—PCV).

Betancourt's views on party formation generated the greatest debate among fellow leftists in the years prior to Gómez's death. In calling for the eventual establishment of a political party, Betancourt jettisoned the discredited and negative image which those organizations had acquired during the nineteenth century in Venezuela, when they were unable to check the disorders and civil wars which only the firm hand of Juan Vicente Gómez succeeded in suppressing. In defining his position on parties, Betancourt rejected two extremes. On the one hand, he opposed working in loose circles lacking in organizing capacity. Such an approach, he wrote to fellow ARDI members, would be too ineffective for "men like us [who are] definitively, biologically propelled to the camp of mass politics."[7] Betancourt's appreciation of party discipline was demonstrated in 1932, when he made it clear to Pocaterra that he could not commit himself to any invasion plan without first consulting fellow ARDI members.

On the other hand, Betancourt's party thinking diverged from orthodox communism. Betancourt, unlike the Communists who founded the PCV in 1931, lacked a fixed dogma and recognized that ARDI's reading of conditions in Venezuela was a mere approximation, adding that "we will not vacillate for one moment in rectifying our program, adding to it, or taking it to a more extreme position, if unforeseen, unpredictable facts invalidate our analysis of Venezuelan society."[8] This more modest and cautious attitude led Betancourt to delay formalization of the party until after returning to Venezuela, when he could observe conditions there firsthand.

Most important, Betancourt, pointing to the minuscule size of the working class, opted for the creation of a multiclass party which would represent workers, peasants, the middle class, and other non-privileged sectors. Nevertheless, Betancourt viewed the working class as playing the lead role in the revolutionary movement, rather than the middle class, as Haya de la Torre envisioned. The defense of the multiclass party model, in the framework of Marxist assumptions regarding the inevitability of class struggle, had major implications which critics within his group were quick to point out. In the first place, Betancourt's closest supporters, including future president Raúl Leoni, feared that a multiclass party would have to make concessions to its middle-class constituents and would thus be less radical than a working-class one.

A second objection to Betancourt's concept of the multiclass party was that it would lack cohesiveness. Each class component would, as Marxism taught, defend its own interests, thus subjecting the party to class conflict within its ranks. Indeed, the Single Front of Classes, which Haya and Betancourt apparently used interchangeably with multiclass party, was admittedly inspired by the Chinese Kuomintang, a loosely structured organization based on solidified factions that subsequently became bitter adversaries. Several leading Venezuelan leftists would write about the disastrous influence that the Kuomintang model had on the nation's left during this period. Betancourt, during his radical years in Costa Rica, recognized that as a result of the Single Front concept "so liberally defined," APRA had also lost its lucidity and had ended up embracing a "muddled and messianic ideology."[9]

As a corrective to party divisiveness and rightist deviation, Betancourt argued for a highly vertical leadership under communist control—"a general staff of intransigent revolutionaries."[10] Subsequently, Betancourt would cease to identify with communism and even Marxism but would retain the notion of a tight-knit party—a logical consequence of the multiclass model which accorded the working class a privileged position. The highly centralized party Betancourt went on to fashion led one Venezuelan historian to call him a Leninist.[11] In any case, the organizational model devised by Betancourt during his leftist period would leave an indelible imprint on the development of populism in Venezuela after 1936.

Two army generals, Eleazar López Contreras (1936–41) and Isaías Medina Angarita (1941–45), ruled Venezuela between the death of Gómez and the creation of a populist democracy in 1945. Both promoted a gradual relaxation of the dictatorship and modest economic reforms. Regime supporters spoke of a "constitutional thread" that would supposedly lead to full-fledged democracy. The PCV, meanwhile, following the Comintern's policies of the popular front and wartime class conciliation, endorsed some of López's actions and then allied itself with the Medina administration.

In 1936 Betancourt united with Communists to form the Partido Demócrata Nacional (National Democratic Party—PDN), which sought to coordinate leftists of various stripes. Betancourt's decision to form the broad-based PDN from already existing organizations was undoubtedly influenced by the communist-promoted "popular front" strategy, which he praised in spite of his differences with international communism. Only in 1938, after two migrations of PDN-istas to the ranks of the PCV, did Betancourt consolidate his control over the PDN, which was left with a small but cohesive and disciplined membership. During the latter part of López's rule, PDN leaders swore adherence to the system of private property as a condition for gaining legal status for the projected AD. Many AD members at all levels of the party, however, assumed that socialism continued to be an unstated goal. This "plan of deception," as one ex-AD leader described it, had originally been formulated by Betancourt during his radical period in Costa Rica. Those who believed that the strategy was still in force lauded Betancourt for his "astuteness" in deceiving the imperialist and oligarchic enemies.[12] In fact, by the early 1940s Betancourt ceased to believe in socialism and, according to one close associate of the time, feared the very word.[13]

This confusion regarding the party's long-term goals is a salient feature of Latin American populist movements. Usually a wide gap existed between the idealistic visions they articulated and the limited structural changes they were prepared to implement. The trajectory of AD leaders, however, contrasted with their populist counterparts elsewhere. Only in Venezuela did leading populists identify with Marxism-Leninism and even communism earlier in their political careers. The ambiguity regarding the party's support for structural changes stemmed from different opinions as to whether these original ideals were still being upheld. In contrast, the top leaders of populist parties in other Latin American nations either never addressed themselves to long-term objectives or offered vague formulas, which (as in the case of Juan Domingo Perón's "Third Position") were subject to varying interpretations.

Like other Latin American populist parties, AD's emergence in 1941 occurred at a time when large numbers of non-privileged Venezuelans were being initiated into political activity, thus creating a legitimacy crisis for the traditional ruling elite. AD embodied the politics of the masses both in its rhetoric, which was designed for popular consumption (as will be discussed below), and the skill with which the party organized mass meetings.[14] Like in other nations, especially Brazil, Peru, and Ecuador, where the leaders came from elite families, AD was led by members of non-privileged classes, specifically the emerging middle sectors, with an important input from representatives of worker and peasant organizations.

The Heyday of Populism in Venezuela

AD leaders conspired with junior army officers to overthrow the Medina administration on October 18, 1945. They claimed their coup was a thorough break with the past, even a second national independence. Rómulo Betancourt became provisional president and implemented many reforms that became part of the Trienio legacy, such as direct universal suffrage and the allocation of 10 percent of the federal budget to the Corporación Venezolana de Fomento (Venezuelan Development Corporation—CVF). Novelist and AD member Rómulo Gallegos became the first popularly elected president of Venezuela, taking office in 1948, shortly prior to the coup that ended the Trienio.

The rural predominance of Venezuela influenced the party's priorities. While the proletarian ideology of the PCV led it to neglect political work in the countryside (an error that party leaders subsequently recognized), AD made a concerted and successful effort to become Venezuela's first truly national party, with headquarters in most towns throughout the country. AD gained control of the urban labor movement at the time it came to power in 1945, but its dominance of the peasant movement was much more absolute and dated from several years before.

AD also became the party of the rural middle class: small merchants *(bodegueros)*, grade school teachers, barbers, and pharmacists. These sectors in turn exercised an important influence over the peasantry as a result of links based on credit (granted informally on the basis of trust) and *compadrazgo* (godparent-godchild relationships). The literacy campaign undertaken during the Trienio was also instrumental in consolidating the party's influence in the countryside. (Similar activity in other Latin American nations during revolutionary periods also mixed educational and political objectives.) During these same years, the Banco Agrícola y Pecuario, which had previously ignored small-scale farming, favored peasants with loans that usually went uncollected.[15] Local government authorities, the Labor Ministry (headed by Leoni), and trade union officials also came to the aid of peasants and in doing so facilitated their partial liberation from the political and economic grip of the hacendados.

The populist coalitions in some Latin American nations took in expansion-minded business sectors, sometimes referred to as the "progressive national bourgeoisie." These businessmen supported (and benefited from) high tariffs and other policies associated with the import substitution strategy which populist governments pursued. In the case of Venezuela, the position of business interests toward AD was complicated by uncertainty surrounding AD's long-term objectives. During the PDN's early years, party members questioned Betancourt's faith in the role of the national bourgeoisie and drafted a resolution denying the PDN's intention of "drawing to its ranks the progressive bourgeoisie as such."[16]

During the Trienio the cabinet positions in charge of the formulation of economic policy were mainly held by party members who lacked formal links to financial groups, unlike the case of AD governments since 1958.[17] Although AD accepted the right of wealthy Venezuelans to join the party on an individual basis, it denied that the progressive wing of the bourgeoisie was explicitly represented in the organization, as were non-privileged sectors. Some AD leaders to this day claim that their party's policy has always been to bar business representatives from the organization's leadership (a practice not completely adhered to in recent years).[18]

Trienio businessmen criticized the AD government for promoting hefty wage increases that only foreign capital could afford to pay. On the other hand, the main business organization, Fedecámaras, praised Betancourt's policies of labor peace and public sector investment in economic development. In the final months of the Trienio, however, Fedecámaras held to an established business tradition of aloofness from political infighting by rejecting Betancourt's request that it issue a statement of support for the democratic regime in the face of the impending military coup.[19]

Betancourt and other party leaders demonstrated great respect for the political rights of women in AD. As far back as the early 1930s Betancourt highlighted the role of women in the struggle against the Gómez dictatorship and hailed their emancipation from traditional gender roles. At the same time, however, he warned against the danger that the political independence of women's organizations would condemn their members to isolation, as had allegedly occurred in Peru and elsewhere. The issue of separatism was debated in the following decade as well. During the Medina administration, AD militants argued against the thesis that until women were granted equal electoral rights (which they later received under the Trienio), they should eschew all party membership. Nevertheless, rhetoric notwithstanding, AD women failed to achieve much importance within the organization, and party leadership remained almost totally male.[20]

Conservative sectors feared AD, not so much because the policies it pursued during the Trienio were detrimental to their interests, but because of its status as a mass-based party and its commitment to a multiplicity of reforms without any fixed date for implementation. Uncertainty reigned as to whether various programs that AD leaders never officially supported, and others they refrained from pushing, would be placed on the party's agenda in the not-too-distant future. The oil companies, for instance, feared that the decision of the government to sell oil royalties on the international market would lead it to enter the business as a permanent competitor, even though this option was not under consideration at the time.[21] Also, AD's oil-worker leaders backed down on the demand to forbid layoffs (an arrangement known as "absolute job security") in the 1946 and 1948 contracts, but it was unclear whether they would insist on this far-reaching proposal in future collective bargaining.

Conservatives were particularly concerned about the pressure exerted on the Trienio government and AD's leadership by the party's rank and file. AD trade unionists, for instance, conducted organizing drives with the active encouragement of the Labor Ministry and were nominated for positions within the party and in Congress, thus enhancing labor's standing as a junior partner in the populist coalition. Most important, it was unclear whether Betancourt and other pragmatic leaders would be able to sidetrack AD's ambitious promises and mass base and contain the prevailing reformist impulse, in response to economic contraction in 1948 after an initial period of postwar prosperity. Businessmen and other conservative sectors were also disillusioned with President Gallegos, who they initially believed would—given his nonpolitical background—distance his government from the party, but who instead ended up naming AD members to almost all cabinet posts.[22]

The modernization project that AD pursued during the Trienio centralized power in Caracas and reduced the authority of various institutions and interest groups. AD leaders viewed such a process as necessary to eradicate vestiges of backwardness and prevent a recurrence of the anarchy that had prevailed in the nineteenth century. The assertion of state power, however, was resisted by diverse sectors which feared encroachment on their decision-making preserves.

The government's promotion of secular education, for instance, alarmed the church, which mobilized its followers against legal measures considered discriminatory against private schools. Similarly, all sectors of the student movement, with the exception of AD, raised the banner of university autonomy in opposition to the government's decision to appoint the authorities of state-financed universities, rather than accepting their election by professors and students. AD insisted that the principles of autonomy and classroom liberty did not rule out the right of the state to intervene in university life in order to guarantee free tuition and provide a patriotic educational orientation. At the same time, AD student leaders attempted to tie the universities to the defense of worker interests and struggles on the streets. Critics, however, feared that these endeavors were a cover for state and party domination of the university system.

Military officers were also wary that an all-powerful government would exercise control over their institution and limit its policy-making capacity. Those who participated in the October 1945 coup, for instance, resented AD's failure to honor its original agreement of providing officers equal representation with AD in the Trienio's first cabinet.[23] The AD's modernizing vision, which implied a shake-up of the armed forces, was expressed by one top party leader in an unpublished manuscript: "The task we have before us is to democratize the army, transform it, extirpate ambitious [officers] . . . , penetrate it with young forces coming from the People, devoid of economic interests, with democratic convictions, liquidating once and for all regional prejudices [and] chauvinism."[24]

AD's support for centralization was demonstrated by its opposition to the direct election of governors and the resident requirements for them proposed by the other parties in the constituent assembly in 1947. AD had previously backed gubernatorial elections, but now argued that the preservation of Venezuela's fledgling democracy required for the time being that the national executive be invested with greater power, including the appointment of governors. AD spokesmen pointed out that in any case governors would be subject to the constraints imposed by the democratically elected state legislatures. President Betancourt actually went further than his party by calling for presidential nomination of governors as an indefinite rather than provisional arrangement and reduction of the authority of the state legislatures to mere administrative functions.

Despite its broad appeal, AD suffered a major limitation when it came to relations with other parties. The political attitudes of Betancourt and his close associates were shaped by the Generation of 1928's absolute condemnation of Juan Vicente Gómez and all those who collaborated with him. AD's principal leaders, ever since their initiation as members of the Generation of 1928, were secure in their faith in their ability to shape Venezuela's future and effect a thorough rupture with the past, without having to rely on the help of those who at one point had a stake in the old order. They could thus not bring themselves to work with politicians who had been allied with Gómez's successors, López and Medina. Since leading members of nearly every other political group had at some time worked with the constituted authorities during the 1930s and 1940s, AD left itself with virtually no allies.

During the 1940s, AD leaders argued that their party was destined to guide the revolutionary process single-handedly. They pointed out that AD drew to its fold the various classes that supported the anti-imperialist, national revolution; was truly national in scope; and instilled in its members a sense of discipline and adherence to the party's nationalistic doctrine. In contrast, rival parties appealed to narrower constituencies. The PCV was a working-class party, COPEI's influence was concentrated in the nation's conservative Andean states, and the Partido Democrático Venezolano (Venezuelan Democratic Party—PDV, pro-Medina) represented mostly government bureaucrats. Furthermore, COPEI and the Communists adhered to foreign models, while the Unión Republicana Democrática (Democratic Republican Union—URD), founded in 1945 by Medina's followers, lacked the doctrinal clarity which allegedly characterized AD. At the outset of the Trienio, Betancourt rejected the proposal of URD's future standard-bearer, Jóvito Villalba, for the formation of a broad-based government of national integration which would take in other parties. AD leaders countered that none of them had a significant following, a claim borne out in the three elections held during the period.[25]

AD's intolerance toward other parties manifested itself in concrete ways. Most important, AD brigades broke up meetings organized by URD and COPEI in the nation's interior, sometimes using rocks and guns. Both parties accused the government and AD's national leadership of being "passive accomplices" in these actions.[26]

Populist Style and Culture

All movements that stand for far-reaching change are challenged to defend their utopian visions, which invariably clash with the values and customs of the majority of the population. Yet they must also temper the radical content of their message in order to reach people at their own level and celebrate popular culture. AD was caught in this predicament during the heyday of populism and in the years following. AD leaders were committed to a thorough reorganization of society, but they utilized language which did not necessarily reinforce these idealistic designs. In the long run, AD abandoned its long-term goals but retained its popular style, which paid dividends, particularly at the polls.

During his early years, Betancourt criticized Communists both for their dogmatic theories and their convoluted verbal style. He once counseled a colleague to avoid "terminology that is familiar to the proletariat of the cosmopolitan West but beyond the reach of our peons and even many intellectuals who sympathize with socialism."[27] Betancourt demonstrated this desire to lower communication barriers when he wrote a leaflet in simple English, with the help of a dictionary, for distribution among striking Jamaican banana workers in Costa Rica. In his articles in *Trabajo,* the official organ of the Costa Rican Communist Party, Betancourt facilitated comprehension by placing between commas the definition of words he used which were basic to Marxist vernacular.

The utilization of readily identifiable symbols was the trademark of AD's style. AD adopted the folk character Juan Bimba, regarded as the quintessence of the humble Venezuelan male, and portrayed him as the typical party member. AD's Juan Bimba was dressed in tattered clothes, kept a piece of bread in his pocket, and wore sandals (*cholas*). Significantly, Juan Bimba was not a factory worker, but rather came from a non-urban area, which in the 1940s was where a majority of the population lived. AD called itself the "party of the *choludos*" (those who wear sandals), a word which conjured up an image as evocative as the Peronist term *descamisados*. Like its Argentine counterpart, *choludo* originally had derogatory connotations, but soon it became a source of pride to AD members.

AD's most prestigious leaders—novelist Rómulo Gallegos, poet Andrés Eloy Blanco (the party's first vice president), and politician Betancourt—committed themselves to projecting AD's image as a "party of the people." Gallegos's novels, whose protagonists were often country folk, reinforced this message. Blanco's poems were among the most popular in Venezuela, and perhaps the most frequently cited in informal gatherings (known as *veladas*) at people's homes. Blanco's speeches, which contained heavy doses of humor, were considered veritable "shows" that entertained the public and broke down class, party, and intellectual barriers.

Betancourt was famous for his concoction of humorous phrases and use of obsolete words. This penchant for colorful imagery, which Betancourt developed in the town of his birth, Guatire,[28] also provoked laughter among people of all backgrounds and increased their receptivity to his ideas. Prior to the 1948 coup, Betancourt's speeches were extremely aggressive, and his frequent attacks against the oligarchy and individual adversaries pleased crowds looking for verbal fireworks.

AD's oratorical style revolutionized political discourse in Venezuela. Particularly significant was the broadcast of constituent assembly speeches on public radio throughout the nation in 1946–47. Indeed, radio kicked off a new era, when politicians modified their style in order to gear it to popular expectations and tastes.

In contrast, COPEI and other rivals continued to employ traditional gentlemanly oration until the late 1950s. They used epithets like "mediocre," "vengeful," and "spendthrift" to denigrate AD's populist style. One critic compared AD leaders Valmore Rodríguez, Luis Lander, Alberto López Gallegos, Andrés Eloy Blanco, and Luis Beltrán Prieto Figueroa with five leading medinistas. The unaccomplished Rodríguez was alleged to be in a different league from the renowned novelist Arturo Uslar Pietri, who had been secretary general of the presidency under Medina. Lander's "hysteria" and "recognized professional failure" were compared to the "technical proficiency" of his medinista counterpart. López Gallegos was referred to as a "former cashier" of a Venezuelan lending institution. Blanco was called an alcoholic, and the lanky Prieto Figueroa was described as possessing a "sinister body."[29] In other writings these negative images were complemented by accounts of AD middle-level leaders who threatened to unleash street violence and incite "collective vengeance" against their party's opponents.[30]

Certain positions of AD leaders on sensitive issues held the party back from exploiting its popular appeal to the fullest. Betancourt and others in the party were closely tied intellectually, politically, and personally to several outstanding Venezuelan intellectuals who upheld positivist assumptions that in many ways represented the antithesis of populism. The two most important were Mariano Picón-Salas and Alberto Adriani, both top leaders of the Organización Venezolana (Venezuelan Organization—ORVE) during its moderate period in early 1936. Betancourt's correspondence with Picón-Salas during their exile under Gómez evidenced great mutual respect and trust. Betancourt had a similar relationship with Adriani and briefly served as his personal secretary in 1936, prior to his unexpected death. On the tenth anniversary of that occasion, a leading AD member called Adriani "the most visible precursor of the October [1945] Revolution."[31]

Both Adriani and (less insistently) Picón-Salas favored mass immigration from Europe in order to whiten Venezuela's racial stock and contribute to its cultural development. Some AD leaders (such as Andrés Eloy Blanco), while rejecting the more overt racist implications of the writings of Adriani and Picón-Salas, viewed miscegenation as a desirable formula. The influence of positivism on AD was also evident in its criticism of López and Medina for failing to encourage sufficiently immigration and the government's vigorous promotion of it during the Trienio.

AD also failed to address important issues related to Venezuela's black population. Party leaders denied the existence of racism among Venezuelans and blamed discrimination on sectors of the elite that were tied to U.S. interests. Moreover, AD stopped short of attempting to heighten national pride by recognizing the black component of the nation's heritage. A more culturally rooted movement would have not only adamantly opposed racist behavior and exalted the nation's mixed racial strain, as indeed Betancourt and other AD leaders did, but would have lauded the historical role and input of blacks. Some scholars (such as Communist anthropologist Miguel Acosta Saignes) by the 1940s began to document this positive African contribution. AD perhaps overlooked these concerns due to its electoral emphasis and the relatively few votes that the Venezuelan black population represented. In addition, AD's limited ethnic and racial consciousness can be explained by the absence of the tensions and contrasts these cleavages produced in other nations with important populist movements, such as Argentina and Peru.[32]

AD's interpretation of Venezuelan history may have also lessened the impact and effectiveness of the party's popular appeal.[33] AD leaders found virtually no figure in the past to identify with, apart from Simón Bolívar, whom they naturally glorified, and a handful of unsuccessful civilian leaders, such as José María Vargas (who was twice forced out of the presidency in the 1830s). As diehard anti-gomecistas, they portrayed nineteenth-century caudillos and their modern dictatorial heirs (including Cipriano Castro, in spite of his confrontations with foreign powers) as backward and malevolent, a corrupt continuum that had to be broken by the Revolution of 1945. To those who pointed to the achievements and positive qualities of various nineteenth-century caudillos of humble extraction, Betancourt retorted that they merely served as props of the feudal system.

The Distinctive Characteristics of Venezuelan Populism

AD has often been likened to Peru's APRA, the party founded in the 1920s by Víctor Raúl Haya de la Torre (see chapter 5). Often described as "sister parties," they were both reformist and anti-Communist. Moreover, Betancourt and Haya had shared many similar experiences and later became personal friends. Nevertheless, Betancourt himself said that his early formation was not shaped by Haya, whom he met for the first time in 1947. The following areas underline the differences between AD and its Latin American populist counterparts such as APRA in the heyday of populism.

Style

AD's style was less manipulative than that of APRA and made fewer concessions to the irrational beliefs of common people. While AD leaders employed colloquialisms and drew on folk symbols such as Juan Bimba to evoke the party's popular concerns, they did not stress millenarian themes the way Haya did.

Cold War Alignment

AD was more independent from the United States at the outset of the Cold War than APRA. AD refused to outlaw the Communist Party or to purge Communists from the labor movement, as other postwar governments did. In addition, AD union leaders identified more with the industrially organized Congress of Industrial Organizations than with the conservative and craft-based American Federation of Labor (AFL), which was attempting to divide the hemispheric workers' movement along Cold War lines. AD labor leaders made efforts to maintain unity at the continental level and refused to join an AFL-promoted splinter organization, which the Apristas were instrumental in creating in 1948. Finally, the Trienio government followed a policy of severing diplomatic relations with recently installed dictatorial regimes, which were the firmest stalwarts of anti-Communism in the hemisphere.

Class Makeup

Since his early Marxist days, Betancourt viewed workers as a vanguard within the party, unlike Haya, who assigned greater revolutionary qualities to the middle class. Many AD trade unionists were convinced that they would assume an increasingly influential role in the nation and the party, leading to its eventual transformation into a labor party. AD peasant leaders also believed that they occupied a special, advanced position in the party and that the struggle for agrarian reform was decisive to the outcome of the revolutionary process. AD thus contrasted with other populist movements that played down rural struggles. AD's mass base also set the party apart from personalistic populist movements, whose leaders were not beholden directly to the rank and file.

Party Alliances and Institutional Relations

While APRA succeeded in entering the government as a result of an alliance with political moderates in 1945, AD refused to draw close to other parties during most of the Trienio. AD's rank and file was particularly adverse to COPEI, which it considered the party of reaction. This partisan aloofness proved fatal in that it contributed to the November 1948 coup. Still, in comparison with APRA and most other populist parties, AD remained firmer in its commitment to a reform program and less willing to make compromises to accommodate other political movements for the sake of short-term political gains.

These four areas of comparison show that AD stood to the left of most Latin American populist parties in the 1940s. They also point to the greater influence of the rank and file in formulating the party's program. This, in turn, may account for the zeal and optimism displayed by AD members. Jorge Gaitán, Colombia's renowned populist leader, remarked on the AD's outstanding esprit de corps during the Trienio. In contrast, he described APRA when it formed part of the Peruvian government during the same period as "burnt out and lacking vitality."[34]

The Populist Legacy after 1958

The trauma of the November 1948 coup left an indelible impression on Betancourt and other AD leaders and influenced their behavior after the restoration of democracy in 1958. Betancourt's presidential campaign of that year focused on convincing conservatives that AD had abandoned its radical populist style in favor of a moderate, cautious approach. Conservatives applauded Betancourt for avoiding heavily charged rhetoric against foreign interests and the oligarchy and, in general, for being more low-keyed than his two opponents.

Wealthy Venezuelans had worried that Betancourt's appetite for power might again threaten the traditional classes and even undermine the entire socioeconomic order. To counter that impression, Betancourt ignored calls of *púllalo* (jump on them), which crowds had frequently shouted out to him during the Trienio to encourage him to attack powerful groups. Instead he typically said, "I have not come here to assail anyone." Betancourt publicly denied that his main opponent, Adm. Wolfgang Larrazábal, former president of the Junta Militar, was making plans to rig the upcoming elections,[35] a position that contrasted with AD's accusations against the government of Medina Angarita in 1945. Perhaps what most calmed the fears of AD's adversaries was Betancourt's appearance of being a reluctant aspirant for the presidency and his alleged preference, which was undoubtedly feigned, for a supra-party candidate acceptable to AD, COPEI, and URD.

During his 1959–64 term, Betancourt managed to distance himself from AD hard-liners more successfully than during the Trienio, when he had occasionally clashed with them over his efforts to appease powerful interest groups. In the early 1960s his government consulted fully with Fedecámaras, the armed forces, and the church on issues directly affecting them. In addition, he urged party leaders to build bridges to political rivals and even to invite them to take positions in the AD administration. Betancourt was particularly adamant about maintaining cordial relations with COPEI leaders, whom he lauded for their honesty and loyalty to his coalition government. This attitude produced some tension in AD—contributing to divisions in 1960, 1962, and 1967—as a result of the traditional anti-COPEI sentiment among the membership.

The internal conflicts and differences that had surfaced in AD's early years underlay the strains that beset the party after 1958.[36] The Machiavellian strategy of concealing ambitious, long-term goals in order to buy time split the party roughly in three after 1958. A left wing, inspired by the restoration of democracy and the triumph of the Cuban revolution, believed that the time was ripe for the party to fight for radical socioeconomic change. In 1960 these militants broke off from AD and formed the Movimiento de la Izquierda Revolucionaria (Movement of the Revolutionary Left—MIR).

A second current, led by the party's secretary general, Jesús Paz Galarraga, held that pressing economic difficulties and the fragility of the nation's democracy obliged AD to defer implementation of its hidden radical agenda. These party leaders agreed with the positions defended by a left-leaning faction within AD known as the ARS, but criticized the poor timing of its break-off from the party in 1962. Nevertheless, when economic and political stability set in by the mid-1960s, Paz's group questioned the need for continued restraint and in 1967 also split off to form the pro-socialist Movimiento Electoral del Pueblo (People's Electoral Movement—MEP). The third current, which remained loyal to Betancourt and included future presidents Raúl Leoni (1964–69) and Carlos Andrés Pérez (1974–79; 1989–93), abandoned AD's original long-term socio-economic objectives in order to take up mainstream positions in Venezuelan politics.

Another legacy of the pre-1948 years that produced tension in AD in the modern period was the party's centralistic structure. Betancourt considered the creation of AD, and his retention of control of it in the face of internal dissension, as the most important accomplishment of his political career. In 1960, 1962, and 1967 he preferred to let the party divide, even at the risk of suffering electoral defeat, rather than allow his own power in it to dissipate. This internal rigidity contrasted with his flexibility toward non-leftist parties and his willingness to compromise with them after 1958.

The most powerful reason for Betancourt to adopt a centralizing strategy in Venezuela after 1958 was to avoid political disorder. Following the restoration of democracy and the subsidence of insurgent threats to the democratic regime in the 1960s, support in the party for mechanisms of rank-and-file participation began to manifest itself. The party machine, imbued with AD's original mentality of vertical control as a corrective to class friction within the party, resisted pressure from below and vetoed measures in favor of internal democratization.

The movement for democratic renovation in Venezuela also involves the decentralization of state authority. On this front as well, AD was initially left far behind. President Jaime Lusinchi (1984–89) of AD at first opposed gubernatorial elections on grounds that such a system would facilitate the resurgence of regional caudillos in the form of governors and thus represented a throwback to the nineteenth century. Lusinchi was merely reflecting his party's traditional distrust of regional centers of power. Betancourt and other AD leaders in the 1940s, like their populist counterparts elsewhere in Latin America, had been in favor of a strong central government capable of promoting economic development and national integration. This position had influenced Betancourt to oppose the direct election of governors and the delegation of authority to the state legislatures. Forty years later, however, the proposed transfer of power to the state level, far from being nationally divisive and retrograde, was a progressive banner that had nearly the entire nation behind it. Lusinchi subsequently backed down, and in 1989 Venezuela held its first gubernatorial elections in the century.

After 1958, AD maintained a centrist position on the political spectrum, with the exception of a short period following the election of the charismatic Carlos Andrés Pérez as president in 1973, when radical populism seemed to be making a comeback. Pérez, taking advantage of OPEC price hikes, decreed popular measures such as wage increases, employment opportunities, and severance pay regardless of the cause of layoffs; nationalized foreign iron and oil interests; and pursued a nationalistic pro–Third World foreign policy. In addition, Pérez went outside the party by naming independents to key positions in his government. By the latter part of his term, Pérez, facing hardened opposition from business sectors and even the conservative Betancourt wing of his own party, lost his nerve and steered the government on a more moderate course. During his administration, Pérez received minimum backing internally from AD's labor bureau, which was closely allied to the Betancouristas, in sharp contrast to the situation prevailing in the 1940s, when AD labor pressured party leaders to take up radical positions.

The adoption of neoliberal economic policies during Pérez's second administration (1989–93) confirmed the weakening of the radical populist tradition in Venezuela formerly associated with AD. As a result of Pérez's political transformation, his personal appeal was no longer underpinned by the values of economic nationalism and social justice associated with Venezuelan populism. Pérez's destitution in 1993 demonstrated the difficulties of combining a populist style with an ideological orientation that emphasized distinct goals.

Historically, populism was closely associated with import substitution industrialization (ISI). Not only did ISI lend itself to reforms that increased the purchasing power of the popular classes (and thus the internal market for traditional commodities), but it bolstered nationalist sentiment, which the populist parties identified with and which their charismatic leaders adroitly exploited. In contrast, neoliberalism in Venezuela, in spite of the expectations it created due to its promises of economic growth and democratic participation, proved incapable of generating the type of enthusiasm that is the mainstay of popular movements. Far from being an innovative model, neoliberal economics was a throwback to the pre–import substitution stage, which populist governments ended. The appeal of neoliberalism was confined to certain privileged sectors of the population, which received an immediate boost from such policies.

For those who defended neoliberalism in Venezuela, populism became a pejorative term synonymous with opportunism and demagoguery. For example, political scientist Aníbal Romero, in *La miseria del populismo,* succinctly defined Venezuelan populism as a "government that knows how to distribute wealth but not create it." Romero accused populists who ran the government after 1958 of squandering the nation's oil income by siphoning it into the public sector without any concern for the nation's long-term development. The import substitution policies favored by populists were equally ill-advised. Contrary to Betancourt's stated intentions, high tariffs threatened to erect a Chinese wall around Venezuela in the name of an "incipient and costly 'national industry.'" Import duties were raised in order to guarantee high levels of employment and profits to local investors, not to promote development. Romero's simplistic identification of populism with state capitalism led him to characterize as populist not only post-1958 AD governments but COPEI ones as well. According to him, just when the populist strategy had apparently exhausted itself, the windfall in oil revenue after 1973 provided the government with the cash to revive it.[37]

Those who sharply attacked populism during the oil-boom period of the 1970s and its immediate aftermath in the 1980s pointed to a crass lifestyle associated with certain AD leaders, which clashed with proper standards of conduct and values. AD critics attributed this behavior to the dubious belief that it paid dividends at the polls. The celebration of mediocrity was reflected in the main campaign slogan of Jaime Lusinchi in the presidential race of 1983: "Jaime is like you." In any case, the economic crisis beginning in the early 1980s reduced the level of general tolerance toward unethical behavior, a change of attitude clearly indicated by the impeachment of President Carlos Andrés Pérez in 1993 on charges of corruption.

The Populist Features of the Chávez Phenomenon

Prospects for a resurgence of radical populism in the 1990s came from an unexpected quarter. On February 4, 1992, a group of middle-ranking military officers attempted to overthrow Pérez, promising to restore patriotism and defend the interests of common Venezuelans. The rebel leader, Lt. Col. Hugo Chávez, emerged as a national hero whose charisma was built on his bold decision to stage the coup attempt against great odds. The group called itself the Simón Bolívar Revolutionary Movement and invoked military symbols and historical figures, singling out three in particular: Bolívar, Simón Rodríguez (Bolívar's mentor and teacher), and Ezequiel Zamora (a nineteenth-century general who had favored distribution of land to soldiers). Chávez's makeshift party for the 1998 national elections was named The Fifth Republic in reference to the three republics founded by Bolívar and the fourth, which emerged following independence. The Fifth Republic party committed itself to the achievement of the national ideals of Venezuela's founding fathers. Chávez ran for president and, unlike his electoral rivals, sharply criticized massive privatization at the same time he raised the banner of the struggle against corruption, even in the armed forces. He won with 56 percent of the vote in December 1998.

The experience of the Hugo Chávez presidency approximates many of the basic characteristics of classical populism, of the 1945–1948 Trienio of AD rule in particular. Most important, the Chávez government and movement exemplifies the inherently conflicted and transitory nature of Latin American populism. Both during the Trienio and since 1999, powerful actors who represented the status quo assumed intransigent positions toward the government, more due to their fear of steady radicalization than their rejection of its announced program of change. Furthermore, in both cases members of the governing party at all levels were convinced that their movement had a hidden agenda in favor of far-reaching transformation. This conviction contributed to the ambiguity over goals that has always been a salient feature of Latin American populism. Chávez's anti-elite discourse, his interventionist economic policies, the sense of empowerment among non-privileged sectors generated by government actions, and the polarization that set in also recall the populist movements in and out of power in the 1930s and 1940s.[38] Finally, Chávez's charismatic leadership has undermined the principle of checks and balances and thereby holds back organizational and institutional development, as Latin American populist leaders have been notorious for doing in the past.

Uncertainty regarding the long-term direction of the Chavista movement has characterized it since its founding in 1982, including at the time of the abortive coup it staged ten years later. When Chávez launched his successful candidacy for the presidential elections of 1998 with an anti-party discourse from a leftist perspective, he even received a degree of support from sectors far away from him on the political spectrum, such as the powerful Cisneros Group and some of the media. The influential newspaper *El Nacional*, which throughout the 1990s had questioned the predominant role of the pro-establishment political parties in Venezuelan politics and society in accordance with pro-neoliberal thinking, provided Chávez with sympathetic coverage.

Both before and after the 1998 elections, Chávez contributed to the lack of definition by vacillating on important issues. During the campaign, for example, he proposed a negotiated agreement on the foreign debt, a position that contrasted with his previous nationalistic rhetoric and that calmed fears regarding a unilateral moratorium. In another gesture designed to dispel concerns about his radical intentions, Chávez unsuccessfully requested a visa from the U.S. government to travel to New York and Washington to explain his economic program to the nation's business and political communities. During his first two years in power after 1998, Chávez concentrated his efforts on institutional political reform embodied in the constitution ratified in 1999 rather than his program of radical socioeconomic change. Chávez also sent mixed signals when he promised the Inter American Press Association to broach the subject of persecution of journalists with Fidel Castro, and at one point he indicated his willingness to consider a U.S. request for permission to fly anti-drug interdiction missions on the Colombian border.[39] These positions resembled the stances of other left-wing populists who, in spite of their confrontations with representatives of the status quo and foreign interests, discarded "left" and "right" labels in order to appeal to broad sectors of the population (as illustrated by Perón's "Third Way").[40]

Chávez embarked on a radicalization course in 2001, signaled by the agrarian reform (Ley de Tierras) and measures reversing the privatization of the oil industry (Ley Orgánica de Hidrocarburos), both promulgated in November of that year. The Chavista movement emerged victorious from three subsequent battles: the coup of April 11, 2002, the general strike promoted by the business organization Fedecámaras in December 2002–January 2003, and the presidential recall election held in August 2004. In the following years, the Chavistas won elections for the National Assembly (2005), Chávez's reelection (2006), gubernatorial-mayoral and state legislature elections (2008), and a proposed constitutional amendment in a national referendum (2009). The Chavistas suffered their first electoral defeat by a slim margin in a referendum on a proposed constitutional reform in 2008.

The institutional and organizational underdevelopment of the Chavista government and movement also resembles populist experiences elsewhere in Latin America. Several factors contribute to this deficiency, as well as the relative inefficiency that characterizes much of the Chavista administration. In the first place, Chavistas in power viewed established structures such as public schools at all levels, the health system, and municipal government as unresponsive to the needs of the popular classes. Rather than abolishing these spheres of activity and facing the risk of hardened resistance from state employees, the Chavistas created parallel structures. The new structures were largely makeshift and lacking in sufficient controls, while the old structures often worked at crosspurposes with the government. In the second place, the support of professional employees for their supervisors who spearheaded the 2002–2003 general strike encouraged the Chavistas to place a premium on loyalty to the revolutionary cause at the expense of competence and experience. Finally, the Chavistas associated the system of checks and balances with the liberal democracy of the old regime that had allegedly worked in favor of the elite. This mentality led the Chavista leaders to overlook the need to guarantee the relative autonomy of the pro-Chávez Partido Socialista Unido de Venezuela (United Socialist Party of Venezuela—PSUV) to serve as a check on the performance of the government. Indeed, the power wielded by ministers, governors, and mayors within the PSUV threatened to convert it into an appendage of the state.

Populist governments are hardly static and often take steps to fill ideological, institutional, and organizational gaps. In the course of their eleven years in power, the Chavistas made advances on the ideological front and in the formulation of goals. In the early part of Chávez's rule, the Chavista movement confronted powerful economic groups but failed to provide a blueprint for structural change that would have limited their power. In January 2005, however, Chávez contributed to ideological clarification by embracing socialism, even while he recognized that the proposed transformation was sketchy and would only be defined through experience.

The emergence of the outlines of a new model based on a mixed economy and limitations on the role of the private sector also represented guideposts for the direction of the Chavista government. The numerous expropriations decreed by the government beginning in 2007 were another important ingredient. The government took control of strategic industries, including oil, steel, telecommunications, and electricity, while state companies competed with oligopolistic private ones in the production and distribution of basic food staples.

On the organizational front, the founding of the PSUV was designed to correct the organizational weakness of the Movimiento Quinta República (Fifth Republic Movement—MVR), which was created to run Chávez's presidential candidacy in the elections of 1998 but remained electorally oriented and lacking in formal links to the movement's rank and file. Even after 2007, however, Chávez's supreme power was undisputed. This arrangement discouraged organizational and institutional complexity as well as the much needed system of checks and balances. Nevertheless, the holding of electoral primaries in 2008, 2009, and 2010 to choose candidates and members of party delegations, and the formation of party cells (referred to as "battalions" and "patrols") to discuss policy issues, promised to diffuse decision making and enhance the party's organizational strength.

Certain basic features shared by Chavismo and AD during its early years are hallmarks of classical Latin American populism, while some of their differences are also important for what they reveal about the impact of the populist phenomenon in two different historical periods. First, both movements promoted the incorporation of previously marginalized sectors, but whereas AD drew in the working class that was in the process of unionization, the Chavista social base of support from the outset was unorganized sectors grouped in smaller economic units in the formal and informal economies. Second, AD's multiclass discourse in favor of national harmony was in line with the tendency of populists to attempt to avoid class confrontation. In contrast, the Chavista rhetoric and policies in the absence of government concessions and compromises galvanized class conflict, including middle-class resistance to certain government measures.

Finally, Chávez's personal style of rule held back organizational and institutional development, as was the case with populist leaders from Perón and Haya de la Torre to Fujimori. In contrast, Betancourt played less of an all-encompassing role in his movement and government.[41] Indeed, Betancourt declined to run for president in 1947 (as he also did in 1973). Nevertheless, Betancourt engineered the 1945 coup without even informing most of his party's leadership. In addition, as provisional president, he bypassed existing institutions by establishing the makeshift Tribunal of Civil and Administrative Responsibility to judge former government officials accused of corruption.

In spite of the contrasts between the two governments, the Chavistas in power promoted such slogans, goals, and strategies as social incorporation, state control of strategic industry, and economic nationalism that were also associated with the classical period of populism in Venezuela. These overlaps demonstrate the continued relevance in the age of globalization of the basic conflicts and challenges that gave rise to populism in Venezuela over half a century ago.

Notes

1. Ruth Berins Collier and David Collier, *Shaping the Political Arena* (Princeton, NJ: Princeton University Press, 1991), 571–73.

2. Jesús Sanoja Hernández, prologue in Arturo Sosa A. and Eloi Lengrand, *Del garibaldismo estudiantil a la izquierda criolla: Los orígenes marxistas del proyecto de A.D. (1928–1935)* (Caracas: Ediciones Centauro, 1981), xiv–xv.

3. Elizabeth Tinoco, *Comedia y tragedia del poder (Manual práctica de Castro a Pérez)* (Caracas: Editorial Panapo, 1994), 38–39; Yolanda Segnini, *Las luces del gomecismo* (Caracas: Alfadil, 1987).

4. Betancourt, July 3, 1931, letter from San José, Costa Rica, published in *Libro Rojo del General López Contreras: Documentos robados por espías de la policía política* (Caracas: Catalá Centauro Editores, 1975), 284–85; Manuel Caballero, *Rómulo Betancourt*, 2d ed. (Caracas: Ediciones Centauro, 1979).

5. Ramón J. Velásquez, "Proyección histórica de la obra de Rómulo Betancourt," in *Betancourt: En la historia de Venezuela del siglo XX* (Caracas: Ediciones Centauro, 1980), 22.

6. Robert J. Alexander, *Rómulo Betancourt and the Transformation of Venezuela* (New Brunswick, NJ: Transaction Books, 1982), 67–78; Alejandro Gómez, *Rómulo Betancourt y el Partido Comunista de Costa Rica: 1931–1935* (Caracas: Universidad Central de Venezuela, 1985), 185–86.

7. Betancourt, June 4, 1932, letter from San José, Costa Rica, published in *El pensamiento político venezolano del siglo 20* (Caracas: Congreso de la República, 1983), 13:195.

8. Betancourt, July 3, 1931, letter from San José, Costa Rica, published in *Libro Rojo*, 284–85.

9. Betancourt, as quoted by Suárez Figueroa in "Los escritos anónimos de Rómulo Betancourt en 'TRABAJO,' vocero del Partido Comunista de Costa Rica (1931–1935)," *Nueva Política* 47 (1991): 218.

10. Betancourt, August 15, 1932, letter from San José, Costa Rica, published in *Libro Rojo*, 178.

11. Manuel Caballero, *Las Venezuelas del siglo veinte* (Caracas: Grijalbo, 1988), 63.

12. Moisés Moleiro, *El partido del pueblo: Crónica de un fraude,* 2d ed. (Valencia, Venezuela: Vadell Hermanos, 1979), 75. According to Raúl Leoni, Betancourt told the left-wing youth faction of AD in 1955: "When in Venezuela, the conditions are ripe for the realization of any revolution, even of the most advanced type, it will not be the Communist Party that carries it out, but Acción Democrática." See also Arturo Sosa A., *Rómulo Betancourt y el partido del pueblo, 1937–1941* (Caracas: Editorial Fundación Rómulo Betancourt, 1995).

13. Steve Ellner, *Los partidos políticos y su disputa por el control del movimiento sindical en Venezuela, 1936–1948* (Caracas: Universidad Católica Andrés Bello, 1980), 74.

14. Judith Ewell, *Venezuela: A Century of Change* (Stanford: Stanford University Press, 1984), 91–92.

15. The AD government was particularly generous in extending credit to rural capitalists. See David Esteller, *Democracia representativa: Apuntes para su historia en Venezuela* (Caracas: Universidad Central de Venezuela, 1996), 36.

16. *El "Partido Democrático Venezolano" y su proceso* (Caracas: Editorial Elite, 1938), 168–69.

17. One exception was Betancourt's minister of agriculture, Eduardo Mendoza Goiticoa, who was the brother of Eugenio Mendoza, one of Venezuela's leading industrialists.

18. Luis Piñerua Ordaz and Carlos Canache Mata were two leading figures in AD who frequently defended this position. Beto Finol (a congressman from Zulia) and Carmelo Lauría (who occupied posts in the cabinets of Carlos Andrés Pérez and Jaime Lusinchi) are examples of prominent AD leaders closely linked to powerful business interests.

19. Samuel Moncada, *Los huevos de la serpiente: Fedecámaras por dentro* (Caracas: Alianza Gráfica, 1985), 227.

20. Eduardo Morales Gil, "El rol de la mujer en el Proyecto Político del joven Betancourt," in *El primer exilio del joven Betancourt* (Caracas: Ediciones Centauro, 1988), 251–67; Betancourt, "Magda Portal y el Voto Feminino (1931)," in *El Pensamiento Político* 12 (1983): 483–87; *Acción Democrática*, February 26, 1944, 2; July 22, 1944, 4.

21. Steve Ellner, *The Venezuelan Petroleum Corporation and the Debate over Government Policy in Basic Industry, 1960–1976* (University of Glasgow Occasional Paper No. 47, 1987), 11.

22. Moncada, *Huevos de la serpiente*, 224.

23. Miguel Tinker Salas, *The Enduring Legacy: Oil, Culture, and Society in Venezuela* (Durham, NC: Duke University Press, 2009), 217.

24. Luis Hurtado, "La lucha popular venezolana de los trabajadores por la democracia," unpublished manuscript (Bogotá, Colombia, 1950), 214.

25. Nelly Arenas and Luis Gómez Calcaño, *Populismo autoritario: Venezuela, 1999–2005* (Caracas: CENDES, 2006), 31–32.

26. Gehard Cartay Ramírez, *Caldera y Betancourt: Constructores de la democracia* (Caracas: Ediciones Centauro, 1987), 111–12.

27. Betancourt, August 15, 1932, letter from San José, Costa Rica, *Libro Rojo*, 186.

28. Alexander, *Rómulo Betancourt*, 24.

29. Roldán Bermúdez, *Aquella farsa (réplica al Dr. M. Pérez Guerrero, Ministro de Hacienda de "Acción Democrática")*, pamphlet (Caracas: n.p., n.d.).

30. Mister X [Germán Borregales], *Rómulo Betancourt: Estadista y diplomático*, 2d ed. (Caracas: Tipografía "El Compás," 1948), 156.

31. *El País*, August 10, 1946, 10 (written by Domingo Alberto Rangel).

32. Winthrop R. Wright, *Café con Leche: Race, Class, and National Image in Venezuela* (Austin: University of Texas Press, 1990).

33. Steve Ellner, *Rethinking Venezuelan Politics: Class, Conflict, and the Chávez Phenomenon* (Boulder, CO: Lynne Rienner, 2008), 30–39.

34. Jorge Eliécer Gaitán, *La revolución venezolana en la opinión extranjera: Declaraciones del ilustre Dr. Jorge . . .* (Caracas: Imprenta Nacional, 1946).

35. Betancourt, *Posición y doctrina* (Caracas: Editorial Cordillera, 1959), 230–31; Manuel González Abreu, *Auge y caída del perejimenismo (el papel del empresariado)* (Caracas: Universidad Central de Venezuela, 1997), 175–76.

36. The thesis that AD's three divisions in the 1960s can be traced back to the 1930s and 1940s is the central argument of Ellner, *Los partidos políticos*.

37. Aníbal Romero, *La miseria del populismo: Mitos y realidades de la democracia en Venezuela* (Caracas: Ediciones Centauro, 1986), 34, 44–45.

38. Steve Ellner, "The Contrasting Variants of the Populism of Hugo Chávez and Alberto Fujimori," *Journal of Latin American Studies* 35, no. 1 (February 2003): 161.

39. Ellner, *Rethinking Venezuelan Politics*, 197.

40. D. L. Raby, *Democracy and Revolution: Latin America and Socialism Today* (London: Pluto Press, 2006), 120–21, 234–38.

41. Ellner, *Rethinking Venezuelan Politics*, 52–53.

7

Populism in Ecuador

From José M. Velasco Ibarra to Rafael Correa

Ximena Sosa

Ecuador has had the second-most intense experience of populism after Brazil. However, Ecuador does not fit the typical mold of Latin American populism nor does the country display all of its characteristics. While the chapter discusses two recent populist presidents, Jaime Roldós and Lucio Gutiérrez, it concentrates on three figures who have dominated the Ecuadorian political scene since the 1930s: a classic populist leader, José María Velasco Ibarra,[1] who was a five-time president between the 1930s and 1970s; a neopopulist, Abdalá Bucaram, who governed for six months in 1996–1997; and a radical populist leader, current president, Rafael Correa, who was first elected in 2006.

This chapter compares these populists primarily through an examination of how they rose to power, how their campaigns appealed to the people, and what they accomplished and failed to do. First, these three charismatic leaders rose to the presidency by presenting themselves as the best alternative during periods of crisis when people had lost trust in the previous president or traditional political parties. Velasco Ibarra and Correa were political outsiders. They effectively organized political movements, Velasquista and Alianza País (AP), rather than political parties. Whereas, even though Bucaram already had been involved in party politics, he formed the new Ecuadorian Roldosista Party as his vehicle to appeal to the people.

Second, all of these populist leaders used confrontational rhetoric. They emerged as prominent figures by identifying the people's unmet needs, wants, and grievances, and then transforming them into political demands, which generated a new political identity not only for the leaders but for the people as well. These populists represented the excluded, the newly enfranchised, those who did not identify with the established structure of power or the dominant ideas and values of the period. Velasco Ibarra stood for freedom of suffrage through fair elections, improved education (especially for women), and expansion of production through the building of roads that would unite the country and expand the market. Bucaram vaguely articulated economic and social reforms that utilized neoliberal policies. Today, Correa fights for better education and health care systems, against corruption, and for an economics of solidarity.

Finally, all three won elections mobilizing well-organized clientelist bases. When their promises could not be fulfilled, however, the political coalitions that brought them to office disintegrated, and their credibility crumbled. This led to Velasco Ibarra being overthrown three times and Bucaram meeting the same fate during his only term in office. Correa remained in power, but his approval rating fell from 80 percent during his first months as president to somewhere between 40 percent and 50 percent at the beginning of 2010, which may signify difficult times ahead for him.

Background

Ecuador is one of the smallest countries in Latin America. After losing a war with Peru over national borders in 1941, Ecuador retained around 280,000 square kilometers. In the 1930s demographers estimated Ecuador's population at a little more than two million, 80 percent of which was concentrated in rural areas. The rural majority was composed of indigenous peoples and *mestizos*. The rest lived in the capital city of Quito, in the main port city of Guayaquil, and in provincial capitals.

Like many other Latin American countries, Ecuador traditionally has relied on exports to support its economy, especially cacao, bananas, and since the 1970s, oil. The Great Depression of the 1930s decimated the prices of Ecuador's raw materials, however, and the Central Bank was flooded with demand for gold bills of exchange to cover imports. Domestic currency then became scarce, causing widespread panic. The lack of government leadership exacerbated the generalized crisis.

Between the 1930s and 1970s Ecuador had an essentially agrarian economy, with scant industry and little national integration. Maiguascha and North have demonstrated that the dominant economic classes were either immersed in family networks or functioned under conditions imposed by the limited markets that then existed. Ecuadorians were not interested in promoting national capitalism through the redistribution of income.[2] While the cacao boom (1860–1920) and later the banana boom (1948–65–1965) presented great opportunities for Ecuador, the surplus was not reinvested in industry. In addition there were limited internal markets, concentration of land in the hands of a few, and weak urbanization. These are the main reasons why Ecuador did not embark on an import substitution industrialization program as other Latin American countries did at the time. And as a result, the economy underwent sharp fluctuations.

In the 1930s the political situation also aggravated an unsteady economy. The two traditional parties, the Conservatives and Liberals, were discredited, and neither had strong candidates. The Conservatives had a disqualified candidate, and the Liberals had been accused of electoral fraud. This crisis presented a good opportunity for a new leader, independent of either party, to rise, and that person was José M. Velasco Ibarra. Unlike many Latin American populists of his time, he did not advocate for industrialization, although he had other characteristics that made him a populist leader.

The Rise of José M. Velasco Ibarra

Velasco Ibarra emerged at the climax of political and economic discontent, when Ecuador needed a "savior."[3] The rationale for his being the best choice was different during each campaign (electoral fraud, conflicts over international boundaries, bad governments, inflation, etc.). All of his presidential campaigns (1933, 1943, 1952, 1959, and 1967) had similar elements. His promises were vague yet offered immediate relief from widespread suffering. Aside from two fixed ideas—public education and road construction—he had no well-defined political or economic program.

He represented himself as a liberal, in the sense that he believed in all sorts of freedoms for the people, and yet his authoritarian way of governing prevented him from forming solid political alliances, which many times caused his downfall.

Velasco Ibarra initiated a process of incorporating into the political arena previously excluded sectors of society. He broke with the tradition of closed-door presidential elections in 1934, when he campaigned by touring the country. Not only did Velasco Ibarra appeal to dissidents of different political parties and movements, but also to well-to-do constituents who had not exercised their right to vote. For dissidents as well as the literate masses, Velasco Ibarra became their representative as a strong critic of the traditional parties. This charismatic figure stood foursquare against the ideology of the power block, which was the political party in control or the opposition party. Velasco Ibarra represented the "people," and either the Conservatives or Liberals or splinters of either party were the power block.

Velasco Ibarra became president of the republic five times (1934–35, 1944–47, 1952–56, 1960–61, and 1968–72). Campaigning as an outsider and yet as

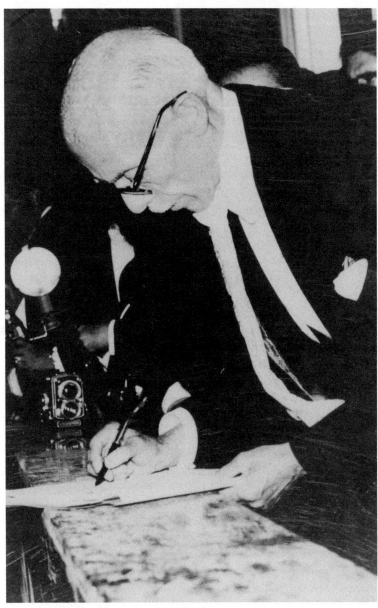

Figure 7.1. President Velasco Ibarra signs a document during his fourth presidency in 1960. (Courtesy of Archivo del Banco Central, Quito, Ecuador)

a unifier, Velasco Ibarra was able to benefit from the divisions among the traditional Conservative and Liberal parties. In 1932 he was known as an anti–status quo newspaper writer who advocated an end to the presidential fraud constantly perpetrated by the Liberals. While in Europe, he decided to accept the offer of the Conservative party to run for Congress. The Conservatives viewed Velasco Ibarra as a potential ally who could defend their presidential candidate, Neptalí Bonifaz. The latter was denied office because he had been born in Peru. However, Velasco Ibarra, who became the vice president of the Congress, supported neither Bonifaz nor the incumbent Liberal president Juan de Dios Martínez, who had been accused of winning the election through fraud. Neither political party was in good shape: the Conservatives suffered from the disqualification of their presidential candidate, and the Liberals had lost public trust because of rumors of electoral irregularities. Therefore, Velasco Ibarra was portrayed as a new type of political figure, independent of any traditional party, who could restore trust in government. He was the atypical strong leader who represented and worked for the people.[4]

His second presidency (1944–47) is the one most remembered by the Ecuadorian people. The Liberal president Carlos Arroyo del Río, like Juan de Dios Martínez before him, was seen as another Liberal who had come to power by fraud. Arroyo del Río's popularity fell further when the unsettled boundary war between Peru and Ecuador resulted in a protocol in 1942 by which Ecuador lost a considerable amount of territory (200,000 square kilometers). The Alianza Democrática Ecuatoriana (Ecuadorian Democratic Alliance—ADE), which included students, workers, and supporters of several political parties, believed that Velasco Ibarra was a strong enough candidate to beat the official Liberal candidate. ADE asked Velasco Ibarra to return to the country after a popular uprising known as *La Gloriosa*. Fearing more fraud from the Liberals, ADE proclaimed Velasco Ibarra as chief of state, and the National Assembly recognized him as the president of the republic. Again he was the unaffiliated person who was able to carry out the ideals of the insurrection: equality before the law, freedom to vote, and justice.

In 1952 a new political party, Concentración de Fuerzas Populares (Concentration of People's Forces—CFP), under the leadership of Carlos Guevara Moreno, was organized. It attracted people of the middle class, who were looking for a leader to represent their interests. Guevara Moreno knew, however, that his regional populist movement was not strong enough to win the presidential election. Therefore, he launched Velasco Ibarra, who was again seen as a unifying figure who could defeat traditional candidates, in particular the Conservative Ruperto Alarcón.

Velasco Ibarra's fourth (1960–61) and fifth presidencies (1968–72) were more challenging. In 1960 Velasco Ibarra confronted two tough opponents, former president Galo Plaza (1948–52) and former secretary general of the Organization of American States, the Conservative candidate, Gonzalo Cordero. The strongest candidate was Plaza. The Liberals ran a campaign that reflected their belief in an easy victory, while the Conservatives advocated more influence by the Catholic Church in government. Velasco Ibarra developed a more sophisticated campaign. According to Menéndez-Carrión, the sub-Velasquismos (supporters of Velasco Ibarra) were born.[5] The regional (mainly coastal and highland) leaders of these support groups campaigned for Velasco Ibarra, and yet again Velasco Ibarra was not linked to any traditional political party.

Finally in 1968, Velasco Ibarra confronted two solid candidates, Liberal Andrés Córdova and his own former protégé, Conservative Camilo Ponce, who had previously been president (1956–1960). Even though Velasco Ibarra resisted, the Partido Velasquista was formed, composed of the Movimiento Unificado Velasquista (United Velasquista Movement), Opción Popular Cívica Ecuatoriana (Ecuadorian Popular Civic Option), and Frente Nacional Femenino (National Feminine Front). Possible electoral fraud by the Conservatives also helped Velasco Ibarra resurrect his clean political image. Once again Velasco Ibarra emphasized that he would save the country while reconciling all Ecuadorians.

Although Velasco Ibarra did not have a very good understanding of economics himself, he continually criticized the government's inability to manage the economy. In 1934 the main issue was confiscation of bills of exchange, which forced all foreign exchange transactions into the Central Bank. Velasco Ibarra claimed that the only thing he and the rest of Ecuador could be sure of was that this caused speculation and thereby induced price increases for basic necessities. In 1944 the issue was inflation caused by an increase in the amount of money in circulation. Velasco Ibarra stated that the financial system was not stimulating the economy, causing widespread unease. Then in 1952, while Ecuador was in the midst of a banana boom, Velasco Ibarra alleged that the government had favored industrialists over the legitimate interests of farmers and ranchers. Reports from the Central Bank proved the opposite.

In 1960 falling world prices for cacao and coffee undermined the economic situation and caused a sharp drop in hard currency reserves. Velasco Ibarra did not miss the opportunity to blame it on government mismanagement. In 1968 the decline of banana exports led to attempts to promote import substitution industrialization by the government. This provoked negative reactions, and once again Velasco Ibarra seized the opportunity to criticize these policies.

Over the long term, public opinion turned against government agencies and their efficacy. Velasco Ibarra encouraged the continued erosion of that faith and argued that if the institutions could not be trusted, then it was time for strong personal intervention. He offered to take control of those institutions so that they worked for the people rather than against them.

The Unstable Continuity of Velasco Ibarra

Velasco Ibarra's unstable continuity created a vicious cycle that allowed him to return to office time after time. It was a form of continuity because it was always the leader returning to office, and unstable because he rarely remained in office for long. His short tenures were because his personalist style prevented him from building a support base or his own institutions, especially a political party.[6]

In five presidential campaigns, Velasco Ibarra was able to win elections with the support of several sectors, joined into coalitions or political parties. In 1933 Nueva Acción Republicana Ecuatoriana (New Republican Ecuadorian Action—NARE) and Junta del Sufragio Libre (Free Vote Junta—JSL) were his main political movements. NARE recruited workers who were interested in better economic and political conditions. JSL included large components of Conservatives and some Liberals. In 1943 ADE was his main political movement. ADE was composed of converts from several political movements: Conservatives, Independent Radical Liberals, Socialists, the Ecuadorian Socialist Vanguard, Communists, the National Democratic Front, and the Democratic University Union of Ecuador.[7] In 1951 the right-wing movement Acción Revolucionaria Nacionalista Ecuatoriana (Ecuadorian Nationalist Republican Action—ARNE) and the populist political party Concentración de Fuerzas Populares (Concentration of People's Forces—CFP) were his main sources of support. ARNE was created by former university students following the 1941 Peruvian-Ecuadorian war. CFP was founded by Carlos Guevara Moreno and dissident Socialists, Liberals, intellectuals, and artists.

In 1959 a number of political movements were formed to support the leader. These groups were known as the sub-Velasquismos, subdivided into the two main regions of the country, highlands and coast. The names of the groups corresponded to the names of their leaders—for example, Araujista Velasquistas, after a leader named Araujo. In 1968 Velasquismo as a political party was finally organized, encompassing several political movements. All of these mechanisms were part of Velasco's strategy aimed at gaining presidential power. And he succeeded.

In his five campaigns, Velasco Ibarra portrayed himself as the honest outsider who was called back by the majority of Ecuadorians to save their country. Carlos de la Torre argues that Velasco Ibarra launched a politics of the masses by addressing his speeches to voters and nonvoters alike. This approach promised the people access to public spaces that had previously been reserved for elites.[8] It also implied that nonvoters should put pressure on voters, so that all Ecuadorians would benefit. Steve Stein has written that the "fundamental distinction between the twentieth century and preceding ones in the history of Latin America has been the growth of the popular masses in size, in importance, and as a potential threat to the status quo."[9] It was this emerging and growing group, made possible by twentieth-century political incorporation of the literate masses, that enabled Velasco Ibarra to energize and bring into his following the persons whose votes ensured his victories.

Velasco Ibarra wielded words in a way that enticed his followers. His speeches and political writings provide evidence of how his addresses made the people feel important, as participants in charting Ecuador's destiny:

> The people, the true working people are those who make the Fatherland great. Architects, engineers, tailors, shoemakers, agricultural workers, all workers, all of them, day by day are forging what we can call the national civilization, they are creating the cities, they are building the highways, they are producing in industry, they are producing in agriculture.
>
> Workers are the foundation of the Fatherland. It is they who maintain the infrastructure of the Republic, who provide the economic base upon which rises the spiritual edifice, the cultural edifice, the international personality of the Republic of Ecuador.[10]

His underlying approach was to touch the emotions of Ecuadorians so that they identified with the leader. It did not matter if the speeches embodied an organized program. In that sense, Velasco fits well into the political discourse described by Álvarez Junco. The populist discourse did not have answers; it provoked responses and calls for action; it did not explain, but persuaded. In contrast, scientific discourse starts from current knowledge and seeks answers that build upon that knowledge.[11]

Populist leaders had little specific interest in ideology. Velasco Ibarra could spout ideas drawn from conservatism, liberalism, socialism, and even communism. The reason was simple: Velasco Ibarra wanted to capture people's attention and ultimately their loyalty. He said things designed to do this rather than to build a coherent doctrine. One of the best examples is his speech on June 4, 1944:

> The current moment is a difficult moment. It is an essentially vital moment. It is the moment in which the communist consorts with the Catholic. It is the moment that demonstrates the basis of the Fatherland. I will not serve any particular ideology. I will not serve any particular party. I

will not be the nation's boss. I will be the servant of the people. I will be the servant of Ecuador, in search of the basis of nationality, of morality, a government of tolerance, of liberalism, of national focus, of cleanliness, of social reform.[12]

This political strategy worked. A common element in all of his campaigns was that the several groups supporting his campaign believed that Velasco Ibarra was the best option. By avoiding the creation of a Velasquista party (except in the last campaign), Velasco Ibarra induced diverse political sectors to trust him to represent their interests. All sectors saw him as a unifying figure.

Velasco's unstable side surfaced when he had to make decisions, however, and inevitably he alienated certain groups. Those betrayed drifted into the opposition. In his first presidency, opposition came essentially from the Liberals. In addition, the students coalesced in opposition to Velasco, largely because he insisted on the right to intervene in public universities, in particular the one in Quito, and closed them for short periods of time. Ultimately, the president was overthrown after less than one year in office.

During his second presidency, Velasco found it impossible to maintain any semblance of unity. As mentioned above, the ADE coalition was a huge mélange. The left wing (socialists and communists) criticized Velasco Ibarra's economic plan, which had created a parasitic bureaucracy. Dissident liberals believed that the administration of government institutions was very inefficient. The right wing, mainly dissident conservatives, thought that the president's cabinet served only his personal interests. Velasco Ibarra's relationship with university students suffered from his perception that they were too dogmatic. His solution was to assume dictatorial powers and to approve a conservative constitution in 1946. These strategies did not work, and once again the president was overthrown in 1947, after three and half years in power.

In his third presidency, Velasco was able to remain in power because of the support of ARNE, a right-wing group that enforced peace in the country through repression. CFP also supported Velasco Ibarra's campaign. Very early in his presidency, however, he exiled the leader of the group, Guevara Moreno.

In his fourth presidency, Velasco Ibarra implemented a tax reform that was not a popular measure. Many sectors of the society, including workers, university students, and bus drivers went on strike. In addition two of his closest collaborators, Manuel Araujo and his own vice president, Carlos Arosemena, joined the opposition and threatened to create a new political movement. For the third time, the president was overthrown after thirteen months in power.

In Velasco Ibarra's final term, university students and union workers formed his main opposition. In order to manage them, the president assumed dictatorial powers to preserve the peace, which had been disturbed in particular by the students, whom he equated with terrorists. He remained as dictator until 1972, when the military overthrew him, a few months short of finishing his term. The real threat was that Assad Bucaram, a regional populist, might win the next presidential elections.

The multiclass, personalist coalitions assembled by Velasco Ibarra allowed him to bypass institutionalized forms of mediation and led to unstable authoritarian and yet formally democratic regimes. Almost every movement and party that campaigned for and supported the leader wound up abandoning him. Labor unions and student organizations felt ignored by him. Even his closest collaborators ended up abandoning him. The military supported Velasco Ibarra until they believed that he broke with constitutional order by assuming dictatorial powers.

That Velasco Ibarra democratically won five of six campaigns (he lost in 1939) demonstrates that he respected elections. In that sense Ernesto Laclau's assertion that "populism is a strategy to include new social groups within the democratic process" fits Velasco Ibarra's inclusion of literate masses to participate in politics through their vote.[13] The president assumed dictatorial power three times, however, believing that citizens had given him the right to do so through their election of him. He believed that he had to protect them, as he embodied the supreme authority of the state, even if his leadership ultimately became dictatorial. The simple fact was that the majority of Ecuadorians usually believed in Velasco Ibarra. They thought he was the person to solve the political and economic problems of Ecuador. When he became authoritarian, however, they lost faith and no longer regarded his administration as legitimate. At this point, Velasco Ibarra would use force to stay in office.

The upshot was that Velasco Ibarra dominated the Ecuadorian political arena for almost forty years, even if it was through an unstable continuity. His disdain for party organization was revealed by his famous claim, "Give me a balcony and I will be President." His rhetoric left no room for party development, professional leadership, or ideology. Ecuadorian society had not achieved political maturity, and he did not remedy the situation. There was no dominant economic policy: Velasco Ibarra simply built roads, schools, health centers, power plants, and potable water systems, all of which provided jobs. He remained in the minds of Ecuadorians as a symbol of honesty, austerity, and strength.[14]

Jaime Roldós and the CFP

While important leaders emerged from the CFP, it had difficulties in becoming a national political movement. It had two Guayaquileño leaders, Carlos Guevara

Moreno and Assad Bucaram, and a national leader, President Jaime Roldós. The latter benefited from the political inclusion of illiterates as citizens and voters.

Guevara Moreno, founder of the CFP, had attracted new groups, particularly farmers who had migrated to the coast because of the banana boom. Guayaquil, one of the cities that benefited from this boom, grew dramatically, especially its peripheral shantytowns known as *suburbios*. In 1950 Guayaquil's *suburbios* constituted 12 percent of the city; by 1965 they had grown to 57 percent. Therefore, the coast, in particular Guayaquil, was the perfect target for the CFP. Guevara Moreno emphasized short-term programs and created an informal clientelist network, which included his wife, Norma Descalzi. They mostly went door to door seeking new members and then integrated them into vertically organized political clubs. Guevara Moreno failed to win the presidential elections in 1956, however, because his lopsided victory in the coastal provinces fell to an even more lopsided victory for Camilo Ponce in the highlands. In addition, Ponce had the significant backing of the Catholic Church and Velasco Ibarra. This showed that the CFP was essentially a regional party.[15]

In 1970 the CFP's new leader, Assad Bucaram, known popularly as don Buca, a Lebanese descendent, became mayor of Guayaquil twice, in 1962 and in 1967. As leader of the CFP, he used mobilization tactics similar to those of Guevara Moreno. When Velasco fell from power in 1972, don Buca wanted to run for president.

The military dissuaded don Buca from even thinking about the presidency. In 1978, while the military still ruled Ecuador, army chief of staff Bolivar Jarrín issued a proclamation disqualifying don Buca. It read: "The existing Organic Law of the Armed Forces stipulates that the President of the Republic is the Commander in Chief of the Armed Forces and therefore must be an Ecuadorian citizen by birth, son of Ecuadorian parents by birth. Consequently, anyone who aspires to nomination and inscription as a candidate for the Presidency or Vice Presidency of the Republic should meet these same requirements."[16]

Even though the CFP denounced this decree as being targeted specifically at Assad Bucaram, it remained in effect. The military and the elite could not, however, eliminate the CFP as a strong political party in the presidential election of 1979, which brought new rules and expanded the voter base. A 1978 referendum allowed Ecuadorians to vote for the return to democracy and for a new constitution, one that permitted illiterates to vote, restructured Congress into a unicameral chamber, and provided for presidential runoff elections.

Since Assad Bucaram could not be a presidential candidate, the CFP selected Jaime Roldós, a thirty-seven-year-old university professor. Because Roldós was married to don Buca's niece Martha, many observers believed that he would be Bucaram's puppet. In fact, some CFP enthusiasts floated the slogan "Roldós to the presidency, Bucaram to power." Early in the campaign, however, Roldós began to put his own stamp on the party with a campaign called "a force for change."

Roldós expanded upon the techniques already developed by CPF leaders. He cultivated an image in the *suburbios* as a CFP stalwart. Members of the party staged rehearsals of the balloting for the benefit of illiterates, who would vote for the first time. They also organized transportation to and from the polls for their supporters. Martha Bucaram was very active in her husband's political campaign. Martha was a lawyer, like her husband, and the couple opened an office to solve problems and answer questions, a practice that they continued when he became president.

Roldós led the voting in the first round. His rival, Social Christian leader Sixto Durán Ballén, regrouped for the runoff, but Roldós and his running mate, Osvaldo Hurtado, garnered 68 percent of the vote, taking all but one province.[17] In his first speech as president, Roldós emphasized his commitment to the poorer sectors of society, especially the indigenous people. He even spoke in Quichua, their main language. He assured the people that this government would uphold democratic participation, respecting everyone's citizenship, even "the downtrodden, the powerless, those who wear the poncho."

Roldós's administrative program contained three main thrusts. First, it guaranteed democracy and respect for all ideologies and sectors of society. Second, it promised economic development. And third, it pledged to pursue social justice. In order to achieve the last two items, he would carry out five reforms, in the political, administrative, agrarian, educational, and tax realms. Political reform entailed encouragement of parties and movements to represent those who had no voice in society. Administrative reform was aimed at eliminating corruption and inefficiency through decentralization. Agrarian reform would increase productivity by investing in rural infrastructure, thereby slowing rural migration to the cities. Educational reform focused on training Ecuadorians whose knowledge was relevant to the needs of the society. Finally, tax reform was intended to raise more revenues from the rich than the poor.[18]

In order to carry out these reforms, Roldós needed congressional cooperation. But Assad Bucaram, who had been appointed president of Congress, began a campaign against the president. Bucaram and Roldós both believed they should control CFP and national policy. Their fight for leadership, called the contest between powers, pitted the executive branch against the legislative. The CFP split into two wings, the loyalists who remained with Bucaram and the Roldosistas, who created their own movement called People, Change, and Democracy. This strengthened the rightist parties in Congress at the expense of the

CFP. The premature death of Roldós in a May 1981 plane crash, followed by Bucaram's death in November of the same year, marked the demise of the CFP. The CFP had been led by three people: Guevara Moreno, Bucaram, and Roldós. The first two were personalistic and paternalistic. Guevara Moreno and Bucaram sought to maintain their own political standing through networks headed by precinct bosses. They appealed to people in the suburbs of Guayaquil, promising immediate material gains. In these characteristics they resembled Velasco Ibarra. Unlike him, though, they never emerged as national leaders.

Roldós and Velasco Ibarra were intellectuals. But unlike Velasco, Roldós used the CFP program to draw people into his party. He appealed not only to the masses but also to the middle classes. Both were lawyers and cared about improving education. Roldós came from a new generation, however, that saw the need to solve the nation's problems through higher moral standards as well as through major structural changes (i.e. his five main reforms). Roldós learned to negotiate with other political parties. His choice of a running mate, Osvaldo Hurtado, from the rival Popular Democratic Party, showed his eagerness to practice participatory democracy.

Abdalá Bucaram: A Neopopulist Leader

In the next fifteen years, a new party emerged, the Partido Roldosista Ecuatoriano (Roldosista Ecuadorian Party—PRE). It was led by Abdalá Bucaram, Roldós's brother-in-law and Assad Bucaram's nephew. When Roldós died, his party was not strong enough to survive. Bucaram saw this as an opportunity to capture Roldos's followers for his own party, which he expanded to include sectors that had previously been ignored, such as informal vendors, mid-level merchants, and even dissidents from traditional political parties.

Abdalá Bucaram was born in Guayaquil in 1952, into a large and poor family. He became involved in politics at an early age, working in the campaigns of Guevara Moreno and don Buca. When he was elected mayor of Guayaquil in 1984, his reputation as an impetuous and passionate politician began. He remained in office for only one year. He openly defied the authority of President León Febres Cordero (1984–88), the armed forces, and the U.S. government. The inevitable warrant for his arrest induced him to flee to exile in Panama.

After two unsuccessful campaigns, Abdalá Bucaram was elected as president in 1996. He defeated his opponent, the Social Christian Jaime Nebot, with a comfortable majority of 54 percent. Bucaram took twenty Ecuadorian provinces; only Pichincha, where Quito is located, went to Nebot.

Bucaram's presidential campaign consisted of promises to reform the political, social, and economic systems of the country. Known as el Loco, or the crazy one, Bucaram used different techniques to capture votes. As Velasco Ibarra did, Bucaram visited numerous towns throughout the country. His speeches were powerful attacks on the rich and the oligarchy. In fact, one of his campaign slogans was, "Only one ideology, against the oligarchy." He promised a better life for the poor, while reminding them of all the material things they did not have and of all of the degradations they had suffered at the hands of the rich. He led them to believe that he represented them and understood them because he himself had grown up as a member of the lower middle class.[19]

Bucaram won in large part because people had lost their trust in the incumbent, Sixto Durán Ballén. The latter's neoliberal economic program, successful at the macroeconomic level, failed to improve the lives of common Ecuadorians. Therefore, Bucaram, as Velasco Ibarra had done in the past, made his mark by criticizing Durán Ballén. Bucaram knew that Ecuadorians were looking for hope, and he provided it. The level of despair was such that Ecuadorians were willing to risk the little they had in the hope that this populist firebrand would fulfill his promises. One of Bucaram's most convincing slogans was, "With me we either sink or swim."

Bucaram improved his chances in the election by choosing Rosalia Arteaga as a running mate. As the first female candidate for vice president, her platform attracted not only women's organizations but also many middle-class voters. Arteaga had resigned as Durán Ballén's minister of education because he wanted to mandate religious education in the public schools. Bucaram proposed to utilize her previous experience by putting her in charge of public health and education issues.

Unlike his predecessors in the CFP, Bucaram was not a political outsider. He represented a new type of leader, a neopopulist.[20] Once in power, he embraced neoliberal policies, such as economic adjustment, including reductions in government spending, shrinking the state bureaucracy, and the privatization of state enterprises. In order to pursue these policies, Bucaram reappointed Augusto de la Torre, a neoliberal technocrat who had served as chairman of the Central Bank since Durán Ballén's presidency and had previously been the International Monetary Fund representative in Venezuela. De la Torre was obsessed with controlling inflation, renegotiating the foreign debt, privatizing enterprises, and downsizing the public sector.

Bucaram attempted to go even beyond this neoliberal program by inviting Domingo Cavallo, a former Argentinean finance minister, to design the economic plan. Cavallo's discussion of convertibility and dollar-pegged currency caused anxiety among the economic elite and tended to divide public opinion into two opposing camps.

On the other hand, Bucaram was eager to live up to his campaign image of paternalism among the poor. His plan promised four hundred thousand low-cost houses and froze the retail price of cooking gas. It also had personalist touches, such as selling Abdalact, inexpensive milk, in Guayaquil's *suburbios*, and providing poor students with free backpacks, books, notebooks, and pencils bearing the president's name.

While the masses supported Bucaram, the elite questioned his attempt to impose currency convertibility. In addition, his bizarre behavior and physical violence were points of tension. Bucaram declared that he had always wanted to be a singer, so he actually recorded a compact disc entitled *A Crazy Man Who Loves*. He also ran for president of the most popular soccer club, Barcelona. These acts led many to conclude that, far from governing, Bucaram was actually destroying the image of the presidency.

Bucaram's verbal aggression caused even more alarm. Probably the most memorable of his many insults was calling former president Rodrigo Borja a donkey. When pressed to apologize, he did so to donkeys. Moreover, his closest collaborators were accused of physical aggression. In particular, Alfredo Adum, minister of energy, was alleged to have insulted people who ignored his orders and assaulted men and women who disagreed with him.

Two other acts evoked the disapproval of intellectuals. Bucaram supported the minister of education, Sandra Correa, even after learning that she had plagiarized her doctoral thesis. And he apologized to Alberto Fujimori, president of Peru, for all of the boundary problems that these two countries had had in the past. Most Ecuadorians thought that these acts demeaned the intellectual community and the dignity of the nation.

The Overthrow of Bucaram

Between late December 1996 and early February 1997, the political situation in Ecuador deteriorated, from the top down. First, Bucaram's austerity plan for the economy met with bitter resistance and led civic and business groups to plan a general strike. The U.S. ambassador spoke out against Bucaram, and major newspapers and public opinion leaders swung massively against the president.[21]

He relented at the last minute, but not soon enough to avert huge public demonstrations (some estimated two million protesters) in all the major cities on February 5. The general cry was "Get out!"

Congress then voted Bucaram's office vacant due to his mental incompetence and chose Fabián Alarcón to replace him. A confusing but nonthreatening succession crisis ensued, during which Ecuador had three presidents: Bucaram, who rejected Congress's resolution; Arteaga, who claimed the right of succession as vice president; and Alarcón, the president of the Congress. After several days, Bucaram surrendered the office to Alarcón and left the country. The case for Arteaga succeeding to the presidency faded, first because she was tainted as a member of the former administration and second due to a printed error in the constitution, which did not specify who succeeded in the president's absence. In a very informal enforcement of the constitution, Arteaga became president for two days; thereafter, she became vice president to Alarcón.

This situation proved the flexibility of the institutions in the country. The goal was to get rid of the president. There was no evidence of his mental incapacity nor were there any legal accusations, and yet Bucaram was overthrown. On the other hand, Arteaga, who had little political support, was also discarded as the legitimate successor. This situation marks the beginning of disregard of constitutional order after the return of the democracy in 1979. It is one thing to formally accuse the president of corruption, in particular in customs or embezzlement of discretionary funds (*gastos reservados*), but it is another to find a way to depose him illegally. The way this situation was handled opened the door for the PRE to find a way for Bucaram to return from exile; it also had a continuing impact on Ecuadorian politics.

Lucio Gutiérrez: The Rise of New Ethnic Color

Lucio Gutiérrez represented the hope for fresh leadership and symbolized the convergence of ethnic and military constituents. Gutiérrez, who came from a lower-middle-class background in the Amazon region, entered the military as a means of social mobility. He built an alliance with another excluded sector, the Indians, while also addressing the expectations of the lower middle classes.

Gutiérrez was part of a new generation of the military that had a stronger relationship with indigenous groups. This was partially a result of the military's decision to work with the civic and reforestation companies, whose purpose was to promote community participation. The indigenous communities provided the land and the military supplied the labor, along with technical training. The program was successful because the indigenous people were able to do the work after receiving training from the military. It also established closer relations between the two groups, which reinforced the idea of the military as protector of the weakest sector, the indigenous.[22] As a result of this relationship, Gutiérrez was able to form the National Salvation Junta in conjunction with Antonio Vargas, president of La Confederación de Nacionalidades Indígenas del Ecuador (Confederation of Ecuadorian Indigenous Nationalities—CONAIE), and Carlos Solórzano, the former president of the Supreme Court. Together they overthrew President Jamil Mahuad in 2000. Mahuad had been elected president in 1998 and was overthrown mainly because of his desperate attempt to solve national economic problems through dollarization of the economy, while simultaneously rescuing corrupt bankers. Even though the junta only lasted a few hours and vice president Gustavo Noboa became president, Gutiérrez and his collaborators had made clear that they were seeking change.

In 2002 Gutiérrez returned to the political arena as a presidential candidate. Congress granted him amnesty for the coup, but he had been forced to resign his military commission. He then formed a party, Sociedad Patriótica (Patriotic Society), with the support of CONAIE, Pachakutik (the indigenous political party), and the leftist political movement Movimiento Popular Democrático. He won the election with a platform of fighting against corruption, mostly characterized as bankers and old political parties. Those groups had assaulted not only national patrimony but the personal savings of citizens when the country was dollarized in 2000. Gutiérrez represented the rise of groups who had not shared political power. He himself was considered a *cholo*, a descendent of an indigenous person who had adopted western ways. Gutiérrez appointed Antonio Vargas as minister of social welfare, because Vargas represented the indigenous group that had gained a political presence since the uprising in 1992 but had never been part of the government. Finally, Gutiérrez stood for the majority of Ecuadorians who were looking for a leader, someone capable of fighting for their rights who did not belong to a traditional party.[23]

Once in power, Gutiérrez, who had declared that he did not believe in any ideology and that his primary fight was to restore the rights of the common people, began implementing unconstitutional policies. He illegally appointed new members to the Supreme Court, the Constitutional Board (which oversees the president, the Congress, and the fundamental rights of the citizens), and the Supreme Electoral Tribunal. By appointing members linked to allied parties, Gutiérrez asserted control over these institutions. Moreover, this allowed him to bring back a strong ally, the neopopulist leader Abdalá Bucaram, who had been in exile in Panama since 1997.

In addition to exceeding his powers, Gutiérrez was accused of nepotism and of having accepted campaign donations from drug traffickers. The press continuously printed information on these issues, causing the president to retaliate by forbidding the press from broadcasting any information about the president. The press accused the president of thwarting the freedom of the press.

In August 2003, after eight months of governing, Gutiérrez broke with one of his main collaborators, Pachakutik, and a year and a half later CONAIE, which withdrew its political support. At this point, Gutiérrez tried a new political alliance with PRE and Partido Renovador Institucional Acción Nacional (Institutional Renewal Party of National Action—PRIAN). The latter, led by millionaire Alvaro Noboa, wanted to bring back Bucaram, now a symbol of corruption. Bucaram returned; however, Ecuadorians felt betrayed. Even though Gutiérrez used populist strategies such as traveling cabinets, pro-government demonstrations, and welfare payments to retain his supporters, in April 2005, after two years and three months, the president was overthrown. Gutiérrez did not keep his promise of fighting against corruption. In fact, the president had an amorphous ideology with no clear political or economic state vision.[24]

Rafael Correa: A Radical Populist

Rafael Correa, a PhD in economics and a leftist, had been a political outsider until his brief appointment as minister of finance during Alfredo Palacio's government (2005–6). Correa appeared to be a clean leader-technocrat who pledged to fulfill promises that Gutiérrez had made but did not carry out. Building on the disillusioned supporters of Gutiérrez, the *forajidos* (outlaws), Correa became their trustworthy leader. Correa, as a radical populist, embodied not only a commitment to break with the past, but most importantly to embrace the twenty-first-century socialism made popular by Hugo Chávez of Venezuela. As had his populist predecessors, Correa promised to build a different type of state, infused with a new identity. This new beginning was meant to recognize citizens as actors who were not linked to any existing political movements. Therefore, the Citizen's Revolution was born to vindicate unmet political demands through participatory democracy and the inclusion of Ecuadorians as protagonists of their own democracy.[25] Correa's slogan "Now the Homeland Belongs to Everybody" encapsulates this belief.

Correa emerged as the presidential candidate of an untainted political movement Alianza PAIS (AP).[26] It was formed in 2005 with five concrete goals: a) constitutional revolution; b) ethical revolution; c) economic revolution; d) educational and health revolution; and e) revolution of integration, dignity, and sovereignty. The constitutional revolution implied decentralizing the state by creating a participatory democracy with the primary goal of convoking a constitutional convention. The ethical revolution implied the reformation of the penal code to stamp out corruption, particularly in taxes, customs, and oil revenues. In addition, the external debt must be paid as long as it does not affect national development. The economic revolution promoted national production, especially through the establishment of cooperatives, small- and medium-size industries, which in turn would generate more employment. It favored the national oil industry instead of foreign ones. The education and health revolution endorsed free instruction and health services. It sponsored the construction of schools and clinics as well as the provision of better services. Finally, the revolution of integration, dignity, and sovereignty fostered more cooperation among Latin American countries by forging economic linkages.[27]

Correa won the presidential election in 2006 and immediately started a campaign for a referendum to approve the election of a constitutional assembly, which won by 82 percent. The next step was to gain approval of the new constitution, proposed by the assembly, whose majority was from AP. Again, 64 percent of Ecuadorians supported the new constitution. As did Hugo Chávez in Venezuela and Evo Morales in Bolivia, Correa needed to solidify his political agenda through the constitution, which symbolized the end of the "long and sad neoliberal night" and the beginning of the socialism of the twenty-first century.

This new constitution stood against inequalities, discrimination, and injustices. It prioritized national production based on equitable distribution of development benefits, means of production, and the generation of dignified and stable jobs. It also provided free health care and education, with the goal of eradicating illiteracy and promoting intercultural instruction. In addition, the state reserved the right to regulate and manage strategic sectors such as all forms of energy, telecommunications, nonrenewable natural resources, transportation, refining of hydrocarbons, biodiversity, genetic heritage, and water supply. While all these principles aimed to protect against prior neoliberal policies, the constitution also expanded the electorate by allowing minors (from sixteen to eighteen years old) and members of the armed services to vote for the first time. The new constitution allowed the president to serve for two consecutive terms, technically allowing Correa to stay in office until 2017.

As anticipated, in 2009 Correa won the presidential election with 52 percent in the first round. With no strong opponents (Gutiérrez had 28 percent) Correa was able to succeed mainly for four reasons. First, his well-thought-out program was aimed to appeal to citizens, the new actors of the society, who felt betrayed by the traditional parties (*partidocracia*). Through AP, Correa launched his five strategic points, which convinced Ecuadorians that he was serious about changing the way politics was done. Then he won the referendum to write a new constitution. These gave Correa credibility as a strong political leader and reinforced the idea that he wanted a participatory democracy, one in which citizens were in charge. Second, his numerous television and radio spots, along with his Saturday broadcasts and his traveling cabinets, strengthened the direct link between the president and citizens of Ecuador. In fact, all broadcasts started with the slogan, "*El gobierno informa a sus mandantes*" or "The government keeps its constituents informed." These methods, mainly inherited from Gutiérrez, underscored the government's accomplishments while putting on the defensive anyone who dared to disagree with the president.

Third, his accomplishments in education, health care, and road building allowed the president to fortify his approval ratings. During his three years in government, Correa built almost four thousand schools, eliminated the twenty-five-dollar school registration fee, and gave free uniforms, books, and even breakfast to poor students. He also doubled spending on health care, eliminated physicians' fees in state hospitals, and promised to increase the number of the medical personnel. In addition, Correa allocated one million dollars for road construction.

Fourth, Correa fostered national production by restricting imports so that domestic goods would be protected. Primarily, the measure was to benefit the textile, leather, and wood products industries. As promised in his campaign, in 2007 Correa defaulted on $3.2 billion of foreign public debt on the grounds that it was illegal and illegitimate because it violated Ecuador's domestic laws, U.S. Securities and Exchange Commission regulations, and general principles of international law. A year and four months later, Ecuador bought back 91 percent of the defaulted bonds at a much lower price, thirty-five cents on the dollar. Therefore, the government reduced 17 percent of the debt and wrote off a third of its debt.[28] Correa portrayed himself as the honest and thoughtful president who preferred to spend this savings on social programs, instead of paying corrupt foreign lenders.

Correa has exhibited successful political tactics, which have contributed to his stability in power. He also has five populist characteristics, however, that are becoming evident as the approval of his current presidency has fallen from 80 percent to 40–50 percent. First, as a radical populist leader, Correa is a socialist of the twenty-first century, who promotes himself as fighting for the majority of poor and exploited Ecuadorians. Because he has won three ballot votes, he is entitled to represent the people, the citizens. Therefore, Correa seems to believe that he is the "savior" of the country. He embodies the good, which fights against the evil, as represented by the *partidocracia* or any other political competitor. His Manichean discourse, highlighted in his 217 media broadcasts, eliminates the possibility of recognized institutionalized opposition in political parties, unions, media, or civil society groups. Correa wants to create his own democracy, only permitting a direct relationship with his followers, who need to agree with his policies in order to receive material benefits. This has been clear in his disagreements with previous supporters like CONAIE, teachers and university professors, union workers, and environmental groups, who have pressed their own agendas and now are distanced from the president. His antagonistic discourse has also alienated former collaborators like Alberto Acosta, former president of the constitutional assembly; Fander Falconi, a former foreign relations minister; and Manuela Gallegos, secretary of citizen participation and social movements.

Second, while Correa has been able to achieve some goals in education, health care, and road building, his policies are populist in the sense of giving material benefits in exchange for citizens' support. This clientelist approach is evident in such policies as doubling welfare payments (*bono de desarrollo humano*) from $15 to $30, doubling credits for housing loans from $1,800 to $3,600, selling subsidized fertilizer to small farmers, and increasing domestic workers' salaries from $120 to $240 per month. While these measures were made possible because of the high price of oil, which constitutes at least 70 percent of government revenues, they also have created a strong connection of loyalty and gratefulness.

Third, Correa has concentrated on patronage for the popular sectors and also targeted the middle class for their support. One way to maintain loyalty is to provide state employment. The government's auditing agency found that between 2005 and 2010, salaries in the president's office rose from $3.3 to $6.59 million.[29] Moreover, the government has increased the number of government cabinet ministries from fifteen to twenty-seven. While Correa claims that the creation of these entities is to facilitate improved service, it certainly provides more employment, particularly for his supporters.

Fourth, even though Correa portrayed himself as an outsider who wanted to lead an ethical revolution against corruption, the facts proved otherwise. He created the position of national secretary of transparency and management, but the occurrence of corruption has not fallen. According to Transparency International, Ecuador still scores quite low in the index of perceived corruption. Between 2007 and 2009 Ecuador's score did not improve, ranging from 2.1 in 2007, 2.0 in 2008, and 2.2 in 2009. The transparency of the national annual budget scored 43, well below the 60 points needed to be considered transparent.[30] These indicators reveal the inefficiency of institutions, which independent of the president can create distrust in government. Even though Correa's administration has passed laws giving priority to local products (textiles and shoes) and subsidizes food staples (wheat, rice, and milk), it also has increased tariffs on almost one thousand industrial and agricultural products. These measures have caused a decline in foreign trade and deterioration in enforcement of copyright law.[31]

Fifth, Correa's personalist, charismatic, and antagonistic political leadership has impeded establishing AP as a political party. AP is a movement that includes six political groups (Movimiento País, Alianza País, Ruptura 25, Alianza Bolivariana Alfarista, Frente de Lucha Ciudadana, and Poder Cívico Ciudadano).

Until March 2010, AP has been only an electoral movement, which does not even have a reliable list of its members. Essentially it has worked with committees whose only task was to recruit followers' votes. Even though the victories in elections have been through AP, the supreme leader has always been Correa. In fact, most voters did not recognize the other AP candidates; they only knew that they had to vote for Correa's movement. Knowing that his movement has gained a majority in the constitutional assembly and the opposition is secondary, Correa feels quite secure in power.[32]

Conclusion

Ecuador's populist experience has been distinctive. As in most Latin American countries, it has gone through three types of populist leaders, classical, neopopulist, and radical. Classic populist Velasco Ibarra did not embark on industrialization, however, nor did he believe in the establishment of his own political party, as his counterparts did. On the other hand, Bucaram and Correa largely fit the populist characteristics in their own way. Bucaram, as a neopopulist, embarked on neoliberal policies, and Correa, as a radical, engaged in an incipient but compelling ideology of twenty-first-century socialism.

Velasco Ibarra, Bucaram, and Correa share similar populist features. They displayed personalist and charismatic leadership, which appeals to multiclass coalitions, while focusing on excluded sectors of the society. They found mechanisms to expand their voters. Velasco Ibarra incorporated the literate constituency, his *chusma*, by reinstating their right to vote. Bucaram targeted the illiterate constituency, and Correa expanded his electorate by including young voters and the military.

All three used antagonistic discourse designed to discredit the enemy, the other, and to create a new identity among their followers that is represented by the populist leader. Velasco Ibarra as well as Correa, political outsiders, targeted the traditional parties as their enemies. For Velasco Ibarra, the Conservatives and Liberals were his major adversaries. For Correa, the enemy was the *partidocracia*, which is an expanded version of the traditional parties from the time of Velasco Ibarra. For Bucaram, paradoxically, the foes were the neoliberals, even though he turned into one of them.

All three appealed to the people by having direct connections with their followers. All toured the country, gave passionate speeches, and promised a new type of government, which would prioritize the lower classes. Velasco Ibarra was the first one to initiate this new tactic, which he combined with radio speeches. Bucaram used his athletic, singing, and dancing attributes to appeal to the voters. Correa marketed a brilliant campaign of radio, television spots, and press releases, which have so far proved to be unbeatable. Once in power, all were reluctant to establish institutions, which might jeopardize their personalist power. While all three were elected democratically, they have shown authoritarian tendencies. Velasco Ibarra became a dictator three times. Bucaram was unable to negotiate with the elite and middle classes. Correa's direct government style, emphasized in his continuous broadcasts, disallowed institutionalized opposition, built-in political parties, unions, media, or civil society groups.

Notes

1. In Ecuador as well as many Latin American countries people often use two last names; the first refers to the father's side and the second to the mother's. Velasco Ibarra usually used both last names.

2. Juan Maiguashca and Liisa North, "Orígenes y Significado del Velasquismo: Lucha de Clases y Participación Política en el Ecuador, 1920–1972," in *La Cuestión Regional y el Poder,* ed. Rafael Quintero (Quito: Corporación Editora Nacional-FLACSO-CERLAC, 1991), 144.

3. Velasco Ibarra was born to a distinguished but economically declining family in Quito. His father, Don Juan Alejandrino Velasco was an engineer, mathematician, and deputy in the national congress. His mother, Doña Delia Ibarra, was a descendent of Simón Bolívar's aide de camp. Velasco Ibarra's passion for politics can be traced to his first mentor, Mons. Federico González Suárez, a historian who was his mother's close friend, and he studied law at the Central University and later at the Sorbonne. However, it became obvious that his passion was writing. He wrote more than fifteen books and hundreds of newspaper articles under the pseudonym of Labriolle. He was married twice, the first time in 1922 to Esther Silva, whom he divorced after eleven years, and the second time to Corina Parral, an Argentine.

4. *El Comercio,* August 14, 1933.

5. Amparo Menéndez-Carrión, *La Conquista del Voto* (Quito: Corporación Editora Nacional and FLACSO, 1986), 102.

6. Ximena Sosa-Buchholz, "Velasquismo: The Most Significant Movement in Modern Ecuadorian History, 1932–72," (PhD diss., University of New Mexico, 1996).

7. "Alianza Democrática Ecuatoriana: Puntos Pragmáticos," *El Universo,* December 18, 1943.

8. Carlos de la Torre, *La Seducción Velasquista* (Quito: Librimundi-FLACSO, 1993), 228.

9. Steve Stein, *Populism in Peru: The Emergence of the Masses and the Politics of Social Control* (Madison: University of Wisconsin Press, 1980), 3.

10. Velasco Ibarra, "El Pueblo frente a la Demagogia Anarquizante: En la Inau-

guración de la Exposición organizada por el Curso de Capacitación del Sindicato Unico de Choferes de Pichincha, el 16 de Mayo de 1955," in *Discursos 1933–56* (Quito: Ed. Santo Domingo, n.d.), 97.

11. José Álvarez Junco, *El Emperador del Paralelo: Lerroux y la Demagogia Populista* (Madrid: Alianza Editorial, 1990), quoted in Ruby Rodríguez Castelo, "Análisis Crítico de la Noción de Populismo" (Tesis de Maestria en Ciencias Políticas, FLACSO, August 1991), 46.

12. Velasco Ibarra, "Síntesis del Discurso del Dr. Velasco Ibarra pronunciado en Guayaquil, el 4 de Junio de 1944," in *Discursos 1933–56,* 32.

13. Ernesto Laclau, *On Populist Reason* (London: Verso, 2005), 167.

14. See Ximena Sosa-Buchholz, "La Memoria Colectiva de Velasco Ibarra y su legado en la cultura política" in ed. Ximena Sosa-Buchholz and William Waters, *Estudios Ecuatorianos: Un Aporte a la Discusión* (Quito: FLACSO/Abya Yala, 2006).

15. See John Martz, "The Regionalist Expression of Populism: Guayaquil and the CFP, 1948–1960," *Journal of Interamerican Studies and World Affairs* 22, no. 3 (August 1980).

16. República del Ecuador, February 27, 1978, 1, quoted by Martz, "Ecuador and the CFP, 1962–81," *Studies in Comparative International Development* 3 (1983): 33.

17. Catherine Conaghan, "Party Politics and Democratization in Ecuador," in *Authoritarians and Democrats: Regime Transition in Latin America,* ed. James Malloy and Mitchell Seligson (Pittsburgh: University of Pittsburgh Press, 1988), 148.

18. Jaime Roldós Aguilera, "Mensaje al asumir el Mando," in *Jaime Roldós y su pensamiento* (Quito: Sendip, 1982), 15.

19. For a discussion on masculine identities, see Ximena Sosa-Buchholz, "Changing Images of Male and Female in Ecuadorian Populist Politics" in *Gender and Populism in Latin America: Passionate Politics,* ed. Karen Kampwirth (University Park: Pennsylvania State University Press, 2010).

20. For a concise characterization see Kenneth Roberts, "Neoliberalism and the Transformation of Populism in Latin America: The Peruvian Case," *World Politics* 48, no. 1 (October 1995): 88.

21. "Señor Presidente, No siga Amurallándose," January 26, 1997, and "La Lección: No Comprar Sueños Baratos," *El Comercio,* January 27, 1997.

22. See Brian Selmeski, "Some of Indians and Indians Sons: Military Service, Familial Metaphors and Multicultural Nationalism," in *Highland Indians and the State in Modern Ecuador,* ed. A. Kim Clark and Marc Becker (Pittsburgh: University of Pittsburgh Press, 2007).

23. See Ximena Sosa-Buchholz, "El cambio del color étnico en el poder en Ecuador: Militares e Inígenas al mando del gobierno," unpublished paper.

24. See César Montúfar, "El populismo intermitente de Lucio Gutiérrez," in *El*

retorno del pueblo: Populismo y nuevas democracias en América Latina, ed. Carlos de la Torre and Enrique Peruzzotti (Quito: FLACSO/ Ministerio de Cultura, 2008).

25. See Raúl A. Sánchez Urribarri, "Venezuela: Turning Further Left," in *Leftovers: Tales of the Latin American Left,* ed. Jorge Castañeda and Marco A. Morales (New York/London: Routledge, 2008), 186–90.

26. See Catherine Conaghan, "Ecuador: Correa's Plebiscitary Presidency," *Journal of Democracy* 19, no. 2 (2008): 46–60.

27. Gustavo Larrea, *Revolución Ciudadana* (Quito: Planeta, 2009), 36–39.

28. Mark Weisbrot and Luis Sandoval, *Update on the Ecuadorian Economy* (Washington, D.C.: Center for Economic and Policy Research, 2009), 17.

29. "Carondelet gasta en 2010 el doble en salarios," *HOY,* March 5, 2010.

30. *www.transparency.org.* See also "Ecuador figura entre los países más afectados por la corrupción," *Vistazo,* November 17, 2009.

31. Office of the United States Trade Representative, "Ecuador" in *2009 National Trade Estimate Report on Foreign Trade Barriers* (Washington, D.C., 2009): 151–57.

32. "Alianza País Guayas analiza su futrro como partido," *El Comercio,* March 22, 2010.

8

Panama for the Panamanians

The Populism of Arnulfo Arias Madrid

William Francis Robinson

On August 17, 1988, hundreds of thousands of Panamanians jammed the streets of the capital city to pay tribute to their most prominent and controversial leader in this century, Arnulfo Arias Madrid. His death a week earlier in Miami raised concerns for the ruling military government. Gen. Manuel Antonio Noriega braced himself for the antigovernment demonstrations he believed would follow the return of Arnulfo's body to Panama. Arnulfo's funeral cortege, buffeted by the grieving throngs, took nearly five hours to travel five miles from the cathedral to the cemetery. No other figure in Panamanian history so deeply stirred the emotions of his fellow countrymen. For over a half century, Arnulfo Arias stood at the forefront of the political scene as a staunch defender of Panamanian nationalism. He embodied the struggle of the middle class against the Panamanian oligarchy and military, while his heightened sense of nationalism led him to undertake initiatives that angered the United States. Also Panama's most accomplished vote-getter, Arnulfo Arias served as president of the Republic on three separate occasions.[1]

Born into a rural lower-middle-class family in Penonomé in the interior province of Coclé in 1901, Arnulfo Arias became a willful, ambitious child who acceded to his mother's wishes to apply himself to his studies in school. His older brother Harmodio had received a scholarship to study in Great Britain and returned to Panama in 1911 with a law degree from Cambridge University and a doctorate from the University of London. Arnulfo also received his professional training abroad: after completion of his studies at a preparatory school in New York, he earned a Bachelor of Science from the University of Chicago, followed by a medical degree from Harvard University. Although he hailed from a rural background of small landholders, Arnulfo Arias's education lofted him into Panama's small upper-middle class.

Nationalist Sentiments

Arnulfo returned to Panama in 1925 and served as a surgeon in the Santo Tomas Hospital until the beginning of the 1930s, when his passion and focus switched to politics. During his first two presidencies (1940–41, 1949–51), he continued to provide free medical services to the needy, though by 1951 his medical career had essentially ended. Arnulfo's interest in Panamanian politics stemmed from his conviction that the political system was corrupt and that the ruling Liberal Party concerned itself with only the well-being of the elite.

Arnulfo Arias saw himself as part of a growing professional class marginalized by a Panamanian oligarchy that thrived on the benefits derived from a cozy commercial relationship with the United States. Independence, gained from Colombia in 1903, came to Panama with an extremely heavy price. The Hay–Bunau-Varilla Treaty of 1903 traded away Panamanian sovereignty and self-determination in exchange for a commitment by the United States to build a canal and to guarantee the independence and security of the new-born republic. The forging of Panamanian independence thus resulted from an alliance between small, mercantile elite in Panama City, who profited from the operation of the canal, and the United States, which enjoyed considerable economic, strategic, and military advantages.

Following independence, Panamanian politics careened from crisis to crisis, relying on the U.S. government to oversee elections and to maintain a semblance of stability. After an initial decade of conservative rule, the Liberal Party imposed one-party rule that converted political elections into personality contests devoid of substantial debate on national issues. Political allegiances were based on politicians' personal interests rather than ideology or conviction.

For many Panamanians involved in politics during the 1920s, government service represented a gateway to personal advancement, and the presidencies of Rodolfo Chiari and his handpicked successor, Florencio Harmodio Arosemena, certainly reached unparalleled levels of corruption, graft, and nepotism. As the nation faced increasing economic and financial crises during the 1920s, the political machine of Chiari's Liberal Party continued to serve the economic interests of a select few. Rodolfo Chiari collected five percent from the salaries of government employees and then placed the proceeds in the Liberal Party coffers. With the National Election Board in their pocket, party bosses amassed a considerable war chest that, combined with electoral dirty tricks, made them invincible at the polls.

Frustrated by a political system dominated by elites and supported by the United States, a group of middle-class professionals met in August 1923 to create a nationalist civic organization known as Acción Comunal. Made up mostly of doctors, lawyers, civil servants, and engineers, Acción Comunal sought to open up the political system and promote national regeneration. Members of Acción Comunal believed that the greatest obstacle to strengthening national identity came from the commercial elites who furthered their own economic positions by allowing foreign domination of the country.

Foremost in the minds of this rising generation of young professionals was the sordid manner in which Panama had been sold out by vested interests at its inception, then forced to suffer a series of injustices. These included U.S. military interventions, importation of tens of thousands of black West Indian laborers, and institutionalized discrimination against Panamanian employees in the Canal Zone. In the eyes of Acción Comunal members, the oligarchy and its U.S. protectors represented a destructive force to incipient Panamanian nationalism.

Arnulfo Arias joined Acción Comunal in November 1930. The organization, with its secret rules and rituals, advocated a defensive style of nationalism captured in the platform slogan "Speak Spanish and count in Balboas." To protect Panamanian national identity, Acción Comunal demanded the implementation of the following measures: educate children in the love of country, teach children to respect the flag, speak proper Spanish, use the national currency (Balboas), avoid businesses with signs in English, limit the number of foreigners in government positions, and refrain from buying from establishments not owned or run by Panamanians. The leadership of Acción Comunal also preached increased state intervention in the economy and the need to replace the Treaty of 1903 with an agreement that recognized Panamanian sovereignty and eliminated U.S. rights to intervene.

An attempt by the administration of Rodolfo Chiari to satisfy some of these nationalist aspirations resulted in a new treaty, initialed in 1926. In secret negotiations led by Ricardo J. Alfaro, Panama ran up against an intransigent U.S. negotiating team that sought only to strengthen the North American strategic and military position in Panama. The Treaty of 1926, rather than making concessions to Panamanian nationalist concerns, instead forced Panama into a closer military alliance with the United States. Acción Comunal vehemently attacked the treaty in its newspaper, in pamphlets, and in public forums.

Harmodio Arias, Arnulfo's brother, though not a member of Acción Comunal, nevertheless served as its voice in the National Assembly and helped turn public opinion against the treaty. Its eventual rejection by the legislature solidified the prestige of Acción Comunal and put Harmodio Arias in the limelight.

Throughout the late 1920s, and especially during the chaotic presidency of Florencio Harmodio Arosemena (1928–31), Acción Comunal intensified its open campaign of defiance against the Liberal regime. Convinced that Arosemena could be removed only by violence, Arnulfo Arias led a daring attack on the presidential palace (Palacio de las Garzas) in the early morning hours of January 2, 1931. Although the coup had been carefully planned with the utmost secrecy, the president of Acción Comunal, Víctor F. Goytía, tried to call off the assault at the last minute, fearing possible U.S. intervention. Even Arnulfo's brother Harmodio wavered in his support as the final hours approached. Fearing all would be lost if the coup were aborted, Arnulfo Arias thrust himself into the leadership of Acción Comunal. His determination to carry through with the assault on the presidential palace, clearly the most dangerous of the three sites attacked by revolutionary forces, resulted in the overthrow of President Arosemena. The fall of the regime represented a turning point in Panamanian history. The coup led by Arnulfo Arias marked the first time since independence that a constitutionally elected government had been violently swept from power.

Political maneuvering in the aftermath of the revolution proceeded quickly. The United States made no attempt to save the corrupt Arosemena regime but insisted that future changes to the Panamanian political landscape occur through constitutional means. Seeking to quell U.S. State Department concerns, the Panamanian Supreme Court engaged in a clever constitutional sleight of hand that placed Harmodio Arias in the presidency on an interim basis until Minister Plenipotentiary Ricardo J. Alfaro could return from Washington to become the next president of Panama.

The choice of Alfaro pleased the United States because his tempered diplomatic skills impressed government officials. Many of Acción Comunal's most loyal adherents, however, pointed to the chaotic search for a new president after the coup as the moment when the momentum of the revolution might be lost. In fact, some argued that the same political insiders that the coup was designed to purge hijacked the revolution at the moment of its inception by placing Alfaro in the presidency.[2] Ricardo J. Alfaro, negotiator of the hated Treaty of 1926, never belonged to Acción Comunal and took no part in the overthrow of Arosemena. He stood out as one of Panama's most distinguished lawyers, however, and enjoyed U.S. support.

Presidential Politics

Harmodio Arias followed Alfaro into the presidency by winning the 1932 election over Francisco Arias Paredes, who hailed from a wealthy family unrelated to the Arias brothers. Arnulfo took up a cabinet position as secretary of agriculture and public works and founded the National Revolutionary Party. Simply put, the party was designed to maintain the Arias family's hold on the presidency until Arnulfo was ready to run in 1940.

Harmodio and Arnulfo shrewdly orchestrated this plan by ensuring the victory of a caretaker candidate in the 1936 election. To elect their candidate, the Arias brothers presided over an election marked by abuses of power and fraud perpetrated by the National Police. The government facilitated distribution of fake voter cards, multiple voting, destruction of ballot boxes, detention of members of the National Election Board, and the stuffing of ballot boxes.[3] With the victory of the Arias candidate, Arnulfo left for Western Europe, where he served as roving ambassador, awaiting his turn to run for the presidency.

The National Revolutionary Party nominated Arnulfo Arias for president at its convention in October 1939. Arnulfo enjoyed the full support of the government throughout his campaign. Returning home from Europe in December 1939, Arnulfo spoke before a large crowd in front of the railroad station in Panama City. He presented a dynamic new political creed. Known as Panameñismo, Arnulfo's political doctrine spoke to the patriotic emotions of his audience: "Panameñismo: sound, serene, based on research and study of our geography, our geology, our flora and fauna, our history, and our ethnic composition. Only in this way can we achieve our goal of well-organized institutions and a perfect government that can produce the greatest happiness possible, security, and sociopolitical stability."

Panameñismo encouraged everything Panamanian, declared the exalted ideal of love of country, and proposed to effect substantive social change through proper education. During the course of the 1940 presidential campaign, Arnulfo Arias elaborated on some of the most salient features of Panameñista doctrine. Using slogans such as "Panama for Panamanians" and "For a Better Panama," he insisted that the nation needed a homegrown doctrine that addressed the specific needs of the Panamanian people. Arnulfo Arias claimed that for revival or rejuvenation to take place, Panamanians needed to change their views concerning government. Service to country had to grow out of patriotism, not out of anticipation of financial advancement. Arnulfo called upon his countrymen to work together to increase economic production in order to raise the standard of living for all. Arnulfo's ideas struck an emotional chord with audiences. Back in 1924, Panama's president and senior statesmen, Belisario Porras, said: "Panama exists because of and for the Canal." Arnulfo Arias crafted Panameñista doctrine to repudiate this very type of thinking. Considered in their entirety, these ideas were not a clearly defined ideology but rather a rough sketch for government reform.[4]

Arnulfo Arias received the presidential sash on October 1, 1940, after his triumph over the Popular Front candidate Ricardo J. Alfaro in an election marred by confrontation and violence. Shortly after the revolution of 1931, members of Community Action divided into different factions—some closing ranks with the Arias brothers to ensure Arnulfo followed Harmodio into the presidency. Other members split off and became intractable opponents.

The Popular Front, an alliance formed to support Alfaro's candidacy, contained many Liberals from the Chiari era, members of the Socialist Party, and Community Action followers opposed to Arnulfo. Tensions ran high with Arnulfista supporters labeling the Popular Front as communistic, while rivals labeled Arnulfo a "Creole Fuhrer," in reference to his apparent fascination with the fascist governments of Adolf Hitler and Benito Mussolini. With the machinery of the government behind him, and with the National Police at his disposal, Arnulfo succeeded in eliminating any possibility of a Popular Front victory. Only days before the election, Alfaro withdrew from the race and allowed his rival an uncontested victory.

President-elect Arias opted at the outset to break with tradition. Previous presidential inaugurations had taken place in the National Theater, which accommodated only several hundred guests of honor. To facilitate a huge popular turnout, Arnulfo transferred his inauguration to the spacious confines of the National Stadium, where he basked in the adulation of the crowd.

Panameñismo in Action

As president, he charged into action with great intensity, determined to shake up Panama's political and economic structures. For years Panamanian politicians had talked about enacting reforms to correct inadequacies in the Constitution of 1904; but although tentative studies had been undertaken, nothing of substance had emerged. In a period of less than two months, President Arias rammed through the National Assembly a new constitution that reflected the tenets of his Panameñista doctrine.

The Constitution of 1941, ratified by referendum, introduced a new concept of social rights that included government protection of the family and salaried workers, programs for social assistance, and national education. At the same time, the Constitution of 1941 stated explicitly that the rights of the state came before the rights of the individual. Believing that the president must have unfettered authority to make rapid decisions to undertake national renovation, Arnulfo Arias included in the constitution provisions to ensure a powerful executive branch. He also provided for state intervention in economic matters.

Other important legislative acts of Arnulfo Arias's presidency included extension of the vote to women, limited agrarian reform, creation of a social secu-

Figure 8.1. New President and Elder Statesman: Arnulfo Arias and Belisario Porras at inauguration ceremony, October 1, 1940. (Courtesy of Jorge Conte Porras)

rity system, government protection of the family, a national campaign in favor of the Spanish language, and protection of Panamanian merchants through a program termed "nationalization of commerce." This last legislation, designed to insulate Panamanian merchants from the competition of foreign shop owners, reflected deep racial and ethnic tensions within Panamanian social and economic life.

From early on in his political career, Arnulfo Arias had expressed feelings, widely held in Panama, of resentment toward black West Indian laborers and Chinese shop owners living on the Isthmus. Viewing the English-speaking West Indian population as a foreign body resistant to assimilation, Arias moved to exclude them from Panamanian citizenship. West Indian blacks had been brought to Panama beginning in the mid-nineteenth century to work on projects such as the Panama Railroad, the Panama Canal, and banana plantations run by the United Fruit Company in the province of Bocas del Toro.[5] While their presence created markets for housing and consumer goods, which benefited Panamanian landlords and store owners, the West Indians also competed with Panamanian laborers for jobs in the Canal Zone. Many Panamanians disliked the presence of a large West Indian population in Panama because they associated this community with U.S. domination. Others simply harbored deep racial prejudices.

President Arias denounced the presence of racial minorities while pushing through legislation prohibiting the immigration of Asians, Middle Easterners, North Africans, and West Indians. While the latter faced restrictions on their citizenship, many Chinese shop owners had their businesses expropriated. These enterprises later reopened under Panamanian ownership. Foreign capital also fell under careful scrutiny, and foreign investments were made subject to the strictures of Panamanian law. Such drastic domestic changes engendered heated debate.

A Sudden Fall

Arnulfo Arias's foreign-policy initiatives likewise triggered huge controversy. Panameñismo clashed with U.S. strategic military interests. President Arias's professed admiration for the authoritarian governments in Germany and Italy raised serious concerns in Washington. Further, despite the outbreak of World War II, Arnulfo refused to cooperate with U.S. defense preparations. Negotiations for leasing defense bases outside the Canal Zone broke down when the Arias government countered U.S. proposals with a list of demands. These included substantial increases in U.S. economic aid, repatriation of West Indians, construction of a bridge over the canal to connect eastern and western Panama, and the return of the lands of the Panama Railroad along with the water and sewer systems of Panama City and Colon.

Arnulfo's attempts to snatch concessions from the United States at a time of international crisis angered U.S. officials. What finally ruptured relations between Panama and the United States was the Arias government's refusal to accede to President Franklin D. Roosevelt's request that Panama arm merchant vessels flying its flag of convenience, most of which belonged to U.S. companies. Arnulfo's intransigence, inspired by his commitment to uphold Panamanian sovereignty against U.S. domination, had dangerous consequences. A combination of rising internal pressures coupled with U.S. opposition sealed the fate of his administration.

On October 9, 1941, President Arias secretly left the country to visit a mistress in Cuba. U.S. intelligence officials in the Canal Zone immediately informed Justice Minister Ricardo Adolfo de la Guardia that the president had abandoned the country. Arnulfo's own constitution required that foreign presidential trips be approved by the National Assembly. Thus began a series of high-level political maneuvers that resulted in a coup that toppled Arnulfo from the presidency.

During his one year in office, Arnulfo had succeeded in alienating many powerful people. Officials of the National Police resented Arnulfo's attempt to dominate the armed forces by replacing some of them with Arias cronies. His authoritarian and impulsive nature even turned his brother into a critic of the regime. Harmodio Arias expressed opposition to his brother's policies in the pages of the family newspaper, *El Panamá América*.

Ricardo de la Guardia assumed the presidency and justified his overthrow of the government by claiming that Arnulfo Arias was a Nazi sympathizer who had seriously jeopardized relations with the United States. Arnulfo's return to Panama a few days later failed to spark any popular uprising on his behalf. Instead, government agents hustled Arnulfo onto a plane and into exile. Shortly thereafter, the Panamanian government rescinded the prohibition against arming Panamanian-flagged merchant vessels and pledged full cooperation with U.S. military needs.

Isthmian Populism

Arnulfo's short and tumultuous administration might best be termed proto-populist. He certainly mounted a campaign that engaged voters in a debate over the role of government and what it meant to be a Panamanian. His style, daring, and ambition resembled other populists in the region, as did his call for citizens from all walks of life to rally behind the nation. The whirlwind constitutional reforms and defiance of the United States echoed Arturo Alessandri and Hipólito Yrigoyen, respectively.

In other ways, however, Arnulfo failed to build a populist coalition and lead it into government. He alienated groups without much reason, behaved imperiously toward established elites and institutions, and did little to bring more people into the political system. In time he might have become a populist in this first term, but his ouster cut short his administration. His second term, however, corrected earlier mistakes and emerged as full-blown populism. Significantly, Arnulfo had spent the previous four years in Buenos Aires, observing the rise of Juan Domingo Perón.

On October 13, 1945, leaflets distributed in Panama City proclaimed, "Ya viene el hombre" ("The man is coming"), referring to Arnulfo Arias's return from exile in Argentina. Arnulfo immediately headed to the emotional epicenter of Panamanian politics, Plaza Santa Ana, where he led an impassioned demonstration against the government. With an eye on the presidential election of 1948, Arnulfo labored to solidify his bases of support among urban workers, rural smallholders, and small business owners. As the campaign approached,

Arnulfo Arias, as the opposition candidate representing the Authentic Revolutionary Party, faced concerted efforts by the government and National Police to ensure his defeat. In an election marked by heightened tensions and outbreaks of violence, Arnulfo won a majority of the popular vote, but his opponent, Domingo Díaz Arosemena, was declared the victor after the National Election Board manipulated the final vote counts. Arnulfo's bid to return to the presidency had been temporarily halted. Arnulfo Arias left for Costa Rica and Guatemala in an unsuccessful effort to organize an armed invasion of Panama with outside backing.

Economic crisis and political turbulence rocked Panama, and the death of President Domingo Díaz on August 23, 1949, further heightened pressures. Demonstrators protested against Chief of Police José Antonio Remón for abusing his powers by intervening in the presidential succession. Filling a power vacuum created by the U.S. policy of nonintervention, the National Police flexed increasing political muscle.[6] The new kingmaker, Colonel Remón, toppled two hapless presidents in rapid succession.

"We Will Return!"

At a moment of national crisis, the complex and muddled world of Panamanian politics witnessed a most unlikely sequence of events. Colonel Remón, an implacable foe of the Arias family, struck a deal with Arnulfo Arias that resulted in Arnulfo becoming the president of Panama for a second time on November 25, 1949. The National Election Board, with embarrassing haste, recounted the tallies of the 1948 election and declared Arnulfo the winner by 2,544 votes. The question in the minds of most Panamanians was whether Arnulfo had mellowed since the fiasco of his first presidency. Out of power, Arnulfo behaved as the consummate statesman, thoughtfully examining Panama's numerous problems and providing concrete suggestions for its future development. While in office, however, Arnulfo seemed to undergo a complete transformation. He made wild statements that led some to doubt his sanity. As president, Arnulfo quickly assumed a "them-and-us" mentality, prompting him to shut down newspapers, revoke constitutional privileges, imprison critics, and rely on the forceful tactics of personal paramilitary organizations.[7]

The new president faced determined opposition and persistent criticism. To strengthen his grip on the government, he removed from office unsympathetic mayors. Liberals in the National Assembly, leftist groups, and students accused him of being a dictator. Arnulfo then unleashed his personal secret police against opposition groups that he characterized as communist-inspired. In addition, the press presented growing evidence that the president involved himself in numerous shady business dealings, misappropriated government funds, and extorted 5 percent from the wages of government employees.

A protracted struggle developed between President Arias and the National Assembly. Rumors spread throughout the capital that Arnulfo's increasingly authoritarian methods would eventually result in his dismissal of the National Assembly. In fact, on May 7, 1951, President Arias announced that he and his cabinet had decided to abolish the Constitution of 1946 and replace it with the Constitution of 1941, dissolve the National Assembly, and suspend the magistrates of the Supreme Court. Panama fell into chaos. On May 8, members of the National Assembly, magistrates of the Supreme Court, and student leaders visited Colonel Remón at his residence to insist on his personal intervention. Remón declined to intervene actively, but he did agree to ask President Arias to reverse the government decree. Arnulfo Arias refused.

The following day the National Assembly met to offer the presidency to Vice President Alcibiades Arosemena. Meanwhile, President Arias telephoned Remón and declared his willingness to drop the Constitution of 1941, but it was simply too late. Arnulfo's dictatorial actions had unleashed tremendous pressures and a widespread public outcry for his resignation. In view of the severity of the political crisis, Remón withdrew his support for President Arias. On May 10, 1951, when two members of the National Police attempted to inform the president of his removal from office by the National Assembly, shots rang out in the presidential palace killing the two officers. In the confusion that followed, an intense gun battle erupted between the followers of President Arias and the National Police. After approximately four hours of skirmishing, Arnulfo and his supporters in the Palacio de las Garzas surrendered. As he left the presidential palace, Arnulfo Arias uttered a cry of defiance: "¡Volveremos!" or "We will return!"

On May 25, 1951, the National Assembly brought formal charges of murder and abuse of presidential power against Arnulfo Arias—the first time in Panamanian history that the legislative branch stood in judgment over the actions of a chief executive. Arnulfo refused to recognize the National Assembly's jurisdiction over him. Rather than participate in the trial, the former president chose instead to sit quietly in the courtroom and read an adventure novel. Shrugging off the protracted hearings, Arnulfo Arias declared in his defense that "The people are the ones who have the last word." At the conclusion of the trial, the National Assembly, serving as a tribunal of justice, formally revoked his presidential powers and permanently disqualified him from holding public office. Found guilty of overstepping the bounds of his constitutional powers, Arnulfo Arias spent nearly ten months in Modelo Prison. But even while incarcerated,

Arnulfo created problems for the government. He rallied support for an early release, and he continued to direct the political actions of his followers. From his jail cell, Arnulfo gave orders for the founding of a new political organization called the Panameñista Party.

Arnulfo learned a great deal during the 1940s, and he managed to stay in office nearly twice as long as his first term. He no longer baited the United States, he respected the interests of the business community, and he left the National Police to its own devices. He clearly enjoyed the support of the vast numbers of people who resonated to his strident speeches and policies. Still, his impetuous character and inability to strike compromises led him into trouble time and again, and the elites simply decided to cut short his embarrassing administration. He was now a populist but not a very successful one, reminiscent of Velasco Ibarra's career.

The 1960s

After he was released from prison in February 1952, Arnulfo remained on the political sidelines for many years. Finally, in 1960 Harmodio Arias, who had ended his feud with Arnulfo, struck a deal with presidential candidate Roberto F. Chiari to trade political support for the restoration of Arnulfo's political rights. In early October 1960 the National Assembly passed a resolution for Arnulfo's political rehabilitation.

Once again Arnulfo jumped into the fray. In January 1964 a bloody clash occurred between U.S. military forces and Panamanian students intent on flying the Panamanian flag alongside that of the United States inside the Canal Zone. Most Panamanians regarded the slain students as martyrs who died for the cause of national sovereignty. Arnulfo Arias, seeking U.S. blessing for his run for the presidency, labeled the students "victims of foreign influences," in a clear reference to international communism. Faced with a growing public outcry, Arnulfo adjusted his position slightly by pointing to the heroism of the students. Nevertheless, Arnulfo continued to demonstrate his extreme anticommunist leanings by warning Panamanians that "international traitors" were using the patriotic passions of the youth for criminal purposes.

Arnulfo Arias ran for president again in 1964 at the head of the Panameñista Party, but an alliance of the oligarchy and National Guard (so renamed in 1953) blocked his probable victory. Arnulfo immediately denounced the electoral process as fraudulent. Having run solely on the strength of his own popular appeal, Arnulfo determined to seek alliances in the next election to guarantee his victory.

In 1968, Arnulfo Arias began to cultivate sectors of Panamanian society that for decades had been his most obstinate enemies. These included the oligarchy, politicians who had participated in the coup of 1951, West Indian voters, and officials of the National Guard.[8] Times had definitely changed since Arnulfo's first run for the presidency in 1940, for in his 1968 campaign he even gained the acquiescence of the U.S. State Department.

Serious political unrest throughout the 1960s accounted for the drastic realignment of political forces in anticipation of the 1968 election campaign. The liberal governments of Roberto F. Chiari (1960–64) and Marco A. Robles (1964–68) responded with violence to protests from workers, students, and the urban unemployed who demanded lower rents and an increased minimum wage. Strikes by transport workers, school teachers, and banana workers created a tense atmosphere of confrontational politics. Disagreement over the government's handling of the economy created a split in the normally unified Panamanian oligarchy. Arnulfo Arias exploited the division, procuring the strong support of several leading industrialists.

His political fortunes rising, Arnulfo moved to terminate efforts by the government to mobilize support for the candidacy of David Samudio. In a preemptive strike, pro-Arias forces in the National Assembly impeached President Robles for illegal interference in the election. The National Guard threw its support behind Robles, enabling him to finish his presidency while triggering yet another confrontation with Arnulfo and his followers.

From the beginning of his election campaign, Arnulfo attempted to avoid alienating the National Guard, which had conspired to depose him twice before. But with the National Guard firmly behind the official candidate, Arnulfo launched a series of public attacks against the military, which retaliated by ransacking his election headquarters and jailing his followers. On May 9, 1968, while on a campaign tour in Darién Province, Arnulfo survived an assassination attempt, declaring defiantly: "Bullets will not prevent our victory." A few days later on May 12, 1968, Arnulfo's political alliance rolled to victory by a substantial margin over Liberal Party candidate David Samudio.

What remained to be seen was whether the National Guard would recognize Arnulfo's claim to the presidency. After the election Arnulfo and the commander of the National Guard, Bolívar Vallarino, reached an uneasy understanding: the armed forces would recognize Arnulfo's victory if Arnulfo and his followers took no reprisals against the military and respected the military hierarchy. Arnulfo's large margin of victory at the polls forced Vallarino to deal. He feared that any attempt to manipulate the vote in favor of the official candidate would be met by an explosive reaction that the military would be hard pressed to control.

On inauguration day, October 1, 1968, ominous conditions prevailed. In his inaugural address, Arnulfo proudly declared that his government would be "of the people, by the people, and for the people" and that sinister "invisible governments" representing special interests would be eliminated. He concluded his speech with the following appeal: "In our political life, there is one lesson we have to learn and can never forget: in the pages of history only those governments that embody the legitimate desires and genuine support of the masses endure—this lesson will guide us every hour and every minute of our mandate."

One of Arnulfo's first acts as president was to call for negotiations leading to the return of the canal to Panama, harkening back to his earliest nationalist efforts on behalf of Panamanian sovereignty. President Arias confidently declared that he would put things back in order. Panama existed in a state of national panic, however, with rumors that the Arias government would return to autocratic methods and that Arnulfo's Panameñista followers would seek revenge on their enemies.

The Military's Shadow

Recognizing that the chaotic political climate lent itself to yet another coup, President Arias broke his agreement with the National Guard and proceeded to tinker with its chain of command in an effort to secure his base of power. On October 11, 1968, after only eleven days in office, members of the armed forces led by Maj. Boris Martínez and Lt. Col. Omar Torrijos overthrew the Arias government and replaced it with a provisional governing junta. Arnulfo Arias fled to the Canal Zone, where he hoped to gain U.S. support for a successful counterattack. Arnulfo claimed that the United States had "a moral obligation to see constitutional democracy restored in Panama, because it had provided the National Guard with arms and had trained it in their use."

Failing to trigger U.S. intervention, Arnulfo then appealed unsuccessfully for the Organization of American States to take action. Finally, from exile in Miami, Arnulfo directed several short-lived guerrilla movements that attacked the National Guard from bases in the provinces of Chiriquí, Veraguas, and his native Coclé. With the opposition quelled, Omar Torrijos emerged as the leader of an authoritarian military government that controlled Panamanian politics for the next twenty-one years.[9]

Arnulfo Arias returned to Panama in June 1978 after a prolonged exile. In 1984, at the age of eighty-two, he ran for president as the representative of a group of political parties under the title Opposition Alliance. Though he probably defeated Nicolás Ardito Barletta, the candidate of the Noriega regime, Arnulfo Arias once again was denied the presidency by the military. Nevertheless, his popular support and charismatic appeal made him a symbol of protest

198 / William Francis Robinson

and a guiding force for the opposition to the military government. Gen. Manuel Noriega considered him a dangerous opponent.

Continuismo

Arnulfismo lives on, however, because Arnulfo's widow, Mireya Moscoso, inherited his party and has maintained control over its diverse constituencies. Promising to battle poverty, slow privatization, improve education, and provide more jobs, Moscoso proved herself a relentless campaigner in two runs for the presidency, walking the neighborhoods of every province to ask for votes. In 1994 she came within a few percentage points of victory, while in 1999 she handily defeated her closest rival, Martín Torrijos, whose father, General Omar Torrijos, toppled Arnulfo in 1968.

By shunning the formality of a ceremony in the National Assembly and taking the oath of office in a new twenty-thousand-seat baseball stadium, Moscoso recalled the style of her late husband. In December 1999 she oversaw the historic U.S. handover of the Panama Canal, declaring triumphantly, "The canal is ours!" But like other populists who made sweeping promises, Moscoso failed to deliver on the structural changes needed for meaningful transformation. Panama's most serious economic and social woes remained unresolved. Instead, allegations of corruption, nepotism, and mismanagement of funds dogged her presidency. Mireya Moscoso will be remembered as her country's first woman president as well as the first president to govern a fully sovereign Panama.

Conclusion

Throughout his long and controversial political career, Arnulfo Arias suffered intense personal attacks, criticism, and slander. Over the years, governments denied him election victories, jailed him, stripped him of his political rights, and forced him into exile. He survived several assassination attempts. While at the center of most political intrigues for over a half century, Arnulfo Arias somehow managed to distance himself from small-scale political infighting. His unwavering self-confidence and charismatic appeal placed him at the forefront of twentieth-century Panamanian political history.

Arnulfo Arias demonstrated populist qualities. He fought for decades to redress popular grievances. Arnulfo drew from eclectic philosophical sources and fashioned a program of government action that promoted Panamanian nationalism, expanded the economy, initiated social security legislation, and directed Panamanian self-discovery in art, folkways, and popular culture. Though he hated compromise, Arnulfo learned from the mistakes of his first presidency and made greater efforts at coalition building. He subsequently worked with Panamanian business interests and actively sought the support of the United States and the West Indian community in his election bids.

Always enjoying a close rapport with "the people," Arnulfo could never parlay his successes at the polls into durable political power. His high-handed tactics and disregard for convention created political crises that prevented him from ever completing a single term in office. In the end, Arnulfo's effectiveness as a populist was diminished simply by his inability to remain in power.

Notes

1. For a synthesis of twentieth-century Panamanian history, see Michael L. Conniff, "Panama Since 1903," in *Cambridge History of Latin America,* vol. 7, ed. Leslie Bethell (Cambridge: Cambridge University Press, 1990), 603–42. Two other very useful overviews are Patricia Pizzurno and Celestino Andrés Araúz, *Estudios sobre el Panamá republicano, 1903–1986* (Colombia: Manfer, S.A., 1996) and Michael L. Conniff, *Panama and the United States: The Forced Alliance,* 2nd ed. (Athens: University of Georgia Press, 2001).

2. For a detailed look at Acción Comunal and the Revolution of January 2, 1931, see Isidro Beluche Mora, *Acción Comunal: Surgimiento y estructuración del nacionalismo panameño* (Panama: Editorial Cóndor, 1981) and Víctor Manuel Pérez and Rodrigo Oscar de León Lerma, *El Movimiento de Acción Comunal en Panamá* (Panama: n.p., n.d.). Both works see the ideals of the revolution as having been compromised in the immediate aftermath of the coup. Peter A. Szok, *"La última gaviota": Liberalism and Nostalgia in Early Twentieth-Century Panamá* (Westport, CT: Greenwood Press, 2001) provides a compelling analysis of Panamanian history from independence in 1903 to the coup of 1931.

3. Jorge Conte Porras, *Réquiem por la revolución* (San José: Litografía e Imprenta LIL, S.A., 1990), 172–73.

4. Felipe J. Escobar, *Arnulfo Arias o el credo Panameñista: Ensayo psicopatológico de la política panameña, 1930–1940* (Panama: n.p., 1946).

5. On the history of the West Indian community in Panama, see Michael L. Conniff, *Black Labor on a White Canal, 1904–1981* (Pittsburgh: University of Pittsburgh Press, 1985) and George W. Westerman, *Los inmigrantes antillanos en Panama* (Panama: n.p., 1980).

6. See Larry LaRae Pippin, *The Remón Era: An Analysis of a Decade of Events in Panama, 1947–1957* (Stanford, CA: Institute of Hispanic American and Luso-Brazilian Studies, 1964) and Thomas L. Pearcy, *We Answer Only to God: Politics and the Military in Panama, 1903–1947* (Albuquerque: University of New Mexico Press, 1998).

7. Richard M. Koster and Guillermo Sánchez, *In the Time of the Tyrants: Panama 1968–1990* (New York: Norton, 1991), 62.

8. Carlos Iván Zúñiga quoted in Conte Porras, *Réquiem,* 363.

9. Detailed analyses of the military government can be found in Steve C. Ropp, *Panamanian Politics: From Guarded Nation to National Guard* (New York: Praeger, 1982), and Margaret Scranton, *The Noriega Years: U.S.-Panamanian Relations, 1981–1990* (Boulder: Lynne Rienner, 1991). George Priestley, *Military Government and Popular Participation in Panama: The Torrijos Regime, 1968–1975* (Boulder: Westview, 1986), argues that Gen. Omar Torrijos exhibited populist qualities. Priestley details the formation of a populist alliance by the Panamanian military designed to legitimize its leadership. Priestley argues that the military's revolution from above, which he claims altered class relations within Panama and Panama's relations with the United States, was made possible by anti-oligarchy and anti-U.S. populist political discourse. Strongly refuting this viewpoint is Koster and Sánchez, *Time of the Tyrants,* which portrays Torrijos as a phony populist seeking legitimacy for a criminal regime engaged in drug and weapons smuggling, torture, and murder. Carlos Guevara Mann, *Panamanian Militarism: A Historical Interpretation* (Athens: Ohio University Press, 1996) places the Noriega regime in the longer history of militarism in Panama.

9
Populism in the Age of Neoliberalism

Kurt Weyland

At the beginning of the 1980s, Latin Americans could look back upon a long history of populist politics. But did populism have a future in the region? The military regimes of the 1960s and 1970s tried to exorcise it on the grounds that it incited instability and radicalism. Would the economic crises of the 1980s deal it the coup de grâce? Populist leaders had always built support by distributing benefits to large numbers of followers. The debt crisis and the resulting scarcity of resources severely constrained any government's generosity. Populist leaders seemingly could not use patronage to attract followers, the way their predecessors had. Thus, the likelihood of a return of populist politics looked slim.

Many democratic thinkers and politicians in Latin America welcomed this prospect. The civilian regimes that were returning to power in the region would be spared the populists' demagoguery, mass manipulation, and administrative incompetence. Populism is based on a quasi-direct but hierarchical relationship between a personalist leader and masses of devoted followers. Populist leaders pursued unrestrained discretion and rule in a personalist fashion. They therefore tried to dominate, bypass, or minimize political parties and interest associations. By contrast, many democratic intellectuals and politicians advocated strengthening such intermediary organizations. Only an independent, vigilant civil society could prevent politicians from overstepping their roles, as well as enforce accountability and responsiveness to citizens' needs. Thus, the expected death of populism was widely seen as beneficial to—if not necessary for—the consolidation of Latin America's new democracies.

Unexpectedly, however, the 1980s saw a stunning revival of populism. Surviving members of the older generation of populists, such as Leonel Brizola and Jânio Quadros in Brazil, returned to power through the ballot box. Moreover, a new generation of populists emerged and temporarily prospered. In 1985 the young and charismatic Alan García won Peru's presidency and led his party, APRA, to victory for the first time in its sixty-year history. In Mexico, Cuauhtémoc Cárdenas posed a severe electoral challenge to the long-entrenched authoritarian regime of the Partido Revolucionario Institucional (Institutional Revolutionary Party—PRI). Raúl Alfonsín in Argentina (1983–89) and José Sarney in Brazil (1985–90) also flirted with populism for some time.

Even more surprisingly, at the end of the 1980s, several leaders who had won presidential elections with typical populist appeals imposed drastic economic restructuring measures when they took office. Carlos Menem in Argentina (1989–present), Fernando Collor de Melo in Brazil (1990–92), and Alberto Fujimori in Peru (1990–2000) all rose as political outsiders, based on their direct appeal to large masses of unorganized voters. Collor and Fujimori emerged out of political obscurity and lacked any solid, organized support. Menem wrested the presidential candidacy away from the leadership of his Peronist party, which he has dominated in a personalistic fashion ever since. All three leaders thus attained power in a clearly populist fashion.

Upon taking office, however, the new presidents imposed harsh programs of economic adjustment. This differed completely from the generous distribution of benefits the classical populists of the 1940s to 1960s had used to reward followers. Menem, Collor, and Fujimori drastically cut government spending, dismissed state employees, privatized public enterprises, raised taxes, and exposed business firms to stiff foreign competition. In doing so, they hurt important sectors of the working, middle, and business classes that classical populists had courted. Nevertheless, Menem, Fujimori, and Collor received high public approval ratings. Menem and Fujimori won midterm congressional and constituent assembly elections and were reelected in 1995. In contrast, Collor's policies failed, his support plummeted, and Congress impeached him on charges of corruption.

The resurgence of Latin American populism in the 1980s challenged all predictions of its demise. The neopopulist leaders' pursuit of market-oriented, neoliberal policies that seemed to threaten their very bases of support, moreover, defied the precedents of classical populism. These and other seeming anomalies will be addressed in this essay, which will also explore the implications of neopopulism for Latin America's democracies of the late 1990s.

Overview

The revival of populism can only be explained by focusing on its political characteristics.[1] Personalistic leaders attained and wielded power by establishing a seemingly direct relationship to the heterogeneous, weakly organized, politically available masses. They used economic and social policies as instruments for attracting support. In their quest for power, they adapted skillfully to prevailing opportunities and constraints. In good times, like the 1940s and 1950s, they distributed benefits. In lean years, as in the late 1980s, they posed as saviors trying to rescue their countries from deep economic crises. Several populist leaders, especially Menem and Fujimori, displayed an enormous capacity for turning economic adversity into political advantage.

Even more surprisingly, several populist leaders adopted neoliberal economic policies, thereby violating the precedents of classical populism. Whereas populism and economic liberalism have often been depicted as polar opposites, they have in recent years proven quite compatible. As a result, the strongest advocates of market-oriented reform—government technocrats, academic experts, competitive business sectors, and international financial institutions—were eager to collaborate with neopopulist leaders. They have discovered many affinities.

Both neopopulists and some neoliberals tried to attract electoral support from the unorganized poor. Both found themselves opposing established interest associations, whose members came mainly from the ranks of the working, middle, and business classes. Both neopopulists and neoliberals have also attacked the so-called political class, made up of traditional elected and appointed officials. Neopopulists identified them as corrupt and unaccountable, while neoliberals condemned them as obstacles to the advent of a free-market economy. At the same time, neopopulists and neoliberals strengthened the apex of the state—especially the presidency. The former did so to boost their personal power, the latter to promote market-oriented restructuring despite opposition from entrenched interests.

Despite their enactment of harsh austerity measures, some neopopulist leaders have continued to enjoy mass support. Many voters accepted the need for painful adjustment in order to prevent total economic collapse. The populist leaders, by carrying out such risky policies, enhanced their aura of leadership and charisma. Success in controlling runaway inflation was necessary for their continued popularity. In addition, to garner further support, both neopopulists and neoliberals also instituted welfare programs for the very poor. Neopopulists used these programs to improve their electoral appeal, while neoliberals wanted to make market-oriented restructuring more palatable.

For these reasons, neopopulism and neoliberalism have proven surprisingly compatible in this time of severe economic challenge. Potentially, this combination of seeming opposites may even survive in the long run.

The Populist Revival of the 1980s

The military leaders who ruled in Latin America in the 1960s and 1970s had sought to eradicate populism, which they identified with disorder and turmoil.

They failed in Peru, Ecuador, Brazil, and Argentina, however, because populism reappeared in the 1980s. Where it did not revive, the causes were other than military influence. In several restored democracies, such as Chile and Uruguay, historic parties with considerable internal strength and voter loyalty made it much harder for personalistic leaders to attract followings. In established democracies with strong parties, like Venezuela and Costa Rica, populist leaders found it difficult to establish a foothold. In authoritarian regimes, such as Mexico's, new populist leaders had to fight entrenched parties with considerable political muscle.

Not only were military regimes unable to stem the revival of populism, but their own policies indirectly promoted it. Most military regimes had pursued rapid economic development. They promoted the modernization of agriculture. They improved their countries' transportation and communications infrastructure. In Brazil and Peru, they established new industries. These socioeconomic changes disrupted the lives of poor people, who became available for political mobilization. Clientelist control of local elites over the rural population slowly diminished. Rural bosses found it more difficult to keep their clients completely dependent.

More important, the economic growth of the 1960s and 1970s spurred the migration of millions of farming people from the countryside to the cities. These migrants hoped to find good jobs in the formal sector of the economy. But since many industries had installed capital-intensive technology, they employed only a small portion of the new migrants. The rest had to find jobs in the informal sector, outside the sphere of government regulation. They worked in repair shops, produced goods in their homes or in illegal shops, provided a wide range of services, from shoe shining to housecleaning to prostitution, or sold cheap goods in the streets.

The masses of people employed in the informal sector were a new phenomenon in Latin America. They were not protected by the legal rules prevailing in the formal sector. Their socioeconomic position was highly precarious. For these reasons, they were difficult to organize into broad-based interest associations, unions, or political parties. They often advanced their interests through clientelist networks in slums and tenement districts. But in most cities, patrons' control over their clients proved much weaker than in rural areas, because alternative patrons were available.

The socioeconomic modernization promoted by military regimes thus produced a mass of people available for political mobilization. At the same time, authoritarian regimes weakened intermediary organizations that could have channeled such participation. They prohibited or strictly controlled political parties and interest associations, which were unable to recruit the newly mobilized groups. In the few cases where military regimes promoted organizations to build popular support, as in Peru (1968–75) and Panama (1968–78), their efforts at control failed. Their attempts to garner popular support actually helped to politicize the masses. The economic crises which many military regimes left behind also weakened interest associations, especially labor unions.

In the course of the 1980s, with the military retreating to the barracks and democracy returning in one country after another, intellectuals and politicians hoped that strong parties and interest associations would soon arise. This would favor the consolidation of democracy and also keep populist leaders from emerging. Such expectations only came true in Uruguay and Chile, where parties already had long-standing acceptance in society. Because of that, personalist leaders, such as "Fra-Fra" Errázuriz in Chile, failed to draw large followings and remained minor political players.

In Peru and Brazil, however, and to a lesser extent in Argentina, political parties had always been weakly institutionalized. In the 1980s, they proved unable to absorb the masses that the outgoing military regimes had unintentionally mobilized. In addition, the new democracies in Brazil and Peru extended the suffrage to illiterates, creating substantial pools of new voters. The presence of a politically available mass and the absence of strong intermediary organizations created enormous opportunities for the revival of populism.[2] Old personalist leaders regained their influence and new ones emerged.

In Brazil, for instance, populist leaders of the 1950s and 1960s, such as Leonel Brizola, Jânio Quadros, and Miguel Arraes, reappeared on the political scene and regained control over their regional strongholds. Brizola re-created a populist party as the vehicle for his ambitions. He ran for president twice and almost reached the runoff in 1989.[3]

The most stunning success story of this first wave of neopopulism was the meteoric rise of Alan García in Peru. In the early 1980s, he took complete control of APRA, which had remained disoriented and divided after the 1979 death of its founder and long-time leader, Víctor Raúl Haya de la Torre. In the presidential campaign of 1985, García appealed especially to the unorganized poor in Peru's huge informal sector, which included about half of the economically active population. His charismatic personality and youthful dynamism inspired hope in people who had benefited little from the country's development and who had suffered most from the economic crises of the late 1970s and early 1980s. (See chapter 5.)

Organized groups, in contrast, were much less susceptible to García's populist appeals. Many labor unions and social movements, in particular, had close links to the United Left coalition. Since these sectors could mobilize support and lobby the government, they found attractive the strategy of collective empowerment advocated by the left. Most poor people in the informal sector, in contrast, lacked such organizational capacity. For them, it made sense to support a personalist leader who offered to serve as their benefactor. As a result, García won the 1985 election by a wide margin.

The policies García enacted resembled those of classical populism. He attempted to deepen and extend the import substitution development model, in which the state helped industries that produced for the domestic market and protected them from foreign competition. His government stimulated growth in order to overcome the bottlenecks that it held responsible for the constant price rises. García thus pursued stabilization by expansionary means. This approach also provided benefits to a wide range of groups, just as the classical populists had done. In order to finance this balancing act, García unilaterally capped interest payments on Peru's huge foreign debt. This decision openly defied the International Monetary Fund (IMF), which tried to induce fiscally responsible approaches to the debt crisis. García reinforced his populist credentials by defying the unpopular IMF, widely regarded as an agent of imperialism. García refused to countenance market-oriented, neoliberal stabilization measures.

García's expansionary economic policies worked for about two years. Strong growth and diminishing inflation guaranteed the president enormous popularity in his crisis-ridden country. But problems soon arose. Peru was cut off from foreign loans. Business doubted that the government could sustain its economic policies and failed to invest as much as García had hoped. As a result, scarcities soon plagued the overheating economy. García responded by nationalizing the banking system in order to gain control over investment capital. This act antagonized much of the private sector and emboldened right-wing opponents.

This fierce opposition induced the government eventually to give up the bank nationalization scheme. This defeat and worsening economic problems weakened the president. As inflation rose, García's popularity plummeted. Tough stabilization measures, adopted belatedly, proved ineffectual. The renewed crisis hurt especially the poor and eliminated the gains they had made earlier. By the time García left the presidency in 1990, his populist experiment had resulted in utter failure.[4]

Argentina and Brazil experienced similar sequences of boom and bust, temporary stabilization and resurgent inflation in the 1980s. Like García, Presidents Alfonsín and Sarney tried to end economic crises without imposing costs on important sectors. At first they seemed to succeed. Poorer strata, especially in the informal sector, made considerable gains in the early phases of these heterodox stabilization programs, especially under the Brazilian Cruzado Plan of 1986. But the Alfonsín and Sarney governments failed to eliminate important causes of inflation, such as deficit spending and debt service. As in Peru, inflationary pressures soon resurfaced. Price freezes proved ineffectual. Rising inflation rapidly eliminated the initial gains made by poorer sectors. Subsequent stabilization attempts also failed, eroding government credibility. In Argentina, runaway inflation triggered social turmoil that forced Alfonsín out of office five months before schedule. Sarney also was weakened by poor economic performance and calls for an early election.

All these disasters dashed the high hopes that citizens had placed in García, Alfonsín, and Sarney. It became obvious that the policies pursued by classical populists in the 1940s and 1950s were no longer viable. The fiscal constraints caused by the debt crisis made the distribution of benefits to a wide range of sectors unsustainable. The scarcity of investment capital rendered expansionary policies untenable. Deficit spending was certain to boost inflation, thereby hurting the poor. There was no easy escape from the debt crisis and its many corollaries. Austerity and other painful adjustment measures had to be taken.

Ultimately, the failed policies of García, Alfonsín, and Sarney undermined faith in the import substitution development model. Could crisis-ridden countries afford to sustain inefficient industries behind high trade barriers? Would noncompetitive enterprises ever produce the foreign exchange required for servicing the debt and for investing in new development? How beneficial was large-scale state intervention in the economy, which encouraged corruption and allowed special interests to gain privileges at the expense of the rest of society? Calls for profound economic restructuring grew ever louder.

By the late 1980s, populism had made a surprising comeback in several countries, yet its capacity for governing seemed exhausted by economic limits. Indeed, while democracy opened the path for populism, the economic crises exacerbated by populist leaders might threaten democracy itself. As political and economic rationality followed different paths, disaster seemed imminent. Either populists would continue to win elections and ruin their economies or democracy would have to be suspended in order to impose economic stabilization.

Neoliberal Neopopulism

Learning from the failures of their predecessors, three new populists in the late 1980s—Menem, Collor, and Fujimori—sought ways out of the dilemma. They used populism to impose liberal economic policies, and they used neoliberalism to reinforce their populist leadership. They tried to make the best of the few opportunities available to them. In fact, they skillfully turned adversity into advantage. Considering the odds against them, they achieved a remarkable degree of success. However strained and forced the combination of neoliberalism and neopopulism, it proved surprisingly viable. Certainly, Menem and Fujimori did not perform miracles. Many of their actions were morally reprehensible, but as politicians exercising power, they were quite successful in unfavorable circumstances. Machiavelli's Prince could have taken some pointers from them.

Collor, Fujimori, and Menem won office in typical populist fashion. As charismatic leaders, they appealed directly (usually on television) to unorganized masses of people, especially in the urban informal sector and the countryside. Menem also drew on the organizational networks of the Peronist Party and labor unions. Many voters were available for renewed populist mobilization. The mid-1980s neopopulism and the continued economic problems had weakened party organizations and interest associations. The failures of the García, Alfonsín, and Sarney governments left many people ready to follow a new savior. As inflation reached exorbitant levels of 30–50 percent per month, bold promises to end the crisis became ever more appealing to poorer sectors who were threatened with disaster.

Collor, Fujimori, and Menem exploited these sentiments to gain widespread support. They depicted themselves as outsiders who would clean up the existing mess. They attacked the incumbent governments, politicians in general, powerful interest groups, and socioeconomic elites. They claimed to be benefactors of the downtrodden. Collor appealed to *descamisados,* using an expression coined by Argentine populist Juan Perón in the 1940s. Fujimori exploited the resentment of Peru's darker-skinned, poor majority (*cholos*) against the country's white elite. Menem promised to favor poor workers and invoked the old Peronist loyalties among the most destitute. As a result, all three leaders won the presidency with disproportional support from the poorest, least organized sectors.[5]

Collor and Fujimori ran as outsiders and eschewed support from other parties. Menem won the presidential candidacy against the wishes of his party's leadership, and he did not rely much on the party apparatus to attract votes. Personal appeals, transmitted especially over television, were decisive for the victories of all three candidates. Collor, Fujimori, and Menem thus attained office in typical populist fashion, as personal leaders with a quasi-direct connection to largely unorganized masses.

Upon taking office, however, all three presidents imposed tough measures of economic adjustment and market-oriented restructuring. In the short term, they tried to break hyperinflation by reducing demand. For this purpose, they took unprecedented steps, including the temporary confiscation of bank accounts. They also slashed public spending. These measures pushed their countries into deep recessions. In the medium-term perspective, they tried to implant a neoliberal development model. They reduced state interventionism in order to give the market freer reign. They opened their economies to foreign trade and investment in order to modernize production and force domestic industry to become more efficient.[6] In these ways, they completely reversed the course followed by the classical populists of the 1940s to 1960s and revived by the neopopulists of the early 1980s.

External constraints exacerbated by the debt crisis and the strong pressures from international financial institutions were largely responsible for the populists' unexpected reversals. Instead of fighting the prevailing currents, they decided to go with the flow. They adjusted their policies to the inevitable. But they used their remaining margin of choice, which was significant,[7] to try to ensure that their neoliberal policies would not limit their personal leadership and undermine their popularity among the masses. Indeed, they showed a striking capacity to use economic challenges and constraints to their own advantage.

As a matter of fact, neoliberal economic policies did not preclude continued populism. They even provided new opportunities for strengthening personal leadership. Despite their high initial costs, they actually boosted leaders' popularity. Only when these harsh measures failed to control inflation, as in Brazil, did strong discontent arise. This economic failure contributed greatly to President Collor's impeachment on corruption charges in late 1992.[8] Where economic stabilization was fairly successful, as in Argentina and Peru, neopopulist leaders retained their mass support. In fact, Menem and Fujimori won immediate reelection in 1995.

Thus, notwithstanding the undeniable tensions between neoliberalism and neopopulism, the two have proven much more compatible than expected. Important affinities between the seemingly polar opposites underlay this apparent contradiction. This may even be seen in two instances where populism was not invoked.

Venezuela's Carlos Andrés Pérez (1989–93) and Mexico's Carlos Salinas de Gortari (1988–94) gained office without using populist appeals because they enjoyed the support of well-established, old parties. Still, Salinas was obliged to use populist tactics to make market-oriented restructuring politically viable. Pérez, in contrast, who imposed drastic adjustment measures without facing an open crisis, failed to attain sufficient political support and was removed from office in mid-1993 as the result of a corruption scandal.

Affinities between Neopopulism and Neoliberalism

Mass Support

Populist leaders traditionally sought support from a wide range of social strata, but they appealed to some of them in particular. Argentina's Perón, for example, gave priority to mobilizing urban workers and lower-middle sectors.[9] His party organized these strata into intermediary organizations, which over time came to acquire some independence. In many countries such autonomous organizations eventually made the working and middle class in the formal sector relatively immune to new populist mobilization.

Neopopulist leaders needed to reach below these strata in the social pyramid. They appealed especially to the unorganized poor in the burgeoning informal sectors and in rural areas. These disadvantaged groups remained excluded from most of the benefits of the import substitution development model. Neopopulist leaders found massive support by answering their desire for inclusion. They thus used the unorganized masses to outflank organized civil society.

Advocates of neoliberalism also identified the unorganized poor as a crucial source of backing for their programs. The informal sector, representing a huge portion of the population, in Peru even a majority, could be a decisive source of support. For example, in his influential book *The Other Path*,[10] Peruvian neoliberal Hernando de Soto praised the informal sector for its pursuit of free-market economics. Unregulated by the state, it generated income for millions of people. Unlike businesspeople in the formal sector, its members had no access to government contracts, subsidies, or tariff protection. In the absence of such special privileges, which were paid by the rest of society, undistorted market rules prevailed among the poor. In the view of de Soto and his followers, the growing size of the informal sector showed that a free-market economy was already emerging in Latin America and that it had widespread popular backing.

Whether for reasons of political expediency or theoretical conviction, influential proponents of neoliberalism agreed with neopopulist leaders on the need to win over the unorganized poor in the informal sector. This surprising affinity yielded crucial political successes. Collor and Fujimori won the presidency with disproportional backing from the unorganized poor. Menem received their support, but also that of Peronist labor unions. To be sure, only Collor had campaigned on a platform of enacting market-oriented restructuring. Yet even after Fujimori and Menem unveiled their neoliberal projects, they retained strong support among the poorest sectors. Opinion polls suggested that both presidents won disproportionate backing from the informal sector that carried over to later congressional and constituent assembly elections. It also led both presidents to immediate reelection in 1995.[11]

Distance from Intermediary Organizations

Both neopopulism and neoliberalism also shared an adversarial relationship with many established intermediary organizations, which found members mainly among the formal working, middle, and business classes. Neopopulist leaders tried to bypass parties and interest associations or to subordinate them to their personal ambitions. Once in office, they marginalized these organizations from decision making in order to expand their own autonomy. Neoliberals, in turn, attacked these organizations' efforts to gain political influence and illicit privileges that undermine market competition.

Collor and Fujimori intentionally distanced themselves from intermediary organizations. They rose out of political obscurity without the backing of any significant party or association. In office, they maintained a high degree of autonomy and kept established interest groups and parties at bay. Both Collor's and Fujimori's parties were purely personal vehicles. Collor even snubbed Brazil's premier business association, the Federação e Centro das Indústrias do Estado de São Paulo (Federation of Industries of São Paulo—FIESP), and ignored its long-standing privilege of consulting with the government. Both presidents also weakened and divided labor unions.

Since Menem could use the Peronist Party and its affiliated labor unions for his own purposes, he did not bypass these intermediary organizations in the same way. His base of support more closely resembled that of classical populists, comprising the working and lower-middle classes and the informal sector. But in typical populist fashion, Menem dominated his party and the Peronist unions and weakened their organizational strength. For instance, he engineered a division in the labor movement in order to undermine a challenge to his policies. Thus, all three neopopulist presidents avoided representing organized civil society and sought to marginalize or dominate its organizations.

Neoliberals also attacked organized interests, accusing them of market-distorting "rent-seeking"—that is, constant lobbying for subsidies and protection.[12] Rather than engaging in fair competition, these special interests exploit privileged business opportunities, which they obtain through shady connections to the state (including corruption). Business sectors, in the neoliberal view, did not prosper through efficient production but instead lived off government subsidies, exemptions from general rules, or special protection from competition.

In order to make universal market rules prevail, neoliberals opposed the hidden influence of organized interests. In their view, most of society benefits from the elimination of such privileges. If producers have to become more efficient, then consumers will find cheaper, better products.

Fittingly, important sectors of the formal working, middle, and business classes and their interest associations were the strongest opponents of neoliberal policies in the early 1990s. Labor unions offered the most open—though often ineffectual—opposition. Public sector unions were particularly hostile because the neoliberal reduction of state interventionism threatened their members' jobs. In Brazil, their resistance slowed down the privatization of state enterprises. Associations of all but the most competitive business sectors paid lip service to neoliberal policies but tried to avoid their impact and lobbied strongly for special exceptions for their own sector.

The resistance of domestic and transnational firms and their associations posed a powerful obstacle to market-oriented reform.[13] In Brazil, for instance, foreign automobile firms strenuously opposed trade liberalization. In Venezuela, important parts of Pérez's neoliberal agenda were blocked by active or passive resistance from business sectors, labor unions, and factions of the president's own party.[14] Thus, the adversarial relationship between neoliberals and established interest associations resulted from opposed interests.

Neoliberals' objection to intermediary associations permitted neopopulist leaders to invoke seemingly rational, technocratic arguments to strengthen their personal leadership. In the name of economic progress, they undermined powerful forces that tried to constrain their autonomy. They used neoliberal policies to weaken labor unions and business groups, which had stalemated their predecessors. With the imposition of market-oriented restructuring, the survival of whole sectors of the economy depended on political decisions. Thus, neoliberal policies gave tremendous power to neopopulist presidents.

Attacks on the "Political Class"

As their favorite target, neopopulist leaders attacked established politicians as a new ruling class that awarded itself enormous privileges at the expense of the people. Neoliberals shared this aversion. They fought against large-scale political interference in the market (state interventionism), which they depicted as the main obstacle to national prosperity.[15]

While neoliberal neopopulists had adversarial relationships with important business sectors, they rarely attacked the most powerful factions, namely internationally competitive industry and agriculture and domestic and international finance. Ironically, these had been the main enemies of classical populists. In the 1990s, these dominant business groups supported market-oriented restructuring. The reduction of state interventionism promised to remove the fetters on their development. Neopopulists' embrace of these business groups arose from the pragmatic recognition of their enormous clout. Defying them could be suicidal, as García's disastrous challenge to the domestic banking sector and to the International Monetary Fund suggested.

Populists needed enemies, however, from which to protect their followers. Their quasi-direct links with the masses required shielding the people from pernicious forces. In the 1990s the main enemy became the special interests that profited under the import substitution development model. This included organized business, labor unions, and the established political elite. State intervention in the economy turned political posts into spigots for acquiring and dispensing wealth, often in illicit ways. Opportunities for demanding kickbacks multiplied when business firms depended on innumerable permits, licenses, regulations, subsidies, protective tariffs, and the like. In fact, many citizens routinely greased the wheels of the public bureaucracy in order to receive the most basic services—like obtaining a driver's license or a retirement pension. Many politicians and state officials, who often owed their appointments to political influence, were notoriously corrupt. Having to pay for services that should be free created tremendous resentment in the population.

Neopopulists tapped into this hostility and focused many of their attacks on politicians and public officials. Anticorruption slogans were among their biggest vote getters. Collor and Fujimori, in particular, blasted their predecessors' administrations as venal. Fujimori started a crusade against Peru's established politicians, which culminated in his closure of Congress. Collor promised to rid the country of the maharajas, politicians who grew rich on government salaries and emoluments. Menem also fueled and exploited the contempt of many Argentines for the political class.

At the same time, these neopopulist leaders depicted themselves as outsiders, untainted by the vices of the political establishment.[16] These tactics enhanced their own power and autonomy and helped discredit the opposition.

Neoliberals shared neopopulists' hostility toward the political class. The association of state interventionism with graft strengthened their demands for market-oriented restructuring. They argued that by reducing political interference in the economy, neoliberal reforms deprived politicians of opportunities to steal. For instance, deregulation reduced chances for public servants to "create difficulty in order to sell facility," as Brazilians characterize the main tactic for extorting bribes. The less businesspeople had to depend on decisions by bureaucrats and politicians, the less the latter could demand kickbacks. Neoliberals thus invoked the unpopularity of the political establishment to support their calls for market-oriented restructuring.

Strengthening the State

Paradoxically, despite their common attack on the political establishment and its pernicious meddling in the economy, neoliberals and neopopulist leaders banded together to strengthen the commanding heights of the state. Neopopulists centralized power in order to bolster their personal authority. Neoliberals needed a concentration of authority to break opposition to their free-market reforms. Ironically, it is the state that has to impose the market.[17]

The neopopulist leaders attempted to use the concentrated power of the presidency to counteract the dispersion of authority inside the bureaucracy. They recognized that their predecessors had failed because state agencies pursued their own organizational goals with little regard for overarching state interests. Societal groups maintained close links to public agencies to protect their interests, thereby undermining central coordination and supervision inside the public bureaucracy. This made it difficult for the government to govern.

When Collor, Menem, and Fujimori took office, they saw this diffusion of power as a threat to their leadership. They tried to reestablish central control inside the state apparatus. Through formal reorganization and appointing close allies to strategic positions, they tried to bring public agencies to heel. They also marginalized or attacked uncooperative branches of government, for instance, through privatization. All three presidents frequently used decree powers to legislate or to force Congress to take up their proposals. Most drastically, Fujimori closed Congress in April 1992, purged the judiciary, and pushed through constitutional amendments to strengthen his powers.

Despite their antistate rhetoric, neoliberals supported concentration of authority in the president's hands. They also wanted the ministry of finance to impose fiscal discipline. More basically, they needed strong presidential leadership to break widespread opposition to market reforms. Paradoxically, the state is the only agency that can implant a free market. In their view, the state must wean businesses from their dependence on government protection and prod them to become entrepreneurial. The state, the protagonist of the old development model, has to induce business to become the engine of the new, market-oriented model.

For these reasons, neoliberals looked to strong presidents to attain their goals. Where governing parties were well organized, as in Mexico, nonpopulist presidents acquired great clout. Yet where intermediary organizations were weak, as in Peru, Brazil, and even Argentina, populism was the most promising avenue for finding powerful executives. Neoliberals therefore eagerly collaborated with neopopulist presidents in strengthening the state in these countries.[18] For instance, Argentine free-market enthusiast Alvaro Alsogaray advised the Menem government, even at the risk of dividing his own party.

Winning Support through Bold Reform

Relying on concentrated presidential authority, neoliberals called for determined attacks on the economic crisis and abandonment of its underlying import substitution model. Neopopulist leaders claimed that such bold measures demonstrated their courage and prevented economic collapse. Therefore, neoliberal policies helped win popular backing for neopopulist leaders.

The economic shock treatments imposed by Presidents Menem, Collor, and Fujimori hurt most citizens. Harsh adjustment caused deep recessions, lower wages, unemployment in the formal sector, and lower demand for the products and services of the informal sector. Cuts in public spending gutted social services for the poor. Poverty initially spread and even surpassed 50 percent of the population in Peru. Since some businesspeople made considerable profits at the same time—for instance, by buying state enterprises on the cheap—socioeconomic inequality probably worsened.

Nevertheless, a majority of the population, including large numbers of poor people, initially supported these painful measures. In the weeks after the imposition of neoliberal shock treatments, presidential popularity reached 85–89 percent in Argentina, 74–81 percent in Brazil, and up to 60 percent in Peru. While Collor's ratings soon began to fall sharply, Menem and Fujimori continued to enjoy high approval ratings. Fujimori, for instance, attained popularity ratings of 60–70 percent between early 1992 and mid-1996.[19]

The reasons for this widespread endorsement were probably twofold. First, tough shock treatments seemed to avert impending catastrophe. Inflation was spiraling out of control, reaching monthly rates of 114 percent in Argentina, 81 percent in Brazil, and 63 percent in Peru during the months before Menem, Collor, and Fujimori took office. Since hyperinflation can destroy people's economic sustenance in a matter of weeks, its end seemed worth the suffering. The price stability achieved by Menem and Fujimori was the main basis for their popularity. Collor's inability to contain inflation planted the seeds for his destruction.

In addition, a crisis provides a golden opportunity for a charismatic leader to prove his or her superior powers. True leadership is only revealed under adversity.[20] Normal politics do not provide the launching ground for heroes. Indeed, when confronting severe threats, many people extend a big advance of support to a daring leader who credibly claims to confront urgent problems head-on, even at enormous transitional cost. In a crisis, citizens may accept a determined leader's decisions and endure considerable hardship in hopes that the situation will improve. Only if the leader does not use this temporary blank check wisely (as Collor did not) will the followers eventually desert.[21]

Voters' preference for risk-taking leaders during crises seemed to explain the existence of broad-based support for painful economic policies. Menem, for instance, announced "surgery without anesthesia" to save Argentina from bankruptcy. The citizenry accepted his tough prescription, even though his chances for success were very uncertain.

Menem and Fujimori succeeded in stabilizing their economies. Inflation in Argentina fell from 3,079 percent to 8 percent between 1989 and 1993, while in Peru it declined from 7,650 percent to under 40 percent between 1990 and 1993. The Argentine economy expanded by 7–8 percent per year from 1991 to 1994, and the Peruvian economy grew by 7 percent in 1993 and a record 12 percent in 1994. These economic successes kept the two presidents' public approval ratings high, despite the draconian measures they enacted, proving that neoliberal neopopulists can, in principle, maintain their mass followings.[22]

Collor, in contrast, did not succeed in ending high inflation. His enormous initial popularity therefore eroded quickly. This failure suggested that he had no special curative powers, so his opponents began attacking his neoliberal program. Like other leaders who could not live up to their extraordinary promises, Collor failed and was removed from office.

The case of Carlos Andrés Pérez suggests that many people will only support a leader's tough decisions if they confront a clear and immediate threat. Pérez imposed harsh economic measures before severe problems were apparent to the common citizens. Many Venezuelans rejected the stabilization program, and large-scale violence erupted in 1989. Support for Pérez's policies, which were quite successful in economic terms, remained low, and he suffered two coup attempts in 1992. He ultimately was impeached on corruption charges in mid-1993. Thus, only an open crisis gives a president the opportunity to find widespread support for painful decisions. This mechanism made neoliberal policies acceptable and even attractive to neopopulist leaders in Argentina, Brazil, and Peru.

Targeted Benefit Programs

Eventually, politicians must provide inducements and rewards for their followers. In order to bolster their electoral support, neopopulist leaders sooner or later enact spending programs to benefit the poor, especially in the informal sector. Neoliberals also advocate antipoverty programs to make market-oriented restructuring politically viable.

Largely for electoral purposes, Menem and Fujimori created spending programs to benefit poor people. They disbursed substantial amounts in highly visible fashion. They insisted on managing the distribution of these funds from the presidency. They used discretionary powers to reward likely followers and punish political opponents. Fujimori, in particular, made personal tours since early 1994 to hand over benefits. In this way, he extracted maximum political payoff from these expenditures. Menem also created a new social fund, the Federal Solidarity Program. The timing of these measures reflected both the precarious nature of the economic recovery in the two countries and the presidents' intention to run for reelection in 1995. This gave them powerful incentives to strengthen support among the poor, who remained most susceptible to their neopopulist appeals.

Neoliberals also proposed public assistance for very poor people. Following the high priest of market economics, Milton Friedman, they advocated targeting benefits to sectors unable to succeed in the market.[23] Likewise, international financial institutions like the World Bank, which press for the adoption of neoliberal reforms in Latin America, also favor antipoverty measures as a way to make market-oriented restructuring politically palatable.

Assistance for the poor also appeals to neoliberals because it is relatively cheap. Given the destitution of the informal sector in countries like Peru, even small benefits can make a big difference. Unlike the indiscriminate subsidies created by classical populists, targeted antipoverty programs do not undermine fiscal equilibrium. Indeed, they can be combined with tough austerity policies and be used to justify spending cuts in other areas.

Posing as saviors of the poor also helped neoliberals muster electoral backing. The votes of the rich and the poor count equally, yet it is much cheaper to buy the support of a poor person. Therefore, antipoverty programs can generate substantial support for leaders enacting market-oriented reforms.

Even autocratic regimes that imposed neoliberal policies, such as those of Augusto Pinochet in Chile and Carlos Salinas in Mexico, created substantial subsidies for the poor. Mexico's National Solidarity Program helped the PRI regime recover from near defeat in the presidential election of 1988.[24]

Ironically, then, the combination of neopopulism and neoliberalism proved surprisingly successful in the 1990s. Neopopulist leaders drew on technical arguments and support from international financial institutions to defend their quasi-direct relationships with the masses. The poor people hurt by the invisible hand of the market, which neoliberals unleashed, received compensatory benefits from the visible hand of the state.

Conclusion

Did the revival of populism and its association with neoliberalism strengthen or weaken Latin America's new democracies? Populism to some extent undermined democracy. Leaders' centralized power limited the accountability of the government. Mass manipulation distorted citizen participation and the government's responsiveness to the people. Where personal leaders prevailed, democratic citizenship was impaired. Neopopulist presidents indeed abused their power on many occasions. For example, Menem's government harassed journalists, and Fujimori shut down Congress and temporarily assumed dictatorial powers.

Populism also eroded the strength of intermediary organizations, like parties and interest associations, which political theorists believe to be important for democracy in modern societies. Populists attacked these intermediary organizations as "political classes" and "special interests." In the most extreme case, Peru, neoliberal neopopulism has created a virtual organizational wasteland. Fujimori's scorched earth tactics make it difficult for democracy to thrive.

Any evaluation of neopopulism, however, must take likely alternatives into account. Latin America's new democracies were imperfect even without the revival of populism. Clientelism persisted, distorting popular participation at least as severely as populism. Also, elite pressure groups representing better-off sectors had much better chances for achieving their interests than the poor. In fact, by mobilizing broad sectors of the masses, populists actually hastened the decline of clientelism and curbed the privileges of special elites. So even the destructive tendencies of neoliberal neopopulism may have beneficial results in the long run, sweeping away obstacles to democracy and encouraging broader-based intermediary associations to arise, after the eventual demise of populism itself.

In the short run, neoliberal neopopulists also achieved some noteworthy accomplishments. Without permanently sacrificing democracy, they carried out painful economic restructuring made necessary by the debt crisis and the new global environment.[25] Many scholars had feared that democracies—especially new, unconsolidated ones—would be incapable of enacting such painful economic reforms. Neopopulism deserves some grudging recognition as the lesser of several evils. Carlos Menem in Argentina fell far short of democratic ideals, but he compared favorably to the dictator Pinochet, who imposed neoliberal reform in Chile. Fujimori acted arbitrarily and temporarily suspended the constitution, yet he pulled the country back from the brink of civil war and put the economy back on a growth track.[26] Perhaps the popularity of the latter-day populists was not altogether unwarranted.

Notes

1. Many authors associate populism by definition with expansionary spending policies, large-scale state intervention in the economy, and generous social programs. See Fernando Henrique Cardoso and Enzo Faletto, *Dependency and Development in Latin America* (Berkeley: University of California Press, 1979), ch. 5; Guillermo A. O'Donnell, *Modernization and Bureaucratic-Authoritarianism: Studies in South American Politics*, 2d ed. (Berkeley: Institute of International Studies, University of California, 1979), 53–57; Rüdiger Dornbusch and Sebastian Edwards, eds., *The Macroeconomics of Populism in Latin America* (Chicago: University of Chicago Press, 1991). Given the strong similarities in the political strategy used by Collor, Fujimori, Menem, and the classical populists, I disagree with such a definition

of populism, which would by fiat preclude any analysis of populism's survival in the age of neoliberalism. I apply instead a purely political concept of populism.

2. Guillermo O'Donnell, "Delegative Democracy," *Journal of Democracy* 5, no. 1 (January 1994): 59–62, characterizes this revived populism as delegative democracy.

3. On the unexpected resurgence of populism in Brazil's new democracy, see Gamaliel Perruci Jr. and Steven E. Sanderson, "Presidential Succession, Economic Crisis, and Populist Resurgence in Brazil," *Studies in Comparative International Development* 24, no. 3 (Fall 1989), especially 40–46.

4. John Crabtree, *Peru under García: An Opportunity Lost* (Pittsburgh: University of Pittsburgh Press, 1992), ch. 5; Carol Graham, *Peru's APRA: Parties, Politics, and the Elusive Quest for Democracy* (Boulder: Lynne Rienner, 1992), ch. 5.

5. José Alvaro Moisés, "Elections, Political Parties and Political Culture in Brazil," *Journal of Latin American Studies* 25, no. 3 (October 1993): 583–93; Edgardo R. Catterberg, *Argentina Confronts Politics: Political Culture and Public Opinion in the Transition to Democracy* (Boulder: Lynne Rienner, 1991), 97–99; Carlos Iván DeGregori and Romeo Grompone, *Elecciones 1990. Demonios y redentores en el nuevo Perú* (Lima: Instituto de Estudios Peruanos, 1991), 42–51, 102–25.

6. For overviews, see Carlos H. Acuña, "Politics and Economics in the Argentina of the Nineties," in *Democracy, Markets and Structural Reform in Latin America: Argentina, Bolivia, Brazil, Chile, and Mexico,* ed. William C. Smith, Carlos H. Acuña, and Eduardo A. Gamarra (New Brunswick, NJ: Transaction, 1994), 30–73; Jeremy Adelman, "Post-Populist Argentina," *New Left Review* 203 (January–February 1994): 82–91; John Crabtree, "The Collor Plan," *Bulletin of Latin American Research* 10, no. 2 (1991): 119–32; Instituto de Economia do Setor Público, *Gestão estatal no Brasil: Limites do liberalismo, 1990–1992* (São Paulo: FUNDAP, 1995); Efraín González de Olarte, "Peru's Economic Program under Fujimori," *Journal of Interamerican Studies and World Affairs* 35, no. 2 (Summer 1993): 51–80; John Sheahan, "Peru's Return toward an Open Economy," *World Development* 22, no. 6 (June 1994): 911–23.

7. See the convincing discussion in Carlos H. Acuña and William C. Smith, "The Political Economy of Structural Adjustment," in *Latin American Political Economy in the Age of Neoliberal Reform: Theoretical and Comparative Perspectives for the 1990s,* ed. William C. Smith, Carlos H. Acuña, and Eduardo A. Gamarra (New Brunswick, NJ: Transaction, 1994), 19–21.

8. Kurt Weyland, "The Rise and Fall of President Collor and Its Impact on Brazilian Democracy," *Journal of Interamerican Studies and World Affairs* 35, no. 1 (Spring 1993): 22.

9. This section draws heavily on my essay "Neopopulism and Neoliberalism

in Latin America: Unexpected Affinities," *Studies in Comparative International Development* 31, no. 1 (Fall 1996): 3–31.

10. Hernando de Soto, *The Other Path: The Economic Answer to Terrorism* (New York: Harper & Row, 1989).

11. For Argentina, see *Análisis de la elección de constituyentes* (Buenos Aires: Centro de Estudios Unión para la Nueva Mayoría, May 1994, Cuaderno 78), 8–10, 27–29; "Menem Exceeds All Expectations," *Latin American Regional Reports—Southern Cone* (June 1, 1995): 2–3; for Peru, see *Informe de Opinión. Lima Metropolitana* (Lima: Apoyo, Sept. 1990), 4, 12; *Imasen Confidencial* 18 (February 1994): 13, 25; and no. 29 (January 1995): 11, 15.

12. See, in general, James M. Buchanan, Robert D. Tollison, and Gordon Tullock, eds., *Toward a Theory of the Rent-Seeking Society* (College Station: Texas A&M Press, 1980).

13. Author interviews with Marcílio Marques Moreira, Brazil's economy minister, Brasília, July 9, 1992, and with former president Fernando Collor, Brasília, June 9, 1995.

14. Moisés Naím, *Paper Tigers and Minotaurs: The Politics of Venezuela's Economic Reforms* (Washington, D.C.: Carnegie Endowment, 1993), 13–17, 74–77, 82–83, 105–6, 128–30, 136, 143; Carlos Guerón, introduction to Joseph S. Tulchin, ed., *Venezuela in the Wake of Radical Reform* (Boulder: Lynne Rienner, 1993), 8–12.

15. See especially Kenneth Roberts, "Neoliberalism and the Transformation of Populism in Latin America: The Peruvian Case," *World Politics* 48, no. 1 (October 1995): 97–99.

16. However, neoliberal neopopulists themselves have been credibly accused of graft, and Collor was forced to resign on corruption charges; Luigi Manzetti, "Economic Reform and Corruption in Latin America," *North-South Issues* 3, no. 1 (1994).

17. For this "orthodox paradox," see Miles Kahler, "Orthodoxy and Its Alternatives," in *Economic Crisis and Policy Choice,* ed. Joan M. Nelson (Princeton: Princeton University Press, 1990), 47, 55.

18. For Peru, see Philip Mauceri, "State Reform, Coalitions, and the Neoliberal Autogolpe in Peru," *LARR* 30, no. 1 (1995): 7–37.

19. Mora y Araujo/SOCMERC, *Anticipo de información 89/5* (Buenos Aires, 1989), 4–5; Datafolha, *Plano Collor I—Avaliação II* (São Paulo: Datafolha, April 1990), 11. In Venezuela, by contrast, where President Pérez imposed tough adjustments before the country's problems led to hyperinflation, popular acceptance always remained low; "Changes Result in Confusion," *Foreign Broadcast Information Service—Latin America* (June 16, 1989): 67; Andrew Templeton, "The Evolution of Popular Opinion," in *Lessons of the Venezuelan Experience,* ed. Louis Goodman et al. (Washington, D.C.: Woodrow Wilson Center Press, 1995), 83–85.

20. See, in general, Max Weber, *Economy and Society: An Outline of Interpretive Sociology*, ed. Guenther Roth and Claus Wittich (Berkeley: University of California Press, 1978), 241–45, 1111–15; for the cases of Argentina, Brazil, and Peru in the late 1980s and early 1990s, see especially O'Donnell, "Delegative Democracy," 63–68.

21. This willingness to give a leader great latitude to combat a crisis has firm psychological roots. Experiments show that people tend to display a high propensity toward risk taking when facing the prospect of losses. Rather than accepting the certainty of a limited loss, they systematically tend to gamble: they prefer an option that holds the possibility of avoiding or recouping all losses, even at the risk of suffering very heavy costs. See Daniel Kahneman and Amos Tversky, "Choices, Values, and Frames," *American Psychologist* 39, no. 4 (April 1984): 341–50. Earlier losses further raise the attractiveness of an option that promises to recoup all losses, however unlikely such "breaking even" may be; Richard H. Thaler and Eric J. Johnson, "Gambling with the House Money and Trying to Break Even," *Management Science* 36, no. 6 (June 1990): 643–60. For an explanation of neoliberal reform in Latin America that draws on these arguments, see Kurt Weyland, "Risk-Taking in Latin American Economic Restructuring: Lessons from Prospect Theory," *International Studies Quarterly* 40, no. 2 (June 1996): 185–207.

22. The immediate reason for Collor's impeachment and forced resignation was corruption, but corruption has not been fatal for more successful leaders, such as Menem; Weyland, "Rise," 22.

23. Milton Friedman, *Capitalism and Freedom*, 2d ed. (Chicago: University of Chicago Press, 1982), 191–94.

24. Carol Graham, "From Emergency Employment to Social Investment," in *The Legacy of Dictatorship: Political, Economic, and Social Change in Pinochet's Chile*, ed. Alan Angell and Benny Pollack (Liverpool: Institute of Latin American Studies, University of Liverpool, 1993), 31–40, 49; Wayne A. Cornelius, Ann L. Craig, and Jonathan Fox, eds., *Transforming State-Society Relations in Mexico: The National Solidarity Strategy* (San Diego: Center for U.S.-Mexican Studies, University of California, 1994). Yet where the population is upset about tough economic measures imposed by a government that did not face a deep open crisis, such as the Pérez administration in Venezuela, even substantial spending on antipoverty programs cannot buy sufficient support; Juan Carlos Navarro, "Reforming Social Policy in Venezuela," paper for XVIII International Congress, Latin American Studies Association, Atlanta, Ga, March 10–12, 1994, pp. 16–31.

25. Cynthia McClintock, "The Breakdown of Constitutional Democracy in Peru," paper for XVIII International Congress, Latin American Studies Association, Atlanta, GA, March 10–12, 1994, 8–10, shows that Fujimori's coup was not

"required" for imposing neoliberal reforms. Also, one of the main reasons for Fuji-mori's coup and the widespread support for it was the profound challenge posed to the Peruvian state by large-scale guerrilla insurgency, especially by the "Shining Path."

26. By contrast, Pérez was not populist enough, failing to bypass established intermediary organizations and create a quasi-direct link to masses of followers: Naím, *Paper Tigers,* 136–38.

Contributors

Jorge Basurto is researcher at the Instituto de Investigaciones Sociales and professor at the Faculty of Political Science of the Universidad Nacional Autónoma de México. His most recent books include *Los movimientos sindicales en la UNAM, La vida política del Sindicato de Trabajadores de la UNAM,* and *La crisis económica en la Revolución Mexicana y sus repercusiones sociales (1913–1917).*

Michael L. Conniff is professor of history at San José State University, where he also directs the Global Studies Program. His most recent books are *A History of Modern Latin America,* with Lawrence A. Clayton; *Política Urbana no Brasil;* and *Panama and the United States.*

Paul W. Drake is professor emeritus of political science at the University of California, San Diego. His most recent book is *Between Tyranny and Anarchy: A History of Democracy in Latin America, 1800–2006.*

Steve Ellner teaches history at the Universidad de Oriente in Puerto La Cruz, Venezuela. His books include *Rethinking Venezuelan Politics: Class, Conflict, and the Chávez Phenomenon; From Guerrilla Defeat to Innovative Politics: Venezuela's Movimiento al Socialismo;* and *Organized Labor in Venezuela, 1958–1991.* He is coeditor of *The Latin American Left; Venezuelan Politics in the Chávez Era: Class, Polarization and Conflict;* and *Venezuela: Hugo Chávez and the Decline of an "Exceptional" Democracy."*

Joel Horowitz is professor of history at St. Bonaventure University. He has published many articles in addition to his books, *Argentine Unions, the State, and the Rise of Perón* and *Argentina's Radical Party and Popular Mobilization.*

Kenneth Roberts is a professor of government and Robert S. Harrison Director of the Institute for the Social Sciences at Cornell University. He is the author of

Deepening Democracy?: The Modern Left and Social Movements in Chile and Peru and the coeditor of *The Diffusion of Social Movements* and *The Resurgence of the Left in Latin America*. His research explores different dimensions of the politics of inequality, including populism, labor and social movements, and the transformation of party systems in Latin America's neoliberal era.

William Francis Robinson is an assistant professor of history and the associate director of the Center for Latin American Studies at Vanderbilt University. He completed his undergraduate studies at Johns Hopkins University and his graduate degrees at the University of Florida and at Auburn University. His research interests include twentieth-century political and social movements, nationalism and populism, and Caribbean diaspora communities.

Ximena Sosa earned her PhD in history as a Fulbright scholar at the University of New Mexico. She teaches at Pontificia Universidad Católica del Ecuador. She was the assistant director of the Center for Latin American and Caribbean Studies at Indiana University and chaired the Ecuadorian Section of the Latin American Studies Association. She has published articles on Ecuadorian populism, indigenous peoples, and gender and populism. She coedited with William Waters a book entitled, *Estudios Ecuatorianos: Un aporte a la discusión*.

Steve Stein is professor of history at Miami University. The author of several works on twentieth-century Peruvian political, social, and cultural history, his major work on populism is *Populism in Peru: The Emergence of the Masses and the Politics of Social Control*. He is presently engaged in a multifaceted study of the history of the Argentine wine industry.

Kurt Weyland, professor of government at the University of Texas at Austin, has written widely about contemporary politics in Latin America. His current book project examines waves of democratic contention in Europe and Latin American during the nineteenth and twentieth centuries.

Index

Quadros, Jânio, 57, 63, 201, 205

Radical Party (Argentina, UCR), 24
Radical Party (Chile), 76
Remón, José Antonio, 193–94
Revolutionary Leftist Group (ARDI), 135–36
Revolutionary Military Government (Peru), 119, 123–24
Roberts, Kenneth, ix–x, 223
Robinson, William Francis, 4, 224
Robles, Marco, 196
Roldós Aguilera, Jaime, 168–71
Roldosista Ecuadorian Party (PRE), 171
Romero, Anibal, 150–51

Sáenz Peña Law, 26
Salinas de Cortari, Carlos, 99–102, 209, 217
Sánchez Cerro, Luis, 111–19
Sarney, José, 202, 206
Seligson, Mitchell, 20–21
SINAMOS. *See* National System for the Support of Social Mobilization
Sistema Nacional de Apoyo a la Movilización Social (SINAMOS). *See* National System for the Support of Social Mobilization
Social Democratic Party (PSD), 53
Socialist Party of Chile (PS), 74–75
Social Progressive Party (PSP), 53
Sosa, Ximena, 4, 224
Stein, Steve, 3, 166, 224

Tamborini, José, 34
Teixeira, Anísio, 51
Torre, Carlos de la, 165
Torrijos, Omar, 197
Trienio, 134, 139–43

UCR. *See* Radical Party (Argentina)
UDN. *See* National Democratic Union

União Democrática Nacional (UDN). *See* National Democratic Union
Unidad Popular (UP). *See* Popular Unity
Unión Cívica Radical (UCR). *See* Radical Party (Argentina)
United Socialist Party of Venezuela (PSUV), 153–54
UP. *See* Popluar Unity
urbanization, 9;

Vallarino, Bolívar, 196
Vargas, Alzira, 54–55
Vargas, Getúlio, 49–50, 52–56
Vargas, José María, 146
Vargas Llosa, Mario, 12
Velasco Alvarado, Juan, 119
Velasco Ibarra, José María, 159–68
Venezuela: 1958 election, 148; 1998 election, 152; coup of 1945, 139, 142; coup of 1948, 147–48; coup of 1992, 151; economic crises, 148–49; Generation of 1928, 134, 142; industrialization, 150; modernization, 141; Plan de Barranquilla, 135; populism in, 4, 132–58; post-2000 elections, 153; Trienio, 134, 139–43
Venezuelan Communist Party (PVC), 136, 143
Venezuelen Organization (ORVE), 145
Venezuelan Revolutionary Party (PRV), 135

Weyland, Kurt, 4, 224
West Indians: in Panama, 190
Wirth, John D., 21
Workers' Party (PT), 64

Yrigoyen, Hipólito, 25–28

Zapatista Army for National Liberation (EZLN), 102
Zedillo, Ernesto, 102–3